Sudoku Programming with C

Giulio Zambon

Apress®

Sudoku Programming with C

ISBN-13 (pbk): 978-1-4842-0996-7

ISBN-13 (electronic): 978-1-4842-0995-0

Managing Director: Welmoed Spahr
Lead Editor: Steve Anglin
Editorial Board: Steve Anglin, Mark Beckner, Louise Corrigan, Jonathan Gennick, Robert Hutchinson, Michelle Lowman, James Markham, Susan McDermott, Matthew Moodie, Jeffrey Pepper, Douglas Pundick, Ben Renow-Clarke, Gwenan Spearing, Steve Weiss
Coordinating Editor: Mark Powers
Copy Editor: Lori Jacobs
Compositor: SPi Global
Indexer: SPi Global
Artist: SPi Global
Cover Designer: Friends in Design GmbH

Distributed to the book trade worldwide by Springer Science+Business Media New York, 233 Spring Street, 6th Floor, New York, NY 10013. Phone 1-800-SPRINGER, fax (201) 348-4505, e-mail orders-ny@springer-sbm.com, or visit www.springeronline.com. Apress Media, LLC is a California LLC and the sole member (owner) is Springer Science + Business Media Finance Inc (SSBM Finance Inc). SSBM Finance Inc is a Delaware corporation.

For information on translations, please e-mail rights@apress.com, or visit www.apress.com.

Apress and friends of ED books may be purchased in bulk for academic, corporate, or promotional use. eBook versions and licenses are also available for most titles. For more information, reference our Special Bulk Sales–eBook Licensing web page at www.apress.com/bulk-sales.

Any source code or other supplementary material referenced by the author in this text is available to readers at www.apress.com/9781484209967. For detailed information about how to locate your book's source code, go to www.apress.com/source-code/.

To Monika, who has put up with me for almost four decades without ever losing her trust in me.

Contents at a Glance

Contents

About the Author

Giulio Zambon's first love was physics, but he decided to dedicate himself to software development more than 30 years ago: back when computers were still made of transistors and core memories, programs were punched on cards, and Fortran only had arithmetic IFs. Over the years, he learned a dozen computer languages and worked with all sorts of operating systems. His specific interests were in telecom and real-time systems, and he managed several projects to their successful completion.

Giulio's career took him to eight cities in five different countries, where he worked as a software developer, systems consultant, process improvement manager, project manager, and chief operating officer. Since early 2008, he has lived in a peaceful suburb a few kilometers north of Canberra, Australia, where he can dedicate himself to his many interests and in particular to writing software to generate and solve numeric puzzles. Visit his web site, `http://zambon.com.au/`, to see the full list of the papers and books he has authored.

Introduction

This is a practical book that will tell you everything you need to know to solve and create Sudoku puzzles in C. My intention is not to teach you how to become a software developer but rather how to use computer programs to deal with Sudokus. Therefore, you will not find here theoretical analyses of algorithms, solvability problems, or complexity theory.

All the code I present and comment on in this book conforms to the ANSI-C standard as described in The C Programming Language by Brian W. Kernighan and Dennis M. Ritchie (2nd ed., Prentice Hall Software Series, 1989). It is a testament to the validity of "K&R" that the book is still in print unmodified since its first publication in 1988. If you don't have it, you should definitely buy it. No C programmer should be without it.

For longer than a decade before writing this book, I developed software exclusively in Java and its derivatives (e.g., JavaScript and JSP). But for this project, I decided to go back to "plain old" C. The main reason was that I didn't want to use object-oriented (OO) technology. In general, I do prefer OO programming, but this book is mainly for people whose primary interest is Sudoku, rather than software development. For such a reader, programming is a means to an end, and writing C statements is easier than defining classes and dealing with things like class inheritance.

Most of this book concentrates on solving the puzzles, but I felt that it would be incomplete if I didn't provide a program to generate them. There is very little information on the World Wide Web about how to generate puzzles. Perhaps it is so because once you have a program to create them, you can also sell them to magazines and newspapers (but good luck with that!).

The two main programs described in this book are the Solver and the Generator. In their development, I gave priority to clarity rather than efficiency. The two qualities are often in conflict, and many programmers make the mistake of trying to be efficient and develop the cleverest algorithms. This is often a bad strategy. First of all, modern compilers, when generating executable code from your sources, take care of any redundancy and make intelligent use of registers. Second, it is always better to write a program that runs like a dog but behaves as needed instead of one that runs very fast but is full of bugs and difficult to fix (I wish that all companies that develop commercial software adopted my priorities).

Once you have a program that works correctly, you can see where it spends most of its execution time and optimize those sections of the code to improve efficiency. But I haven't done anything in that direction concerning my Sudoku software. The main reason is that its purpose is to show you how to solve and generate puzzles with C. Any optimization would have made it more difficult to understand.

Some of the algorithms I implemented are far from trivial. In fact, some of them are among the most difficult code I have developed. In those cases, besides explaining the code in the book, I have added some comments in the code on key points.

Chapter 1 tells you how to model a Sudoku puzzle in C and introduces you to the Solver and the Generator.

Chapter 2 lists and explains the strategies implemented in the Solver program. Although the intent is to get you to understand the the structure of the program, it also is a great little introduction to solving Sudoku puzzles in a systematic manner.

Chapter 3 describes the structure of the Solver and its general utilities.

Chapters 4 to 13 explain the implementation in C of the solving strategies described in Chapter 2.

Chapter 14 describes how the Solver accepts input from a file to solve many puzzles one after the other.

Chapter 15 describes the Generator program in detail.

Chapter 16 analyzes the puzzles that the Generator creates and explains how and explains how to create more puzzles.

Chapter 17 shows how to can create special puzzles.

Chapter 18 shows how to build multi-grid Sudokus.

Appendix A explains how to use the code provided with the book within Eclipse.

Appendix B lists abbreviations and acronyms.

■ ■ ■

CHAPTER 1

Modeling a Sudoku Puzzle in C

The purpose of this book is to teach you how to write computer programs to solve and generate Sudoku puzzles. This chapter introduces you to the Solver and the Generator programs and describes the notation I use throughout the book for Sudoku puzzles and how I represent Sudoku grids in C.

Solving a Puzzle

Each blank cell in a Sudoku puzzle offers nine possible candidates. You solve a Sudoku by applying a series of strategies that let you remove candidates from the puzzle's cells. The solution is complete when only one candidate remains in each cell.

Some strategies are simple. Perhaps the simplest one of all is that once you have solved one cell with a particular number, you can safely remove that number from all other cells that belong to the same row because you know that each number between 1 and 9 can only appear once in each row.

Other strategies are significantly more complex. Your ability to recognize the patterns that let you apply difficult strategies is what makes you an accomplished Sudoku solver.

I just searched the Web for "sudoku strategy" (without double quotes) and Google returned about 3,350,000 links. How many strategies are there? Many, but some of them are so difficult that no unaided human mind would probably be able to apply them. Also, beyond a certain level of complexity, the distinction between a "logical" strategy and a "trial and error" strategy becomes blurred.

In this book, I describe the 15 strategies that I believe an extremely capable human solver might be able to use with only the help of pencil and paper. To be honest, I doubt that I would be able to apply them all. But then, that's just me.

The Solver implements all 15 strategies.

Some of the strategies belong to "families" of strategies. That is, they are conceptually identical but apply to increasing numbers of candidates in cells, numbers of rows, or other quantities. Once you have familiarized yourself with the code, you should be able to extend the Solver by adding more complex strategies to one or more of the "families."

If the Solver runs out of strategies before completing the solution, it uses a 16th strategy, "backtracking," which is an elegant name for "trial and error," also called "brute force." Thanks to backtracking, the Solver is guaranteed to solve any puzzle.

Generating a Puzzle

When generating a Sudoku puzzle, you must satisfy two criteria: it must be solvable and the solution must be unique.

The first criterion requires some qualifications, as the term "solvable" is too broad.

Obviously, you can solve any valid puzzle (i.e., without internal inconsistencies) by trial and error, but the key question is, which puzzles require it? The better you are at solving Sudoku, the fewer are the puzzles that force you to guess.

In the section "Solving a Puzzle," I stated that there are 15 strategies that, in my opinion, an expert player can possibly be able to apply. It therefore makes sense to define as solvable, or, more precisely, "analytically solvable," all and only the puzzles that the Solver program can complete without resorting to backtracking.

The second criterion, uniqueness is pretty obvious: if you generate a puzzle and provide its solution, you don't want anybody to come up with a different one.

To generate a puzzle, the Generator starts by filling up a 9 x 9 Sudoku grid with random numbers in such a way that no number appears twice in any row, column, or box.

It then proceeds to remove clues (i.e., clear cells) according to your preferences (see below) and checks that the puzzle, using the remaining clues, admits a unique solution.

When executing the Generator, you can decide how many clues you want to remove (or eliminate as many as possible). You can also choose to remove clues individually or, to generate pleasingly symmetrical puzzles, two or four at a time.

For simplicity, the Generator uses brute-force approaches whenever possible. For example, to fill in the initial grid, which represents the solved puzzle, it just inserts one random number (1 to 9) at a time and keeps trying until it finds a valid combination.

It would have been possible to optimize the choices and obtain a valid grid more efficiently, but why bother? To save a fraction of a second in computing time?

After completing the removal of the clues, the Generator checks the uniqueness of the solution (see Chapter 15 for a detailed explanation of how to do that).

What the Generator doesn't do is determine how difficult the new puzzle is. For that, you need to run the puzzle through the Solver. There is another way of applying a brute-force approach: generate hundreds or thousands of puzzles and then run the Solver "in batch" to measure their difficulties.

Modeling the Puzzle

A Sudoku puzzle is a partially filled grid of 9 x 9 cells. Therefore, the obvious way of representing it is to define a matrix of nine rows by nine columns, as in

```c
char grid[9][9];
```

Figure 1-1 shows how you identify each cell with a pair of numbers indicating row and column. As in C, the indices start with zero, so grid[3][6], as an example, refers to the seventh cell of the fourth row.

	0	1	2	3	4	5	6	7	8
0	0,0	0,1	0,2	0,3	0,4	0,5	0,6	0,7	0,8
1	1,0	1,1	1,2	1,3	1,4	1,5	1,6	1,7	1,8
2	2,0	2,1	2,2	2,3	2,4	2,5	2,6	2,7	2,8
3	3,0	3,1	3,2	3,3	3,4	3,5	3,6	3,7	3,8
4	4,0	4,1	4,2	4,3	4,4	4,5	4,6	4,7	4,8
5	5,0	5,1	5,2	5,3	5,4	5,5	5,6	5,7	5,8
6	6,0	6,1	6,2	6,3	6,4	6,5	6,6	6,7	6,8
7	7,0	7,1	7,2	7,3	7,4	7,5	7,6	7,7	7,8
8	8,0	8,1	8,2	8,3	8,4	8,5	8,6	8,7	8,8

Figure 1-1. *Cell numbering*

You might wonder why, when defining cells, I use the type char instead of int. After all, we are talking about integer numbers, aren't we? It is true, but the type char is stored in a single byte, consisting of eight bits. This is more than enough to contain the 1 to 9 Sudoku numbers, which only require four bits, and I have learned that being economical often leads to better programs.

Usually, there is a trade-off between memory and speed. It could be that defining everything of type int would result in slightly faster processing, but, in practical terms, it would also probably be irrelevant, as we are talking anyway about a small amount of data. On the other hand, arrays of characters have the advantage that you can initialize them more easily. It's almost a matter of taste more than of anything else.

Anyhow, the simple grid with one character per cell will not do. The reason is that a Sudoku cell contains a single number only when you have solved it. In general, while you are in the middle of solving the puzzle, each cell contains a number of candidates. This means that a Sudoku program must be able to store more than one number in each cell. Figure 1-2 shows an example of a partially solved Sudoku with all its candidates.

Best-effort transcription of the partially-solved Sudoku grid (Figure 1-2). Large digits are solved cells; numbers in parentheses are the candidate marks shown in the cell.

	0	1	2	3	4	5	6	7	8
0	4	9 (2,8)	7	(2,6,8)	1	(5,6,8)	(5,6)	(5,6)	3
1	(1,3,7)	5 (3,8)	4	(6,8,9)	(6,9)		2	(6,7,9)	(1,7,9)
2	(1,2,7)	6	(1,7)	5	(2,8,9)	3	(7,8)	4	(1,7,9)
3	(2,3)	7	8	6	1	4	9	(3,5)	(2,5)
4	(1,6)	(2,3)	(1,6)	9	5	8	4	(3,7)	(2,7)
5	9	5	4	3	7	2	1	8	6
6	(5,6,7)	1	3	8	4	(6,7,9)	(5,6,7)	2	(5,7,9)
7	(5,6,7)	4	2	1	(6,9)	(6,7,9)	3	(5,6,7,9)	8
8	8	9	(6,7)	2	3	5	(6,7)	1	4

Figure 1-2. *Partially solved Sudoku*

For example, cell $(7,7)$ has four candidates: 5, 6, 7, and 9. The maximum number of candidates, as unlikely as it can be, is nine, when you have no clue at all about the number that solves the cell.

The simplest solution to keep track of the candidates is to replace a single character with an array of characters, as in

```
char grid[9][9][10]
```

There are many ways in which you could use an array to memorize what candidates are present. I have chosen to use each element of the array as a flag, with 1 meaning that the candidate is present and 0 that the candidate is not present. For example, assuming that you already have initialized the array to all zeroes, to memorize the two candidates of cell $(7,4)$, you could write the following two lines of code:

```
grid[7][4][6] = 1;
grid[7][4][9] = 1;
```

Additionally, I decided to use the first element (i.e., the 0th) of the array to store the number of candidates in the cell. You would do this with the following assignment statement:

```
grid[7][4][0] = 2;
```

I could have used the array as a list of candidates rather than a list of flags in fixed positions. If I had done so, you would record the two candidates as follows:

```
grid[7][4][1] = 6;
grid[7][4][2] = 9;
```

There is nothing wrong with that, but it would force you to compact the list every time a strategy removes candidates. For example, for a cell containing the candidates 3, 5, 7, and 9, the array would contain 4, 3, 5, 7, 9 in its first five elements, where the 4 in first position tells you the number of valid numbers that follow. If you then needed to remove, say, the 5, you would have to change the array to 3, 3, 7, 9. It means that you would have to copy the third number to the second position and then the fourth number to the third position. Not elegant.

But there is also another reason for using flags. With flags, if you need to check for the presence of a candidate in a cell, you only need to see whether the corresponding flag is set. For example, in the statement

```
if (grid[r][c][5]) { },
```

the block following the if condition only executes if the 5 is a valid candidate for the cell in row r and column c. Quite neat! Remember that in C, any integer different from zero is considered to be true. With the list-based solution, you would have to scan the list every time.

You could use a bit instead of a character, but this would force you to use bit operations, which are less readable. Moreover, you would no longer have the possibility of using the 0th element to count the candidates. The candidate counter is very useful to check whether a cell has been solved or not: you only need to check whether grid[r][c][0] is set to 1.

So far so good, but you are not yet done with defining your Sudoku grid. The reason is that in Sudoku there are three types of groups of cells that you must consider: rows, columns, and 3 x 3 boxes. They are generically referred to as *units*. To make the programming of solving strategies easier, you need to be able to identify a generic unit, so that you can use a single function to operate indifferently on a row, on a column, or on a box. In other words, it would be a badly designed piece of software if you had to develop three separate functions to check whether a candidate of a cell is unique within its row, its column, or its box.

Before I explain how you can resolve that issue, though, it is appropriate that you are 100% clear on how you identify the boxes. For that, please refer to Figure 1-3.

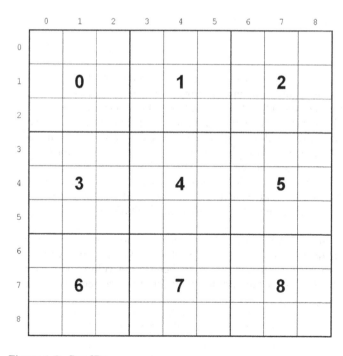

Figure 1-3. Box IDs

As you can see, you identify the boxes with numbers between 0 and 8, like you do with rows and columns. So, for example, the cell (3,5) belongs to box 4. Sometimes, in the course of this book, I will identify a cell with three coordinates (row,column,box) instead of only two (row,column). Obviously, the third coordinate is redundant and you could easily calculate it from the first two, but additional information (as long as it is consistent with the rest!) sometimes makes things more clear.

Here is how you calculate the box ID of a cell for which you know the row and column:

```
box = row / 3 * 3 + column / 3;
```

This calculation takes advantage of the fact that in C, when you divide an integer by another integer, the result is truncated (not rounded) to an integer value. So, for example, the box ID of the cell (7,2) is calculated as 7/3*3 + 2/3 = 2*3 + 0 = 6.

To avoid having to develop unit-specific code, you can use arrays to index the Sudoku grid, as shown in Listing 1-1.

Listing 1-1. Indices of Rows, Columns, and Boxes

```
char grid[9][9][10];
char row[9][9][2];
char col[9][9][2];
char box[9][9][2];
  for (int k = 0; k < 9; k++) {
    for (int j = 0; j < 9; j++) {
      row[k][j][0] = k;
      row[k][j][1] = j;
      col[j][k][0] = k;
      col[j][k][1] = j;
      box[k/3*3+j/3][k%3*3+j%3][0] = k;
      box[k/3*3+j/3][k%3*3+j%3][1] = j;
      }
    }
```

To understand how it works, concentrate first of all of the lines highlighted in bold, which refer to the rows. The outermost loop, with control variable k, goes through all the rows, while the innermost loop, with control variable j, goes through the columns (i.e., the cells) of the current row. The statements row[k][j][0] = k and row[k][j][1] = j will save the row and column ID of the cell (k,j) in the row array. It means that the jth element of row k identifies the cell with coordinates (k,j). Now, this will probably seem trivial and useless: why should you use the two elements of row[k][j] to affirm that the coordinates of the cell are indeed (k,j)? If you only had rows, you would be right. But look at what happens when you examine the column-related statements. This time, the row ID (i.e., k) is stored in col[j][k][0], while the column ID (i.e., j) is stored in col[j][k][1]. That is, the indices in the matrix col are swapped compared to those we used for the matrix row. In plain language, this means that the kth element of column j is the cell with coordinates (k,j).

Perhaps you find the use of k and j confusing. But this code lets us treat a row and a column the same way, without even knowing whether you are dealing with a row or with a column. To see how this works, let's look at an example. Suppose that you want to check whether number x has been found within a particular row. I know, it is not an exciting example, but it will serve our purpose. To do the check, you could create a function called x_found(), as shown in Listing 1-2.

Listing 1-2. Example: x_found()

```c
int x_found(int x, char unit[9][2]) {
  int result = 0;
  for (int i = 0; i < 9 && !result; i++) {
    int iR = unit[i][0];
    int iC = unit[i][1];
    char *cands = grid[iR][iC];
    result = cands[0] && cands[x];
  }
  return result;
}
```

To find out whether, say, the number 5 has been found in row 3, you would then execute the function x_found() as follows:

```c
int yes = x_found(5, row[3]);
```

The code of the function is pretty straightforward: you loop through all the elements of the row (control variable i), determine the row and column and use those values to access the corresponding element of the grid. If the number of candidates is 1 and the flag for x (i.e., 5 in the example) is set, it means that the number has been found. At that point, you break out of the loop and return to the calling function.

Now, what if you want to check column 6 instead of row 3? Easy: you just execute the following:

```c
int yes = x_found(5, col[6]);
```

The function also works with boxes. If you go back to Listing 1-1, you see that as you go through all the cells of a box, from left to right and from top to bottom, the second index of the matrix box goes from 0 to 8. Let's look, for example, at box 5. It consists of the cells $(3,6)$, $(3,7)$, $(3,8)$, $(4,6)$, $(4,7)$, $(4,8)$, $(5,6)$, $(5,7)$, and $(5,8)$. If you calculate the second index of the matrix box, you obtain the following:

k	j	index
3	6	3%3*3 + 6%3 = 0*3 + 0 = 0
3	7	3%3*3 + 7%3 = 0*3 + 1 = 1
3	8	3%3*3 + 7%3 = 0*3 + 2 = 2
4	6	4%3*3 + 6%3 = 1*3 + 0 = 3
4	7	4%3*3 + 7%3 = 1*3 + 1 = 4
4	8	4%3*3 + 8%3 = 1*3 + 2 = 5
5	6	5%3*3 + 6%3 = 2*3 + 0 = 6
5	7	5%3*3 + 7%3 = 2*3 + 1 = 7
5	8	5%3*3 + 8%3 = 2*3 + 2 = 8

Therefore, to check whether, say, digit 7 has been found in box 4, you can execute the following:

```
int yes = x_found(7, box[4]);
```

Now, if you are familiar with C, you will be probably asking yourself why I didn't use pointers. For example, I could have defined the following arrays:

```
char row[9][9][10];
char *col[9][9];
char *box[9][9];
```

and then initialized col and box with the addresses of the appropriate elements of the row. Initially I actually did it like that, but I couldn't get it to work properly, because the compiler treated, say, row[3] and col[6] differently when I passed them to a function. I kept getting compile-time warnings, and I want my code to be warning free. If you find a way to do it without getting warnings, please let me know!

You might argue that C++ could have made it simpler to define Sudoku puzzles. You could have defined Row, Column, and Box as subclasses of a Unit class. It is true, but I also wanted to write a book that people without extensive knowledge of programming would be able to fully understand. Unfortunately, as schools are still in the process of introducing computing as a core subject, most people have some difficulties in getting around OO concepts (despite the fact that OO programming more closely reflects how we think). Plain C, given its availability and its widespread use, was the most appropriate choice.

Summary

In this chapter, I introduced you to the Solver and the Generator and described how to identify the rows, columns, and boxes of a Sudoku puzzle. I also explained how you can represent a Sudoku in C and warned about alternative solutions that would cause problems. In the next chapter, I describe all the strategies used by the Sudoku Solver.

CHAPTER 2

■ ■ ■

The Strategies

Not all strategies are created equal. When solving a Sudoku puzzle manually it makes sense to use simpler strategies as long as they result in candidate removals and cell solutions, and only then move to more complex strategies. Obviously, there is no reason for making the same distinction when writing a computer program to solve Sudokus. And yet, that is precisely how I structured my Sudoku-solving program. The reason is that I want to use the Sudoku Solver to estimate the difficulty of Sudoku puzzles. If the program applied more complex strategies before achieving what is possible with simple ones, it would be impossible to know whether the complex strategies were needed at all.

Let's go about this systematically.

I group Sudoku-solving strategies in five levels of increasing complexity, which I number from 0 to 4.

Level 0 Strategies

Level 0 strategies are those that every Sudoku beginner knows and applies. They are *naked single, unique,* and *cleanup* (my naming convention).

The Strategy Naked Single

If a cell only has a single candidate, that candidate solves the cell. This is obvious: if there are no other possible candidates in a cell, the only one present must be it. I hesitated before including this strategy in the list because it is trivial. But I then decided to mention it because if you decided to modify the Solver or the Generator, perhaps to make them more efficient, you might choose to flag solved cells in a special way. By flagging the cell, you would effectively be implementing naked single. Being aware of it could help you to structure the software more consistently.

The Strategy Unique

If you find a candidate for a particular number in a single cell of a unit, the candidate must solve the cell. For example, suppose that looking at all cells of box 4 you find out that the only candidate 2 of the box is in $(5,3)$. As there must be a 2 in every box, it means that the 2 in $(5,3)$ must be the 2 for that box, and you can remove all other candidates from that cell.

The Strategy Cleanup

When you solve a cell, the number that solves it cannot be a candidate anywhere else in any of the units to which the cell belongs. For example, if $(0,4)$ solves to a 3, you can remove the candidate 3s from all the cells of row 0, column 4, and box 1.

Usage of Level 0 Strategies

When removing a candidate from a cell, it could be that it was one of only two candidates in that cell. If that is the case, by removing it, you leave the cell with a single candidate, which means that the naked single strategy applies. For example, if $(2,7)$ contains two candidates, 1 and 3, and you remove the 3, it is clear that 1 must solve the cell.

It could also be that the candidate you have removed was one of only two candidates for a particular number in a unit. In that case, the unique strategy applies to the remaining candidate. For example, if you remove a 3 from cell $(2,7)$, it could be that only one candidate 3 is left in column 7, say, in $(8,7)$. In that case, 3 must solve $(8,7)$, otherwise there wouldn't be any 3 at all in column 7.

Obviously, you must do a cleanup whenever you solve a cell. Otherwise, there is a good chance that you keep considering as possible some candidates that are not.

All in all, it makes sense to apply naked single and unique whenever you remove a candidate, followed by a cleanup if naked single or unique solves a cell. This often results in a chain of removals that can completely solve easy Sudokus. (See, for example, Figure 2-1).

	0	1	2	3	4	5	6	7	8
0	2 3 / 8 9	8 9	2 3 / 8 9	**1**	3 / 5 6 / 8	2 3 / 5 6 / 8	**7**	**4**	6 / 8
1	1 / 8	**5**	1 / 7 8	4 6	**9**	6 / 8	1 / 6 / 8	**3**	**2**
2	1 2 3 / 4 / 8	1 / 4 / 8	**6**	**7**	3 / 4 5 / 8	2 3 / 5 / 8	**9**	5 / 8	1 / 8
3	**4**	1 / 7 9	1 3 / 7 9	**8**	1 3 / 5 6 / 7	1 2 3 / 5 6	2 / 6	2 / 7 9	3 / 6 / 7 9
4	3 / 5 6 / 8 9	**2**	3 / 7 8 9	3 / 4 5 6	3 / 4 5 6 / 7	3 / 5 6	4 / 6 / 8	**1**	3 / 4 6 / 7 8 9
5	1 / 3 / 6 / 8	1 / 7 8	1 / 3 / 7 8	2 3 / 4 6 / 7	1 3 / 4 6 / 7	**9**	2 / 4 6 / 8	2 / 7 8	**5**
6	1 2 / 8 9	1 / 8 9	**4**	5 6 / 9	1 / 5 6 / 8	**7**	**3**	2 / 5 / 8 9	1 / 8 9
7	**7**	**3**	1 / 8 9	5 / 9	**2**	1 / 5 / 8	1 / 4 5 / 8	**6**	1 / 4 / 8 9
8	1 2 / 8 9	**6**	**5**	3 / 9	1 / 3 / 8	**4**	1 2 / 8	2 / 7 8 9	1 / 7 8 9

Figure 2-1. An easy Sudoku

And following is the beginning of the Solver's log:

```
unique_unit: 5 in (4,0) is unique within the column
unique_unit: removed 3 from (4,0)
unique_unit: removed 6 from (4,0)
unique_unit: removed 8 from (4,0)
unique_unit: removed 9 from (4,0)
cleanup_unit [row of (4,0)]: removed 5 in (4,3)
```

```
cleanup_unit [row of (4,0)]: removed 5 in (4,4)
cleanup_unit [row of (4,0)]: removed 5 in (4,5)
unique_unit: 4 in (2,1) is unique within the box
unique_unit: removed 1 from (2,1)
unique_unit: removed 8 from (2,1)
cleanup_unit [row of (2,1)]: removed 4 in (2,4)
...
```

I don't show the whole log because it is 158 lines long. But you get the idea: the functions unique_unit() and cleanup_unit() keep executing until all candidates have been removed, without any need of more complex strategies. The log doesn't show any entry marked "naked single" because when a single candidate remains in a cell, besides "cleaning up" around it, the program doesn't need to execute any additional function.

Level 1 Strategies

Level 1 strategies are those that most Sudoku players easily discover on their own. They are *naked pair*, *hidden pair*, *box-line*, and *pointing line*.

The Strategy Naked Pair

If two cells in the same unit only contain the same two candidates, it means that one of those candidates will solve one of the two cells, and the other candidate will solve the other cell. Therefore, you can remove the same candidates from all other cells of the unit.

For example, suppose that box 3 has reached the point shown in Figure 2-2.

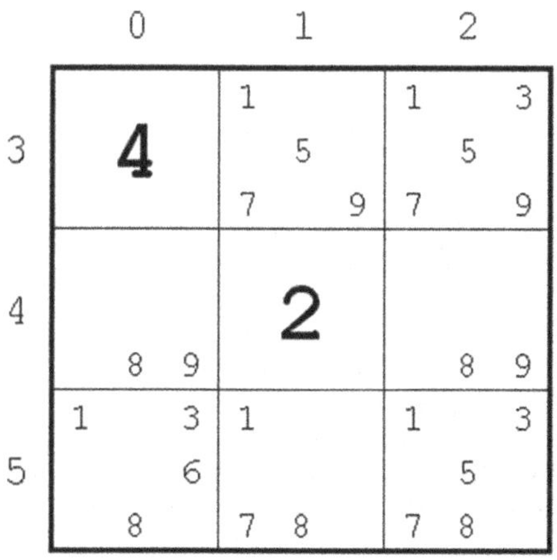

Figure 2-2. A naked pair

The two cells (4,0) and (4,2) contain the naked pair 8 and 9. If 8 solves (4,0), then 9 must solve (4,2). On the other hand, if 8 solves (4,2), then 9 must solve (4,0). In either case, both 8 and 9 are used. Therefore, you can remove the 8s in cells (5,0), (5,1), and (5,2) as well as the 9s in cells (3,1) and (3,2).

The Strategy Hidden Pair

If two candidates only appear in two cells of a unit, it means that one of those candidates will solve one of the two cells, and the other candidate the other cell. Therefore, you can remove all other candidates in the two cells.

Consider for example the row shown in Figure 2-3.

0	1	2	3	4	5	6	7	8
1 2 3 1 4 8 8	6	7	4 5 8	2 3 5 8	9	5 8	1 8	

Figure 2-3. A hidden pair

Notice that the candidates 2 and 3 only appear in column 0 and 5. Either the 2 is in 0 and the 3 in 5 or vice versa. In either case, cell 0 cannot contain either 1 or 8, and cell 5 cannot contain either 5 or 8. It means that you can "strip" the 2–3 pairs in columns 0 and 5 and leave them naked. The name "hidden" comes from the fact that the two candidates of the pair are hidden among other candidates.

The Strategy Box-Line

When a specific candidate within a row or a column only occurs in a single box, one of those occurrences must be a solution. Therefore, you can remove the same candidate from all other cells of the same box.

To understand how this strategy works, refer to the partial Sudoku shown in Figure 2-4.

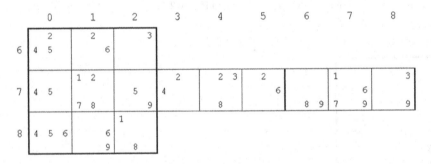

Figure 2-4. A box-line configuration

All 5s of row 7 are within box 6. Therefore, 5 must solve either (7,0) or (7,2). Otherwise, there would be no 5 in row 7. As a result, you can remove the 5s from (6,0) and (8,0).

The Strategy Pointing Line

This strategy is often named pointing pair, but I prefer to call it pointing line because the action of pointing might actually be done by a triple instead of a pair. It works as follows: when all the cells containing a particular candidate within a box belong to the same line (row or column), you can remove the candidates for the same number that appear in the line but outside that box. I know, it sounds complicated. Let's look at the example shown in Figure 2-5.

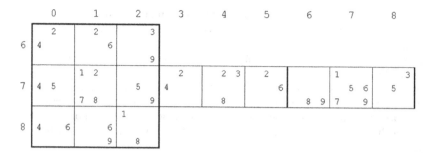

Figure 2-5. *A pointing line configuration*

All 5s of box 6 are within row 7. Therefore, 5 must solve either $(7,0)$ or $(7,2)$. Otherwise, there would be no 5 in box 6. As a result, you can remove the 5s from $(7,7)$ and $(7,8)$ because there cannot be more than one 5 in row 7, and you know that either $(7,0)$ or $(7,2)$ is a 5.

This strategy is in a sense *symmetrical* to the box-line strategy that I described in the previous section. Both strategies rely on a candidate that appears in the three-cell intersection of a box with a line, but box-line lets you remove some candidates from the box when the candidates do not appear anywhere else in the intersecting line, while pointing line lets you remove some candidates from the line when the candidates do not appear anywhere else in the intersecting box.

Level 2 Strategies

Level 2 strategies are more complex than level 1 strategies. The patterns of candidates that let you apply the strategies are not easy to identify. The strategies are *naked triple, hidden triple, lines-2, naked quad,* and *Y-wing*.

The Strategies Naked Triple and Naked Quad

These are extensions of the naked pair strategy to triplets and quadruplets of candidates.

Naked triple: if three cells in the same unit only contain the same three candidates, it means that one of those candidates will solve one of the three cells, another candidate will solve a second cell, and the third candidate will solve the remaining cell. Therefore, you can remove the same candidates from all other cells of the unit.

Naked quad: if four cells in the same unit only contain the same four candidates, it means that one of those candidates will solve one of the four cells, another candidate will solve a second cell, yet another candidate will solve a third cell, and the fourth candidate will solve the remaining cell. Therefore, you can remove the same candidates from all other cells of the unit.

Now, theoretically, you could have a naked strategy with more than four cells, but they are so unlikely that it isn't worth considering them.

The Strategy Hidden Triple

This is an extension of the hidden pair strategy to triplets of candidates. If three candidates only appear in three cells of a unit, it means that one of those candidates will solve one of the three cells, another candidate will solve a second cell, and the third candidate will solve the remaining cell. Therefore, you can remove all other candidates in the three cells.

It sounds very similar to naked triple, but hidden triple lets you remove candidates from the cells that contain the triplets of candidates, while naked triple lets you remove candidates from the cells of the unit that do not contain the triplets.

The situations in which you can apply this strategy are very unlikely—so unlikely, that it would be unreasonable to consider a hidden quad strategy.

You might argue that, unlike us humans, a program wouldn't mind scanning a Sudoku for very unlikely strategies. Sooner or later, it might be the only way of solving a difficult Sudoku without having to guess. Perhaps, but I don't like the idea of programming strategies that a human being would never apply. In one of the next chapters, you will see the code for hidden pair and hidden triple. I'll leave it up to you to write hidden quad, if you feel like it.

The Strategy Lines-2

This strategy is also called X-wing. If you find a particular candidate in the same two rows (i.e., positions) within two columns, you can remove that candidate from the other cells of those two rows. (See Figure 2-6 for an example.)

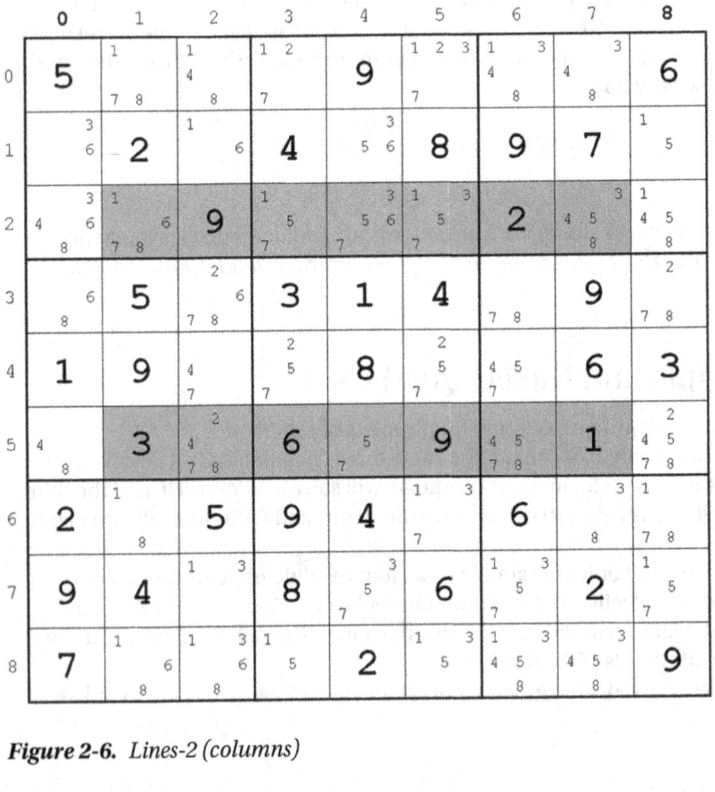

Figure 2-6. *Lines-2 (columns)*

Notice that in columns 0 and 8 all candidates for 4 are in the two rows 2 and 5. That is, there are candidates for 4 in the four cells $(2,0)$, $(2,8)$, $(5,0)$, and $(5,8)$. If the 4 of column 0 is in $(2,0)$, it means that there cannot be a 4 in either $(2,8)$ or $(5,0)$. Therefore, there must be a 4 in $(5,8)$. If, on the other hand, the 4 of column 0 is in $(5,0)$, it means that the 4 of column 8 is in $(2,8)$. In either case, you have identified cells in row 2 and row 5 whose solution must be a 4. As a result, you can remove all the candidates for 4 in rows 2 and 5 that are not in columns 0 and 8. These are the grayed cells in Figure 2-6. To be completely clear, you can remove the 4 from $(2,7)$, $(5,2)$, and $(5,6)$.

Obviously, the same applies if you swap rows and columns: if in two rows all the cells that contain a particular candidate are in the same two columns, you can remove that candidate from the other cells of those two columns.

The Strategy Y-wing

On the web there are many explanations of the Y-wing strategy, but none seems to go to the core of the issue. The only clear statement I found was that Y-wing doesn't solve cells but only eliminates possible candidates. Correct, but not of much help.

To apply the Y-wing strategy you need to look for cells that contain only two candidates each. Among those cells, you need to find three cells that satisfy the following two conditions:

- The arrangement of candidates in the cells is AB, AC, and BC. That is, no two cells have the same pair of candidates.

- The cells are in two intersecting units. This is equivalent to say that the two wing cells cannot share any unit, and it can only happen in two ways: row+column (one of the cells shares the row with one of the other two cells and the column with the third one) and line+box, where "line" stands for either "column" or "row" (one of the cells shares the line (row or column) with one of the other two cells and the box with the third one).

In other words, you can apply Y-wing when you find a chain of three cells containing all possible different pairs that can be formed with three candidates, whereby two cells are said to be "chained" when they belong to the same unit and one (and only one) of their two candidates is identical.

You will see in the next section of this chapter that if the chain of cells is longer than three, Y-wing becomes the more general strategy XY-chain.

When both conditions are satisfied, you have one of the two configurations shown in Figures 2-7 and 2-8.

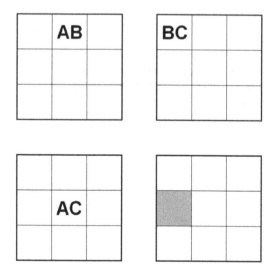

Figure 2-7. Y-wing row+column

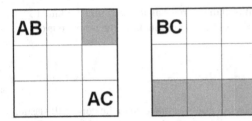

Figure 2-8. *Y-wing line+box*

The four boxes shown in Figure 2-7 can be adjacent to each other or not. Regardless of what numeric candidates correspond to A, B, and C, one of the candidates appears in both of the two "wings." In the example, it is C. If, at a later stage, you find out that the solution for the intersection cell (i.e., the cell that, at this stage, contains the candidates A and B) is A, C must be in the bottom-left cell. If, on the other hand, the intersection cell turns out to solve into B, C must be in the top-right cell. In either case, the grayed cell cannot contain C.

In the example in Figure 2-8, the line containing one of the pairs is in the top row of a box, and the box is the left one. But the row could be in the middle or at the bottom of the box, and the box could be on the right. Also, you could rotate the diagram by 90 degrees and have column-box configurations. You can easily verify that regardless of whether the intersection cell turns out to solve into A or B, the grayed cells cannot contain a C.

Level 3 Strategies

Level 3 strategies are complex, and only clever Sudoku solvers can discover them on their own. They are *XY-chain*, *rectangle*, *lines-3*, and *lines-4*.

The Strategy XY-Chain

As I already mentioned, XY-chain is a generalization of Y-wing. Essentially, instead of looking for a chain of three pairs, you look for longer chains in which the intersection cell of the Y-wing is expanded to a chain. The chain can be surprisingly long, as shown in Figures 2-9 to 2-11.

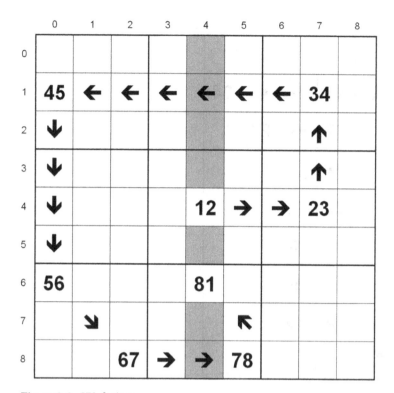

Figure 2-9. *XY-chain 1*

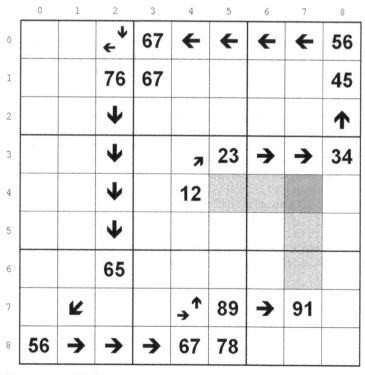

Figure 2-10. *XY-chain 2*

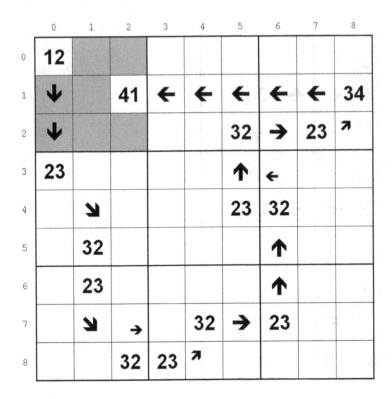

Figure 2-11. *XY-chain 3*

In Figure 2-9, the cells highlighted in gray are the cells from which you can remove candidates for 1. If cell (4,4) contains a 1, the grayed cells cannot contain 1s. If, on the other hand, cell (4,4) contains a 2, it means that cell (4,7) must contain a 3, (1,7) a 4, ..., and (6,4) a 1. Therefore, again, the grayed cells cannot contain 1s. Without knowing whether the 1 of column 4 is in row 4 or in row 6, you can safely remove all 1s from the grayed cells.

In Figure 2-10, you can only exclude the presence of a 1 in cell (4,7). But notice that the chain consists of 14 cells. Also note that some of the cells contain the same pair. In fact, it is possible for most of the cells of a chain to contain the same candidates. The fact that the chain is so long shouldn't deter you from attempting to apply this method. You only need to ignore all cells that contain more than two candidates (and, obviously, the cells that are already solved); start from the top-left cell, see whether you can chain it to another cell with two candidates, and keep going until you hit a cell of which the second candidate is identical to the first one of the first cell of the chain.

Obviously, it will often happen that you don't manage to build a chain. If so, look at the next cell with exactly two candidates and try again.

Figure 2-11 shows another example.

Notice that most pairs are identical. I have only written them alternatively as 23 and 32 to highlight the chain.

There is still one thing I would like to tell you about chains: they are not always unique. Look, for example, at Figure 2-12.

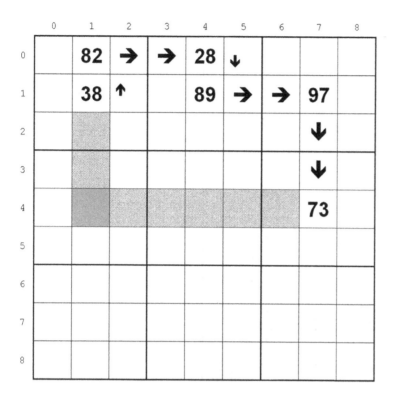

Figure 2-12. *Chain with redundant cells*

To connect $(1,1)$ with $(4,7)$, there was no need to go from $(1,1)$ to $(0,1)$, $(0,4)$, and $(1,4)$. The chain could have gone directly from $(1,1)$ to $(1,4)$. So, why take the detour? There is no reason. It might be argued that the alternate chain, being shorter, is "nicer," but either chain is perfectly valid.

The Strategy Rectangle

If the cells containing a particular candidate outline a rectangle with its vertices in four different boxes, the vertices cannot contain the candidate. For example, consider the configuration shown in Figure 2-13 (only the candidates for 5 are shown).

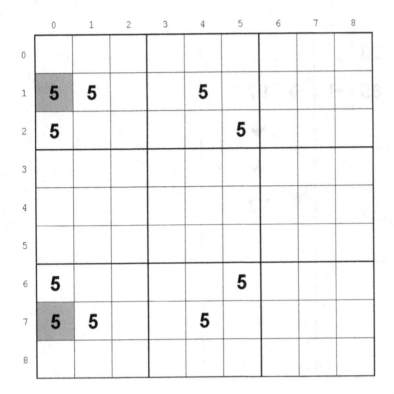

Figure 2-13. *The rectangle strategy*

If (1,0) contains a 5, then (1,4) cannot. Therefore, (2,5) must. Then, in box 7 there can only be a 5 in (7,4), and in box 6 there can only be a 5 in (6,0). But, as column 0 would end up with two 5s (one in row 6 and the initial one in row 1), your premise must be wrong, and (1,0) cannot contain a 5. Similarly, (7,0) cannot contain a 5 either.

Notice that there can be many more 5 candidates, but, for the strategy to apply, it seems that the candidates in the four boxes with the vertices of the rectangle must be on the edge of the rectangle, as highlighted in Figure 2-14. But that is actually not always true, as shown in the example in Figure 2-15.

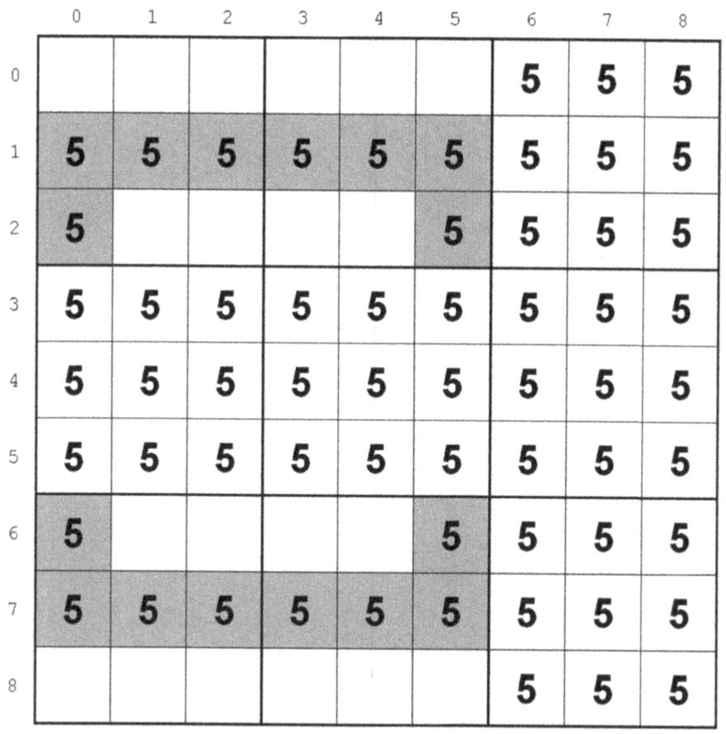

Figure 2-14. *A full rectangle*

Figure 2-15 is almost identical to Figure 2-13. I only moved the candidate from (6,0) to (6,1), but the candidate for 5 in (7,0) can still be removed although (6,1) is inside the rectangle. There is a difference, though: the candidate in (1,0) can no longer be removed.

	0	1	2	3	4	5	6	7	8
0									
1	5	5			5				
2	5					5			
3									
4									
5									
6		5				5			
7	5	5			5				
8									

Figure 2-15. *A not-hollow rectangle*

To complete the section on the rectangle strategy, I would like to show you that there are some cases in which a candidate can be outside the rectangle without invalidating the strategy, as shown in Figure 2-16.

The candidate in `(7,1)` can be removed although there are nine candidates outside the rectangle: `(0,1)`, `(0,5)`, `(6,0)`, `(6,5)`, `(7,0)`, `(8,0)`, `(8,1)`, `(8,2)`, and `(8,5)`.

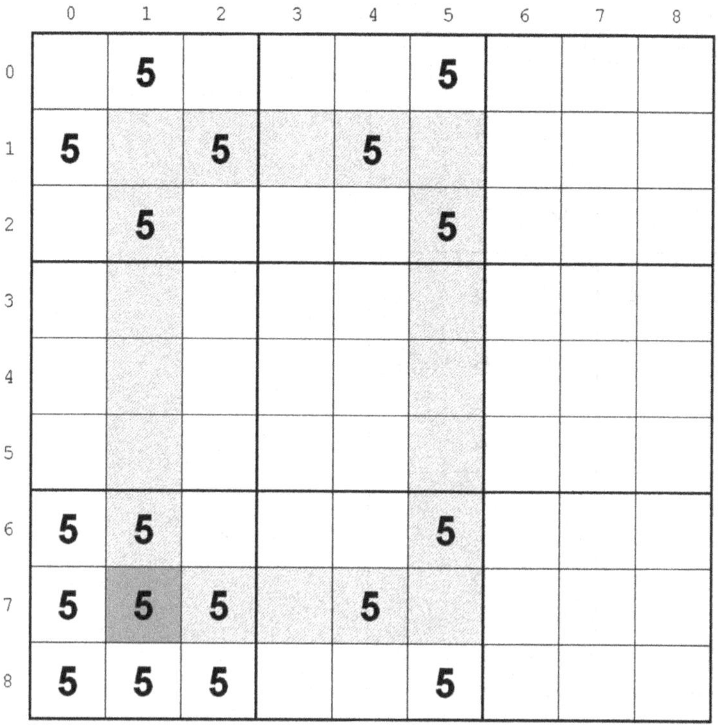

Figure 2-16. *A rectangle with something more*

The Strategies Lines-3 and Lines-4

These two strategies are generalizations of the level 2 strategy lines-2. Lines-3, which is also known as Swordfish, applies to three lines what lines-2 applies to two. If you find all the cells with a particular candidate in the same three rows (or columns) of three columns (or rows), you can remove that candidate from the other cells of those three rows (columns). See Figure 2-17 for an example, this time with rows instead of columns.

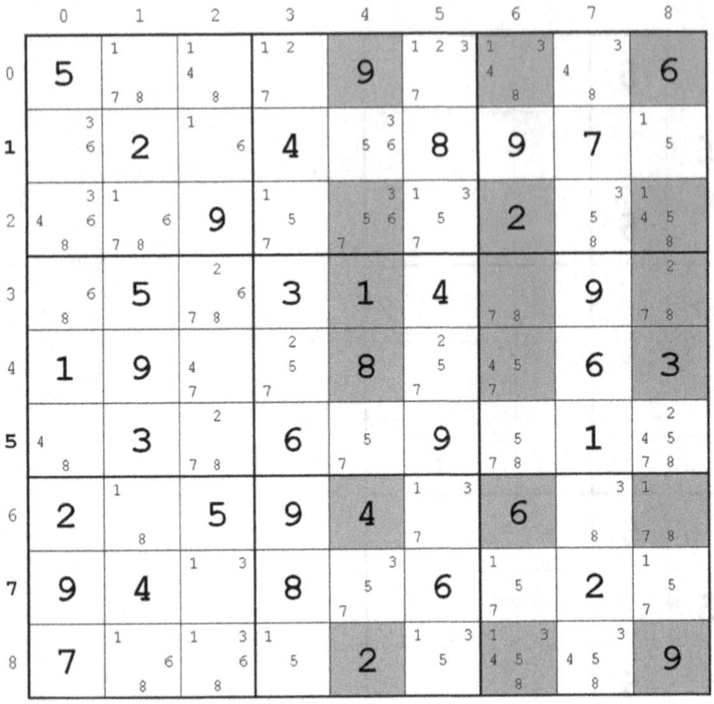

Figure 2-17. Lines-3 (rows)

Notice that in rows 1, 5, and 7 the candidates for 5 are in the three columns 4, 6, and 8. You can examine all possibilities by building a small table in which you list the column IDs of the 5s for each one of the three rows (see Table 2-1, where A, B, C, and D are arbitrary names to identify the possibilities).

Table 2-1. Lines-3 Possibilities

	row 1	row 5	row 7
A	4	6	8
B	4	8	6
C	8	4	6
D	8	6	4

As you can see, regardless of how you choose the columns in which to place the 5s in the three rows (e.g., in case A, you choose to place the 5s in column 4 of row 3, column 6 of row 5, and column 8 of row 7), there is always a 5 in column 4, one in column 6, and one in column 8. How could it be otherwise? You need a 5 in each row and you have exactly three columns to choose from! Notice that in row 1 the 5 can only be in two of the three columns, but that is OK. The important thing is that the 5s of each row are confined to the same three columns. It doesn't matter that one or more of them are missing.

I am going into so much detail because this strategy is not easy to visualize. In any case, as you know that the columns 4, 6, and 8 already have a 5 in one of the rows 1, 5, and 7, you can remove the 5s from all the other cells of columns 4, 6, and 8 (grayed in Figure 2-17) —that is, from (2,4), (2,8), (4,6), and (8,6).

Lines-4 is like lines-2 and lines-3 but with four rows (or columns). If you find four rows (or columns), each with two, three, or four candidates for a particular number and all the candidates are in the same four columns (rows), you can remove the candidates for the same number from all other cells of the same columns (rows).

Level 4 Strategies

There is only one level 4 strategy, and that is *backtrack*. Backtrack is nothing more and nothing less than trial and error, and it is the last resort when everything else fails. It is not so satisfying to resort to random choices and see whether they lead to a solution, but—brace yourself—there are Sudokus that cannot be solved with any combination of the strategies I listed in the previous sections. Perhaps they could be solved with strategies of which I am not aware. If you discover or hear of a strategy that I have not included, I would like to know about it.

What about Coloring?

You might have read about coloring as a strategy for solving Sudokus. But coloring is only a way of making the discovery of chains easier. That's why I haven't introduced it as a separate strategy.

Strategy Selection

The only reason for dividing strategies into levels of complexity is to select them separately when solving a puzzle. As you will see, the Sudoku Solver keeps trying all strategies of one level before attempting any individual strategy of a higher level. That is, it only attempts a strategy of a certain level of complexity when no strategy of a lower level succeeds in removing a single candidate (let alone solving a cell). This ensures that the Solver only attempts more complex strategies when strictly necessary.

Summary

In this chapter, I described the strategies that the Sudoku Solver applies and explained how they work. In Chapter 3, I'll talk about the Solver's main program and general utility functions.

CHAPTER 3

The Solver Program

The main program, sudoku_solver.c, accepts the Sudoku to be solved, performs some checks, solves the Sudoku, and presents the final result. It is the module that binds together all the various functions of the program.

Several of the modules listed in this and following chapters include commented-out pieces of code whose purpose is to display partial or final results of algorithms. If you enable them by removing the enclosing /* and */, they will help you to better understand how the program works and to modify the code if you so wish.

Before talking about the main program itself, you need to study def.h (see Listing 3-1), the header file that contains definitions and declarations used throughout the program.

Listing 3-1. def.h

```
/* def.h
 *
 * Definitions and declarations
 *
 * Copyright (C) 2015  Giulio Zambon  - http://zambon.com.au/
 *
 */
#ifndef DEF
#define DEF

// General definitions
#define FALSE 0
#define TRUE  1

// Definitions for logging
#define LOG_FOOTPRINT
#define LOG_HIDDEN_PAIR
#define LOG_NAKED_QUAD
#define LOG_HIDDEN_TRIPLE
//#define LOG_IN_OUT
#define LOG_LINES
#define LOG_NAKED_PAIR
#define LOG_NAKED_TRIPLE
#define LOG_POINTING_LINE
#define LOG_RECTANGLE
#define LOG_REMOVE_CANDIDATE
#define LOG_BOX_LINE
```

```c
#define LOG_UNIQUE
#define LOG_XY_CHAIN
#define LOG_Y_WING

// Definitions to distinguish between Y-wing and XY-chain when invoking
// pairs_find()
#define DEF_Y_WING  0
#define DEF_XY_CHAIN 1

// Structure and typedef to build chains of cell coordinates.
// It makes possible to develop functions that return lists of cells.
#define MAX_INTER_N 13
typedef struct rc_struct *rc_p_t;
typedef struct rc_struct {
  int row;
  int col;
  rc_p_t next;
  } rc_struct_t;

// Strategy functions
typedef int (*f_ptr_t)(void);
extern f_ptr_t *strat_all[];
extern char **strat_all_names[];
extern int n_strat_all[];
extern int n_levels;

// List of strategies used in a solution
// 0 means 'unique', 40 means 'backtrack'
// Other strategies: (strat level) * 10 + (strat ID within the level)
extern int strats_used[];
extern int n_strats_used;

// Used in some strategies for clarity
#define ROW 0
#define COL 1
#define BOX 2
extern char *unit_names[3];

// Sudoku declarations in sudoku_solver.c
extern char grid[9][9][10];
extern char row[9][9][2];
extern char col[9][9][2];
extern char box[9][9][2];

// Flags
extern int problem_found;
extern int silent;
extern int backtracking;
```

```
// Patch because Windows doesn't recognize srandom() and random()
#ifdef __WIN32__
#define srandom srand
#define random rand
#endif

#endif
```

The first two lines and the last line ensure that multiple inclusions of def.h will not cause any problem:

```
#ifndef DEF
#define DEF
...
#endif
```

This is a mechanism that, to be on the safe side, you should use in all header files: if an identifier matching the name of the header file is undefined, define it and do the rest. Otherwise, do nothing.

The definitions of FALSE and TRUE deserve a couple of comments. The use of symbolic names for *true* and *false* makes for more readable code, but you have to keep in mind that in C the condition (an_integer == TRUE) succeeds only if an_integer is equal to 1, while the condition (an_integer) succeeds when an_integer is not equal to zero. That is, (an_integer == TRUE) and (an_integer == FALSE) are *not* mutually exclusive. If a variable gets corrupted (e.g., because you write outside the boundaries of an array) and an_integer is assigned a value other than 0 or 1, (an_integer == TRUE) fails, while (an_integer != FALSE) succeeds!

I developed the Solver on a Mac. When I tested the code on a PC, I discovered that stdlib.h didn't declare srandom() and random() and that the linker didn't find them in the libraries.

By choosing to use srandom() and random() instead of srand() and rand(), I had made my code not portable to Windows! I decided to stick to my choice because srandom() and random() work better, and add to def.h the following 'patch':

```
#ifdef __WIN32__
#define srandom srand
#define random rand
#endif
```

The definitions for logging allow you to selectively switch out the displaying of messages when some events occur, as in

```
#ifdef LOG_UNIQUE
  if (!silent) {
    printf("unique_unit: %d in (%d,%d) is unique"
          "within the %s\n",
        i, kR, kC, what
        );
  }
#endif
```

In this example, you also see the use of the global variable silent. By setting it to TRUE, you can completely suppress logging. Also, and most important, you can change silent at runtime. It allows you to temporarily suppress logging while doing the initial cleanup of a Sudoku and while backtracking.

Ignore for the moment the definitions associated with pairs_find(). You will learn about them in Chapters 10 and 11, which explain the implementation of the strategies Y-wing and XY-chain.

The definition

```
typedef int (*f_ptr_t)(void);
```

and the declarations

```
extern f_ptr_t *strat_all[];
extern char **strat_all_names[];
extern int n_strat_all[];
extern int n_levels;
```

make it possible to execute sequences of strategies of any particular level of difficulty without having to call them one by one. The Solver initializes the arrays strat_all, strat_all_names, and n_strat_all in the main program (sudoku_solver.c) as follows:

```
// Arrays of strategies
//
// Trivial strategies (level 0)
f_ptr_t strat0[] = {unique_loop};
char *strat0_names[] = {
    "unique-loop"
    };
//
// Easy strategies (level 1)
f_ptr_t strat1[] = {naked_pair, hidden_pair, box_line, pointing_line};
char *strat1_names[] = {
    "naked-pair", "hidden-pair", "box-line", "pointing-line"
    };
//
// Intermediate strategies (level 2)
f_ptr_t strat2[] = {naked_triple, hidden_triple, lines_2,
    naked_quad, y_wing
    };
char *strat2_names[] = {
    "naked-triple", "hidden-triple", "lines-2", "naked-quad", "Y-wing"
    };
//
// Complex strategies (level 3)
f_ptr_t strat3[] = {rectangle, xy_chain, lines_3, lines_4};
char *strat3_names[] = {
    "rectangle", "XY-chain", "lines-3", "lines-4"
    };
//
// All strategies
f_ptr_t *strat_all[] = {
    &strat0[0], &strat1[0], &strat2[0], &strat3[0]
    };
char **strat_all_names[] = {
    &strat0_names[0], &strat1_names[0], &strat2_names[0], &strat3_names[0]
    };
int n_strat_all[] = {
```

```
    sizeof(strat0)/sizeof(f_ptr_t),
    sizeof(strat1)/sizeof(f_ptr_t),
    sizeof(strat2)/sizeof(f_ptr_t),
    sizeof(strat3)/sizeof(f_ptr_t)
    };
int n_levels = N_LEVELS;
```

First, you initialize the group of strategies of a particular level of difficulty, as in the following example for level 1:

```
// Easy strategies (level 1)
f_ptr_t strat1[] = {naked_pair, hidden_pair, box_line, pointing_line};
char *strat1_names[] = {
    "naked-pair", "hidden-pair", "box-line", "pointing-line"
    };
```

Then, you initialize the arrays for all levels.

As all functions that implement strategies have no parameters and return an int value, you can execute all the strategies of a particular level with a simple loop like in the following example, in which k_level is a non-negative number smaller than n_levels:

```
for (int k_strat = 0; k_strat < n_strat_all[k_level]; k_strat++) {
  printf("Executing %s...\n", strat_all_names[k_level][k_strat]);
  int result = strat_all[k_level][k_strat]();
  printf("...%s happened\n", (result)?"something":"nothing");
  }
```

For improved readability of the code, you could also decide to use pointers as in

```
f_ptr_t *strats = strat_all[k_level];
char **strat_names = strat_all_names[k_level];
int n_strat = n_strat_all[level];
for (int k_strat = 0; k_strat < n_strat; k_strat++) {
  printf("Executing %s...\n", strat_names[k_strat]);
  int result = strats[k_strat]();
  printf("...%s happened\n", (result)?"something":"nothing");
  }
```

strats_used and n_strats_used make possible for the Solver to save a list of all strategies it needs to solve a particular Sudoku puzzle. Such summaries of strategy usage are useful when the program solves many puzzles one after the other. (More about this in Chapter 14).

In the remaining statements of def.h, only the declarations of problem_found and backtracking require some explanation, but it would be confusing to explain them here. You will find their description in Chapter 13, concerned with the implementation of backtracking.

Now that you know most of what def.h does, you can look at the main program. Its first part consists of "include" statements, as shown in Listing 3-2.

Listing 3-2. sudoku_solver.c–Part 1: Includes

```
/* sudoku_solver.c
 *
 * Main program.
 *
 * Copyright (C) 2015   Giulio Zambon   - http://zambon.com.au/
 *
 */
#include <stdio.h>
#include <stdlib.h>
#include <string.h>
#include "backtrack.h"
#include "box_line.h"
#include "cleanup.h"
#include "count_candidates.h"
#include "count_solved.h"
#include "def.h"
#include "display.h"
#include "display_strats_in_clear.h"
#include "display_string.h"
#include "hidden_pair.h"
#include "hidden_triple.h"
#include "inconsistent_grid.h"
#include "init.h"
#include "lines_2.h"
#include "lines_3.h"
#include "lines_4.h"
#include "naked_pair.h"
#include "naked_quad.h"
#include "naked_triple.h"
#include "pointing_line.h"
#include "rectangle.h"
#include "solve.h"
#include "unique_loop.h"
#include "xy_chain.h"
#include "y_wing.h"
```

Notice that the includes are in alphabetical order. This is possible because their order is irrelevant. To rely on the order of includes is a very bad programming practice that can only result in disaster!

After the includes, come the definitions of two configuration parameters.

```
//#define USE_FILES
#define N_LEVELS 4  // levels of strategies
```

The Solver looks for the definition of USE_FILES to decide whether to solve multiple puzzles contained in a file or a single one passed to the program via an input argument. In the previous code, the comment before the definition renders it inactive.

Then, the definitions of global variables follow (see Listing 3-3). These are the variables declared in def.h.

Listing 3-3. sudoku_solver.c–Part 2: Global Variables

```c
// Sudoku grid and Sudoku indexing arrays
char grid[9][9][10];
char row[9][9][2];
char col[9][9][2];
char box[9][9][2];

// Unit names used for display in clear
char *unit_names[3] = {"row", "column", "box"};

// Easy strategies (level 1)
f_ptr_t strat1[] = {
    naked_pair, hidden_pair, box_line, pointing_line
    };
char *strat1_names[] = {
    "naked-pair", "hidden-pair", "box-line",
    "pointing-line"
    };
int n_strat1 = sizeof(strat1)/sizeof(f_ptr_t);

// Intermediate strategies (level 2)
f_ptr_t strat2[] = {
    naked_triple, hidden_triple, lines_2,
    naked_quad, y_wing
    };
char *strat2_names[] = {
    "naked-triple", "hidden-triple", "lines-2",
    "naked-quad", "Y-wing", "XY-chain"
    // Warning: appended "XY-chain"
    };
int n_strat2 = sizeof(strat2)/sizeof(f_ptr_t);

// Complex strategies (level 3)
// WARNING: Keep XY-chain in the first position
//          because strategy() depends on it to set
//          strats_used
f_ptr_t strat3[] = {
    xy_chain, rectangle, lines_3, lines_4
    };
char *strat3_names[] = {
    "XY-chain", "rectangle", "lines-3", "lines-4"
    };
int n_strat3 = sizeof(strat3)/sizeof(f_ptr_t);

// List of used strategies (never seen more than 19)
int strats_used[50];
int n_strats_used;

// Global flags, to 'pop out' from nested calls
int problem_found = FALSE;
int silent = FALSE;
```

After that, the executable statements begin, and the Solver follows different paths depending on whether you have defined USE_FILES or not. You achieve this with an ifdef directive to the C preprocessor:

```
int main(int argc, char *argv[]) {

#ifdef USE_FILES
... Code to process multiple puzzles read from file.
... See Chapter 14.
#else
... Code to process a single puzzle obtained from an input argument.
#endif
```

Listing 3-4 shows how the Solver obtains a puzzle definition from an input argument and checks that it is correct.

Listing 3-4. sudoku_solver.c–Part 3: Checks

```
#else

  // Check for the presence of an input Sudoku string
  if (argc < 2) {
    puts("*** You need to provide a sudoku string");
    return EXIT_FAILURE;
    }

  // Check that the Sudoku string is 81-chars long
  if (strlen(argv[1]) != 81) {
    puts("*** The sudoku string must be 81 characters long");
    return EXIT_FAILURE;
    }

  // Check that the Sudoku string consists of digits between 0 and 9
  for (int k = 0; k < 81; k++) {
    if (argv[1][k] < '0' || argv[1][k] > '9') {
      puts("*** The sudoku string must only contain 0 to 9 digits");
      return EXIT_FAILURE;
      }
    }
```

These are not exhaustive and foolproof checks, but they catch some major mistakes that would prevent the program from working.

They ensure that you launch the program with at least one argument, that the string contained in the first argument is 81 characters long (i.e., equal to the number of cells in a Sudoku), and that it consists of digits between 0 and 9 (1 to 9 for the clues and 0 for the empty cells of the puzzle). Obviously, it doesn't mean that the string represents a valid Sudoku puzzle, because not all sequences of digits admit one (and only one) solution, but it is better than no check at all. More about this argument in the section "Input/Output."

The last part of sudoku_solver.c is where you do the interesting work (see Listing 3-5).

Listing 3-5. sudoku_solver.c–Part 4: Solving the Sudoku

```c
// Print the Sudoku string
if (argc > 2) {
  printf("--- \"%s\"\n", argv[2]);
  }
printf("--- \"%s\"\n", argv[1]);

// Initialize the Sudoku arrays
init(argv[1]);
display();

// Remove the impossible numbers with an initial cleanup without
// displaying any logging messages
printf("sudoku: the initial grid contains %d solved cells\n",
    count_solved()
    );
silent = TRUE;
cleanup();
silent = FALSE;
printf("sudoku: after the initial cleanup, the grid"
       " contains %d solved cells\n", count_solved()
       );
display();

// Execute the strategies
solve();

// Backtrack if necessary
if (count_solved() < 81) {
  backtracking = TRUE;
  backtrack(0);
  backtracking = FALSE;
  }

// Check that everything is OK
if (inconsistent_grid()) {
  printf("*** The grid is inconsistent\n");
  }

printf("sudoku: the final grid contains %d solved cells\n ",
       count_solved()
       );
display();
display_string();
prinf("Strategies used %d: ", n_strats_used);
/*
for (int k = 0; k < n_strats_used; k++) {
  printf(" %d", strats_used[k]);
  }
printf("\n");
*/
```

```
  display_strats_in_clear();

#endif

  return EXIT_SUCCESS;
  }
```

sudoku_solver.c does its work by executing four functions, highlighted in bold in Listing 3-5. The following sections describe the first three of them in detail. For the description of the function backtrack() refer to Chapter 13.

init()

This function initializes the Sudoku arrays and fills in the grid with the input Sudoku string (see Listing 3-6).

Listing 3-6. init.c

```
/* init.c
 *
 * Copyright (C) 2015  Giulio Zambon  - http://zambon.com.au/
 *
 */
#include <stdio.h>
#include <stdlib.h>
#include "def.h"
#include "init.h"

void init(char *arg) {
#ifdef LOG_IN_OUT
  printf("--- init >>>\n");
#endif

  // Initialize the sudoku arrays
  for (int k = 0; k < 9; k++) {
    for (int j = 0; j < 9; j++) {
      grid[k][j][0] = 9;
      for (int i = 1; i <= 9; i++) {
        grid[k][j][i] = TRUE;
        }
      row[k][j][0] = k;
      row[k][j][1] = j;
      col[j][k][0] = k;
      col[j][k][1] = j;
      box[k/3*3+j/3][k%3*3+j%3][0] = k;
      box[k/3*3+j/3][k%3*3+j%3][1] = j;
      }
    }
```

```
  // Save the sudoku string into the array
  for (int k = 0; k < 81; k++) {
    int kR = k / 9;
    int kC = k - kR * 9;
    if (arg[k] != '0') {
      for (int i = 1; i <= 9; i++) {
        grid[kR][kC][i] = FALSE;
        }
      grid[kR][kC][arg[k] - '0'] = TRUE;
      grid[kR][kC][0] = 1;
      }
    }

/*
  // Display the allocated numbers
  for (int k = 0; k < 9; k++) {
    for (int j = 0; j < 9; j++) {
      if (grid[k][j][0] == 1) {
        int i = 0;
        do {
          i++;
          } while (grid[k][j][i] == 0);
        printf("%d", i);
        }
      else {
        printf(".");
        }
      }
    printf("\n");
    }
*/
#ifdef LOG_IN_OUT
  printf("<<< init ---\n");
#endif
  }
```

The first set of for-loops is independent of the input string. It sets up the arrays row, col, and box so that they point to the correct cells of the Sudoku grid (i.e., the array grid). At the same time, it also initializes each cell of the grid to contain all nine possible candidates.

The second set of for-loops examines each character of the input string, and when it is non-zero, it sets the corresponding element of the grid to that number.

Straightforward, really.

cleanup()

This function uses the level 0 strategies naked single and cleanup to remove as many candidates as possible from the initial Sudoku. As you can see from Listing 3-7, it simply executes the function cleanup_around() for each cell of the grid.

Listing 3-7. cleanup.c

```
/* cleanup.c
 *
 * Copyright (C) 2015  Giulio Zambon  - http://zambon.com.au/
 *
 */
#include <stdio.h>
#include <stdlib.h>
#include "cleanup.h"
#include "cleanup_around.h"
#include "def.h"

void cleanup() {
#ifdef LOG_IN_OUT
  printf("--- cleanup >>>\n");
#endif
  for (int k = 0; k < 9 && !problem_found; k++) {
    for (int j = 0; j < 9 && !problem_found; j++) {
      if (grid[k][j][0] == 1) cleanup_around(k, j);
      }
    }
#ifdef LOG_IN_OUT
  printf("<<< cleanup ---\n");
#endif
  }
```

Notice that both for-loops are aborted when the variable problem_found is not FALSE. As I already said, I will explain how you use problem_found in Chapter 13.

The function cleanup_around() (see Listing 3-8) executes the function cleanup_unit() for the row, column, and box containing the specified cell.

Listing 3-8. cleanup_around.c

```
/* cleanup_around.c
 *
 * Copyright (C) 2015  Giulio Zambon  - http://zambon.com.au/
 *
 */
#include <stdio.h>
#include <stdlib.h>
#include "cleanup_around.h"
#include "cleanup_unit.h"
#include "def.h"
```

```
void cleanup_around(int k, int j) {
#ifdef LOG_IN_OUT
  printf("--- cleanup_around (%d,%d) >>>\n", k, j);
#endif
  cleanup_unit("row", k, j, row[k]);
  if (!problem_found) cleanup_unit("column", k, j, col[j]);
  if (!problem_found) cleanup_unit("box", k, j, box[k/3*3+j/3]);
#ifdef LOG_IN_OUT
  printf("<<< cleanup_around (%d,%d) ---\n", k, j);
#endif
  }
```

You now have to look at cleanup_unit() (see Listing 3-9).

Listing 3-9. cleanup_unit.c

```
/* cleanup_unit.c
 *
 * Copyright (C) 2015  Giulio Zambon  - http://zambon.com.au/
 *
 */
#include <stdio.h>
#include <stdlib.h>
#include "cleanup_around.h"
#include "cleanup_unit.h"
#include "def.h"
#include "remove_candidate.h"

void cleanup_unit(char *what, int kElem, int jElem, char unit[9][2]) {
#ifdef LOG_IN_OUT
  printf("--- cleanup_unit (%s) for (%d,%d) >>>\n", what, kElem, jElem);
#endif
  char *elem = grid[kElem][jElem];
  if (elem[0] == 1) {
    int i = 0;
    do { i++; } while (elem[i] == FALSE);
    for (int j1 = 0; j1 < 9 && !problem_found; j1++) {
      int kR = unit[j1][ROW];
      int kC = unit[j1][COL];
      if ((kR != kElem || kC != jElem) &&
          grid[kR][kC][i] != FALSE
          ) {
        char mess[40];
        sprintf(mess, "cleanup_unit [%s of (%d,%d)]",
                what, kElem, jElem
                );
        remove_candidate(mess, i, kR, kC);
        if (grid[kR][kC][0] == 1 && !problem_found) {
          cleanup_around(kR, kC);
          }
        }
      }
    }
```

```
      }
#ifdef LOG_IN_OUT
  printf("<<< cleanup_unit (%s) for (%d,%d) ---\n", what, kElem, jElem);
#endif
      }
```

If cleanup_unit() finds that the cell with coordinates (kElem, jElem) is solved (i.e., elem[0] == 1), it removes from the given unit all the candidates for the number i that solve the cell. It does so by executing the function remove_candidate(). The bit highlighted in bold is worth examining in more detail: if removing a candidate from the cell (kR, kC) leaves the cell with a single candidate, the function executes cleanup_around() for that cell. This is how it applies the strategy naked single, but the interesting bit is that cleanup_around(), as you have seen, executes cleanup_unit(). It means that cleanup_unit() executes itself recursively through cleanup_around().

You can only execute a function recursively if there is a well-defined termination condition, to ensure that the recursion doesn't continue forever (i.e., until the stack overflows and the program crashes). This is certainly true in the Solver's case, because you only execute cleanup_around() recursively when you solve a cell, and there are only 81 cells in a puzzle.

remove_candidate() is straightforward (see Listing 3-10).

Listing 3-10. remove_candidate.c

```
/* remove_candidate.c
 *
 * Copyright (C) 2015  Giulio Zambon  - http://zambon.com.au/
 *
 */
#include <stdio.h>
#include <stdlib.h>
#include "def.h"
#include "remove_candidate.h"

void remove_candidate(*caller, int i, int k, int j) {
  grid[k][j][i] = FALSE;
  grid[k][j][0]--;
#ifdef LOG_REMOVE_CANDIDATE
  if (!silent) {
    printf("%s: removed %d from (%d,%d)\n", caller, i, k, j);
    }
#endif
  if (grid[k][j][0] < 1) {
    if (!silent) {
      printf("*** No candidates left in (%d,%d)\n", k, j);
      }
    problem_found = TRUE;
    }
  }
```

The statements highlighted in bold are the key ones: the first one sets the ith digit of the cell (k, j) to FALSE, and the second one decrements the counter of candidates. Notice that remove_candidate() doesn't check whether i is indeed a candidate present in (k, j). You must do it before executing the function. The execution of remove_candidate() for a candidate that is not present in the specified cell would cause an erroneous decrement of the counter of candidates of the cell (i.e., grid[k][j][0]), with catastrophic results.

solve()

The function solve() keeps executing strategy functions until all 81 cells are solved or until two successive executions of the strategies are unable to remove a single candidate (see Listing 3-11).

Listing 3-11. solve.c

```
/* solve.c
 *
 * Copyright (C) 2015  Giulio Zambon  - http://zambon.com.au/
 *
 */
#include <stdio.h>
#include <stdlib.h>
#include <string.h>
#include "count_candidates.h"
#include "def.h"
#include "display.h"
#include "display_string.h"
#include "execute_strategies.h"
#include "keep_going.h"
#include "solve.h"

void solve() {
#ifdef LOG_IN_OUT
  printf("--- solve >>>\n");
#endif
  if (!backtracking) n_strats_used = 0;
  int n_candidates = count_candidates();
  int n_candidates_old = n_candidates + 1;

  while (keep_going()  &&  n_candidates < n_candidates_old) {
    n_candidates_old = n_candidates;
    if (keep_going()  &&  !execute_strategies(0)) {
      if (keep_going()  &&  !execute_strategies(1)) {
        if (keep_going()  &&  !execute_strategies(2)) {
          execute_strategies(3);
          }
        }
      }
    n_candidates = count_candidates();
    }
#ifdef LOG_IN_OUT
  printf("<<< solve ---\n");
#endif
  }
```

keep_going() is a one-line function defined to improve readability (see Listing 3-12).

Listing 3-12. keep_going.c

```
/* keep_going.c
 *
 * Copyright (C) 2015  Giulio Zambon  - http://zambon.com.au/
 *
 */
#include <stdio.h>
#include <stdlib.h>
#include "count_solved.h"
#include "def.h"

int keep_going(void) {
  return (count_solved() < 81  &&  !problem_found);
  }
```

Therefore, the main loop continues executing as long as some cells are still unsolved, the puzzle remains consistent, and the previous loop execution has removed at least one candidate.

The core of solve() is in the four lines highlighted in bold (note that the braces are syntactically unnecessary and are only present to make the code more readable). Each line contains the execution of execute_strategies() (see Listing 3-13) for increasing levels of difficulty, from 0 to 3.

But, because execute_strategies() only returns TRUE if a strategy has removed at least one candidate, solve() only tries more difficult strategies when the easier ones have had no effect at all. For example, if execute_strategies(1) returns TRUE, it means that one of the level 1 strategies has succeeded in removing at least one candidate. Then, the condition of the third if fails, and solve(), instead of proceeding with execute_strategies(2), updates n_candidates and starts a new loop iteration with level 0 strategies. If execute_strategies(1) returns FALSE, it means that no level 1 strategy has managed to remove any candidate, and solve() tries level 2 strategies by invoking execute_strategies(2) within the condition of the if that follows.

Listing 3-13. execute_strategies.c

```
/* execute_strategies.c
 *
 * Copyright (C) 2015  Giulio Zambon  - http://zambon.com.au/
 *
 */
#include <stdio.h>
#include <stdlib.h>
#include "count_candidates.h"
#include "count_solved.h"
#include "def.h"
#include "display.h"
#include "display_string.h"
#include "execute_strategies.h"
#include "keep_going.h"
#include "unique_loop.h"

/*
 * It returns TRUE when at least one candidate is removed.
 *
 * It goes through all the strategies of the level, but only as long as no
```

```
 * candidate is removed.  When that happens, it aborts the loop and returns.
 */
int execute_strategies(int level) {
#ifdef LOG_IN_OUT
  printf("--- execute_strategies >>>\n");
#endif
  f_ptr_t *strats = strat_all[level];
  char **strat_names = strat_all_names[level];
  int n_strat = n_strat_all[level];
  int n_candidates = count_candidates();
  int n_candidates_initial = n_candidates;
  for (   int k = 0;
          k < n_strat && keep_going()  && n_candidates == n_candidates_initial;
          k++
          ) {
    (void)strats[k]();
    n_candidates = count_candidates();
    if (n_candidates < n_candidates_initial) {
      if (!backtracking) {
        strats_used[n_strats_used] = level * 10 + k;
        n_strats_used++;
        }
      if (!silent) {
        printf("strategy: after '%s' the grid contains "
            "%d solved cells\n\n", strat_names[k], count_solved()
            );
        }
      if (!silent) { display(); display_string(); }
      }
    }
#ifdef LOG_IN_OUT
  printf("<<< execute_strategies ---\n");
#endif
  return (n_candidates < n_candidates_initial);
  }
```

To guarantee that the program solves a puzzle with the simplest possible strategies, the while-loop in solve() must restart from level 0 strategies whenever any strategy removes at least one candidate. To see how this happens, look at the for-loop in execute_strategies() (see Listing 3-13) and in particular to the end condition highlighted in bold: the loop terminates as soon as a strategy causes the number of candidates to decrease. The decrease of the number of candidates also causes the function to return TRUE, which, as you have already seen, forces the while-loop in solve() to restart from level 0 strategies.

If no strategy of the given level removes candidates, the for-loop runs to completion and execute_strategies() returns FALSE, thereby forcing solve() to attempt more difficult strategies until it reaches level 3.

Counting

In the previous sections, you have already seen that there are two counting functions: count_solved() (see Listing 3-14) and count_candidates() (see Listing 3-15). Their names say it all.

Listing 3-14. count_solved.c

```c
/* count_solved.c
 *
 * Copyright (C) 2015  Giulio Zambon  - http://zambon.com.au/
 *
 */
#include <stdio.h>
#include <stdlib.h>
#include "count_solved.h"
#include "def.h"

int count_solved() {
#ifdef LOG_IN_OUT
  printf("--- count_solved >>>\n");
#endif
  int result = 0;
  for (int k = 0; k < 9; k++) {
    for (int j = 0; j < 9; j++) {
      if (grid[k][j][0] == 1) result++;
      }
    }
#ifdef LOG_IN_OUT
  printf("<<< count_solved ---\n");
#endif
  return result;
  }
```

Listing 3-15. count_candidates.c

```c
/* count_candidates.c
 *
 * Copyright (C) 2015  Giulio Zambon  - http://zambon.com.au/
 *
 */
#include <stdio.h>
#include <stdlib.h>
#include "def.h"

int count_candidates() {
#ifdef LOG_IN_OUT
  printf("--- count_candidates >>>\n");
#endif
  int result = 0;
  for (int k = 0; k < 9; k++) {
    for (int j = 0; j < 9; j++) {
      result += grid[k][j][0];
      }
    }
```

```
#ifdef LOG_IN_OUT
  printf("<<< count_candidates ---\n");
#endif
  return result;
  }
```

As you can see, the only difference between count_solved() and count_candidates() is that count_solved() adds 1 for each cell that has a single candidate, while count_candidates() adds up the counter of candidates of all cells. You could have written a single function and used an argument to choose between the two statements, as in the following:

```
int count(int what) { // what: 0 for counting solved, otherwise counting candidates
  int result = 0;
  for (int k = 0; k < 9; k++) {
    for (int j = 0; j < 9; j++) {
      if (what) result += grid[k][j][0];      // count candidates
      else if (grid[k][j][0] == 1) result++; // count solved
      }
    }
  return result;
  }
```

The only advantage of having two separate functions is that you are more likely to avoid confusion and can more easily insert printf()s for debugging purposes. Not a big deal either way.

Checking Consistency

You probably noticed in Listing 3-5 the invocation of inconsistent_grid(). This function (see Listings 3-16 and 3-17) ensures that the grid does not contain empty cells (i.e., without candidates at all) or units with more than one cell solved by the same number (e.g., two 7s in the same row).

Listing 3-16. inconsistent_grid.c

```
/* inconsistent_grid.c
 *
 * Copyright (C) 2015  Giulio Zambon  - http://zambon.com.au/
 *
 */
#include <stdio.h>
#include <stdlib.h>
#include "def.h"
#include "inconsistent_grid.h"
#include "inconsistent_unit.h"

int inconsistent_grid() {
  int result = FALSE;
  for (int k = 0; k < 9 && !result; k++) {
    result |= inconsistent_unit("row", k, row[k]);
    if (!result) {
      result |= inconsistent_unit("column", k,
                                  col[k]
                                 );
```

```
      if (!result) {
        result |= inconsistent_unit("box", k, box[k]);
        }
      }
    } // for (int k..
  return result;
  }
```

inconsistent_grid() executes inconsistent_unit() for every row, column, and box of the Sudoku, and aborts the execution immediately if one of the units is inconsistent.

Listing 3-17. inconsistent_unit.c

```c
/* inconsistent_unit.c
 *
 * Copyright (C) 2015  Giulio Zambon  - http://zambon.com.au/
 *
 */
#include <stdio.h>
#include <stdlib.h>
#include "def.h"
#include "inconsistent_unit.h"

int inconsistent_unit(char *what, int kG, char unit[9][2]) {
  int result = FALSE;
  int i_vect[10] = {0};
  for (int k = 0; k < 9 && !result; k++) {
    int kR = unit[k][ROW];
    int kC = unit[k][COL];
    char *elem = grid[kR][kC];
    if (elem[0] < 1) {   // we have an empty cell
      result = TRUE;
      if (!silent) {
        printf("*** (%d,%d) has %d candidates\n", kR, kC, elem[0]);
        }
      } // if (elem[0]..
    else if (elem[0] == 1) {
      int i = 0;
      do { i++; } while (!elem[i]);
      if (i_vect[i] == FALSE) {
        i_vect[i] = TRUE;
        }
      else {   // we have a duplicate solution
        result = TRUE;
        if (!silent) {
          printf("*** More than a single %d solution in %s %d\n", i, what, kG);
          }
```

```
        } // else..
      } // else if (elem[0]..
    } // for (int k..
  problem_found = result;
  return result;
}
```

Input/Output

You have become used to interacting with computer programs via smart dialog boxes and flashy graphics. In fact, the graphical user interface (GUI) is what drives the specification and a large portion of the design of most applications. But a program to solve and generate Sudoku puzzles is a different type of program, because it doesn't require much interaction with the user. In particular, the Solver program only needs one input: the initial Sudoku. And as outputs, it only needs to list what candidates it eliminates and why, followed by a display of the solved puzzle.

You are interested in solving Sudokus, not in fancy graphics. Aren't you?

Therefore, the Solver accepts a puzzle as a string of 81 characters, representing the contents of the cells scanned from left to right and from top to bottom, with empty cells represented by zeroes. For example, you would input the partially solved Sudoku of Figure 1-2 with the following string:

409701003005400200060503040078614900000095840095437218601384002004210030889023501 4

To provide a Sudoku to be solved in the form of a string of characters might seem awkward, but it is in fact more convenient than having a fancy input interface that forces you to fill in a Sudoku grid by hand. Typing a command-line directive often is much more efficient than clicking on dialog buttons.

The information the program generates also has a very simple format. The program sends one or two lines of text to the standard output every time something happens (i.e., when the application of a strategy results in solving a cell or removing candidates). It also shows the current state of the puzzle it is solving. Not with graphics but with ASCII characters. For example, the program would display the puzzle of Figure 1-2 as shown in Figure 3-1.

```
         0    1    2    3    4    5    6    7    8
    ++===+===+===++===+===+===++===+===+===++
    ||   | 2 |   ||   | 2 |   ||   |   |   ||
  0 || (4) |   | (9)|| (7) |  6| (1)|| 56| 56| (3)||
    ||   | 8 |   ||   | 8 |   || 8 |   |   ||
    ++---+---+---++---+---+---++---+---+---++
    ||1 3|  3|   ||   |   |   ||   |   |1  ||
  1 ||   |   | (5)|| (4)|  6|  6|| (2)|  6|   ||
    ||7  | 8 |   ||   | 89|  9||   |7 9|7 9||
    ++---+---+---++---+---+---++---+---+---++
    ||12 |   |1  ||   | 2 |   ||   | (4)|1  ||
  2 ||   | (6)|   || (5)|   | (3)||   | (4)|   ||
    ||7  |   |7  ||   | 89|   ||78 |   |7 9||
    ++===+===+===++===+===+===++===+===+===++
    || 23|   |   ||   |   |   ||   | 3 | 2 ||
  3 ||   | (7)| (8)|| (6)| (1)| (4)|| (9)| 5 | 5 ||
    ||   |   |   ||   |   |   ||   |   |   ||
    ++---+---+---++---+---+---++---+---+---++
    ||123| 23|1  ||   |   |   ||   | 3 | 2 ||
  4 ||  6|   |  6|| (9)| (5)| (8)|| (4)|   |   ||
    ||   |   |   ||   |   |   ||   |7  |7  ||
    ++---+---+---++---+---+---++---+---+---++
    ||   |   |   ||   |   |   ||   |   |   ||
  5 || (9)| (5)| (4)|| (3)| (7)| (2)|| (1)| (8)| (6)||
    ||   |   |   ||   |   |   ||   |   |   ||
    ++===+===+===++===+===+===++===+===+===++
    ||   |   |   ||   |   |   ||   |   |   ||
  6 || 56| (1)| (3)|| (8)| (4)|  6|| 56| (2)| 5 ||
    ||7  |   |   ||   |   |7 9||7  |   |7 9||
    ++---+---+---++---+---+---++---+---+---++
    ||   |   |   ||   |   |   ||   |   |   ||
  7 || 56| (4)| (2)|| (1)|  6|  6|| (3)| 56| (8)||
    ||7  |   |   ||   | 9|7 9||   |7 9|   ||
    ++---+---+---++---+---+---++---+---+---++
    ||   |   |   ||   |   |   ||   |   |   ||
  8 || (8)| (9)|  6|| (2)| (3)| (5)||  6| (1)| (4)||
    ||   |   |7  ||   |   |   ||7  |   |   ||
    ++===+===+===++===+===+===++===+===+===++
```

Figure 3-1. Sudoku display

The solved digits are highlighted by round brackets and placed in the middle of their cells. See Listing 3-18 for the full code of the function that does the display.

Listing 3-18. display.c

```c
/* display.c
 *
 * Copyright (C) 2015  Giulio Zambon  - http://zambon.com.au/
 *
 */
#include <stdio.h>
#include <stdlib.h>
```

```
#include "def.h"
#include "display.h"

void display() {
  char *h =
        "  ++---+---+---++---+---+---++---+---+---++";
  char *hh =
        "  ++===+===+===++===+===+===++===+===+===++";
  int jBase[] = {2, 6, 10, 15, 19, 23, 28, 32, 36};
  printf(
        "    0   1   2   3   4   5   6   7   8\n"
      );
  for (int k = 0; k < 9; k++) {
    if (k%3 == 0) {
      printf("%s\n", hh);
      }
    else {
      printf("%s\n", h);
      }
    //        000 000 111  111 122 222  223 333 333
    //        234 678 012  567 901 345  890 234 678
    char top[42] =
          "||   |   |   ||   |   |   ||   |   |   ||";
    char mid[42] =
          "||   |   |   ||   |   |   ||   |   |   ||";
    char bot[42] =
          "||   |   |   ||   |   |   ||   |   |   ||";
    char *displ[42] = {top, mid, bot};
    for (int j = 0; j < 9; j++) {
      if (grid[k][j][0] == 1) {
        int i = 0;
        do { i++; } while (grid[k][j][i] == 0);
        mid[jBase[j]] = '(';
        mid[jBase[j]+1] = '0'+i;
        mid[jBase[j]+2] = ')';
        }
      else {
        for (int i = 0; i < 9; i++) {
          if (grid[k][j][i+1] != 0) {
            displ[i/3][jBase[j] + i%3] = '0' + (i+1);
            }
          } // for (int i..
        } // else..
      } // for (int j..
    printf("  %s\n", displ[0]);
    printf("%d %s\n", k, displ[1]);
    printf("  %s\n", displ[2]);
    }
  printf("%s\n", hh);
  }
```

For each row of the grid, display() prepares three character arrays (top, mid, and bot) and then fills them in with the candidates. The tricky bit is to make the line offsets defined in jBase point to the sequences of empty spaces in top/mid/bot. To make sense of it, refer to the offsets of the empty spaces listed as comments above the character arrays.

Notice that some closed braces are followed by a comment indicating what block they are closing. This is a practice that makes the source code easier to read when you nest more than a couple of block statements and/or the open and close braces are at a certain distance from each other. Software development environments have made it almost redundant, because they highlight for you the open brace that corresponds to the closed brace you click on (and vice versa), but the little comments are still useful when reading a listing, especially when you print it out.

Finally, the program can display a Sudoku puzzle as a string of 81 characters, via the function display_string() (see Listing 3-19).

Listing 3-19. display_string.c

```c
/* display_string.c
 *
 * Copyright (C) 2015  Giulio Zambon  - http://zambon.com.au/
 *
 */
#include <stdio.h>
#include <stdlib.h>
#include "def.h"
#include "display_string.h"

void display_string() {
  printf("****** ");
  for (int k = 0; k < 9; k++) {
    for (int j = 0; j < 9; j++) {
      char *elem = grid[k][j];
      if (elem[0] > 1) {
        printf("0");
        }
      else {
        int i = 0;
        do { i++; } while (!elem[i]);
        printf("%d", i);
        }
      }
    }
  printf("\n");
  }
```

Summary

In this chapter, I have explained the main program of the Sudoku Solver, together with its utility functions to initialize the Sudoku arrays, solve the puzzle, and display information. The next chapter is the first one of a series of chapters dedicated to the implementation of the solving strategies. First up: the level 0 unique strategy.

CHAPTER 4

■ ■ ■

Implementing "Unique"

The "unique" strategy looks for candidates that are unique within a unit. This happens when all other candidates for the same number are removed from the unit (see Figure 4-1).

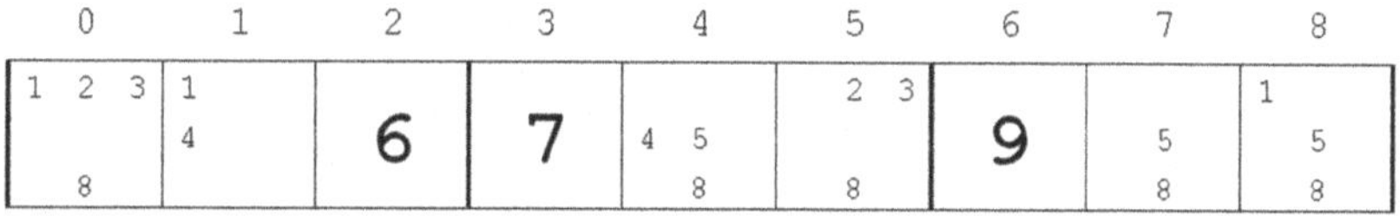

Figure 4-1. *"Unique" within a row*

If Solver, while applying another strategy, happens to remove the candidates for 5 from cells 7 and 8 of Figure 4-1, the 5 in cell 4 becomes unique within the row and, as a result, the candidates for 4 and 8 in cell 4 can be removed.

To be consistent, the name of this strategy should have been hidden single, but I started with the name unique and then couldn't bring myself to rename all the modules and the references to the strategy. It doesn't really matter, though.

To implement the strategy, you need three functions that call each other: unique_loop(), unique(), and unique_unit(). The following sections go through them beginning with the innermost function.

unique_unit()

This is where the whole work is done. It checks for unique candidates within a unit (see Listing 4-1).

Listing 4-1. unique_unit.c

```
/* unique_unit.c
 *
 * Copyright (C) 2015  Giulio Zambon  - http://zambon.com.au/
 *
 */
#include <stdio.h>
#include <stdlib.h>
#include "cleanup_around.h"
#include "def.h"
#include "remove_candidate.h"
#include "unique_unit.h"
```

```c
int unique_unit(char *what, char unit[9][2]) {
#ifdef LOG_IN_OUT
  printf("--- unique_unit (%s) >>>\n", what);
#endif
  int result = FALSE;
  int r[10];
          for (int i = 0; i < 10; i++) { r[i] = -1; }
  int c[10];
  for (int j1 = 0; j1 < 9; j1++) {
    int kR = unit[j1][0];
    int kC = unit[j1][1];
    char *elem = grid[kR][kC];
    if (elem[0] > 1) {
      for (int i = 1; i <= 9; i++) {
        if (elem[i] != FALSE) {
          if (r[i] == -1) {
            r[i] = kR;
            c[i] = kC;
            }
          else {
            r[i] = -2;
            }
          } // if (elem[i]..
        } // for (int i..
      } // if (elem[0]..
    } // for (int j1..

  for (int i = 1; i <= 9 && !problem_found; i++) {
    if (r[i] >= 0) {
      result = TRUE;
      int kR = r[i];
      int kC = c[i];
#ifdef LOG_UNIQUE
      if (!silent) {
        printf("unique_unit: %d in (%d,%d) is unique"
               " within the %s\n", i, kR, kC, what
               );
        }
#endif
      char *elem = grid[kR][kC];
      for (int ii = 1;
           ii <= 9 && !problem_found;
           ii++
           ) {
        if (elem[ii] != FALSE && i != ii) {
          remove_candidate("unique_unit", ii, kR, kC);
          }
        }
      if (!problem_found) cleanup_around(kR, kC);
      } // if (r[i]..
    } // for int i..
```

```
#ifdef LOG_IN_OUT
  printf("<<< unique_unit (%s) ---\n", what);
#endif
  return result;
  }
```

To find unique candidates, unique_unit() relies on two vectors (i.e., one-dimensional arrays): r is used to store row IDs, and c to store column IDs. Each vector contains ten elements, and the elements of the r vector are initially set to -1. In a first pass, unique_unit() goes through the cells of the unit and stores into the two vectors the coordinates of the first candidate of each number—that is, the first candidate it encounters. For example, suppose that unique_unit() is processing the box shown in Figure 4-2.

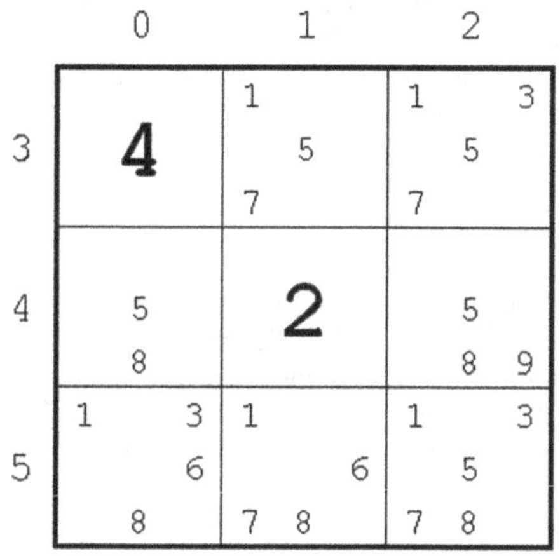

Figure 4-2. *"Unique" within a box*

To build up the r and c vectors, after skipping (3,0) because it is already solved and checking that the relevant elements of the r vector contain the value -1, unique_unit() processes (3,1) by doing the following:

```
r[1] = 3;
c[1] = 1;
r[5] = 3;
c[5] = 1;
r[7] = 3;
c[7] = 1;
```

unique_unit() then processes (3,2). Before saving the row and column IDs of the candidate for 1, it checks the values stored in r[1] and discovers that it is *not* set to -1. This means that the candidate for 1 in (3,2) is not the first one encountered in the scan. It cannot therefore be unique within the unit. unique_unit() therefore sets r[1] to -2 and proceeds to the next candidate of (3,2), which is a 3. After completing the processing of (3,2), the two vectors r and c look as follows:

```
     0    1    2    3    4    5    6    7    8    9
r:  -1   -2   -1    3   -1   -2   -1   -2   -1   -1
c:  -1    1   -1    2   -1    1   -1    1   -1   -1
```

unique_unit() then checks (4,0), skips (4,1) and checks (4,2), (5,0), (5,1), and (5,2). At the end of the checks, r and c look as follows:

```
    0    1    2    3    4    5    6    7    8    9
r: -1   -2   -1   -2   -1   -2   -2   -2   -2    4
c: -1    1   -1    2   -1    1    0    1    0    2
```

Element 0 was never meant to be set, because the Sudoku numbers are 1 to 9, and has remained untouched. It is only there to avoid having to subtract 1 when indexing the numbers 1 to 9. Elements 2 and 4 have also remained set to their initialization values of -1, because the corresponding numbers were already solved before executing unique_unit(). The row IDs of 1, 3, 5, 6, 7, and 8 were set to -2 when unique_unit() found further candidates after the first one. The corresponding column IDs were set when the first candidate was found and not changed after that. Only the element of r for the number 9 is set to a non-negative value. This is because the 9 of cell (4,2) is indeed unique within the unit.

unique_unit() in the for-loop with control variable i goes through the r vector as you have just done, and removes the candidates for 5 and 8 from (4,2).

unique()

This function (see Listing 4-2) executes unique_unit() for each row, column, and box of the whole Sudoku. As you saw in Chapter 3, the Solver restarts from level 0 strategies as soon as the application of any strategy of any higher level of difficulty removes (or solves) one (or more) candidates. But unique is a level 0 strategy. Therefore, Solver keeps attempting it as long as it produces a result. That's why unique() applies unique_unit() to all 27 possible units (9 rows, 9 columns, and 9 boxes) and, as you will see shortly, unique_loop() keeps doing it as long as unique numbers exist.

Listing 4-2. unique.c

```c
/* unique.c
 *
 * Copyright (C) 2015  Giulio Zambon  - http://zambon.com.au/
 *
 */
#include <stdio.h>
#include <stdlib.h>
#include "def.h"
#include "unique.h"
#include "unique_unit.h"

int unique() {
#ifdef LOG_IN_OUT
  printf("--- unique >>>\n");
#endif
  int result = FALSE;
  for (int k = 0; k < 9; k++) {
    result |= unique_unit("row", row[k]);
    result |= unique_unit("column", col[k]);
    result |= unique_unit("box", box[k]);
    }
```

```
#ifdef LOG_IN_OUT
  printf("<<< unique ---\n");
#endif
  return result;
  }
```

unique_loop()

This function (see Listing 4-3) keeps executing unique() as long as it succeeds in removing candidates.

Listing 4-3. unique_loop()

```
/* unique_loop.c
 *
 * Copyright (C) 2015  Giulio Zambon  - http://zambon.com.au/
 *
 */
#include <stdio.h>
#include <stdlib.h>
#include "def.h"
#include "unique.h"
#include "unique_loop.h"

int unique_loop() {
#ifdef LOG_IN_OUT
  printf("--- unique_loop >>>\n");
#endif
  int found;
  int something = FALSE;
  do {
    found = unique();
    something |= found;
    } while (found && !problem_found);
#ifdef LOG_IN_OUT
  printf("<<< unique_loop ---\n");
#endif
  return something;
  }
```

Summary

In this chapter, you have learned how to implement the level 0 unique strategy. In the next chapter, I explain how to implement the "naked" strategies: "naked pair" at difficulty level 1 and "naked triple" and "naked quad" at level 2.

CHAPTER 5

Implementing "Naked" Strategies

The three naked strategies, naked pair, naked triple, and naked quad, work on the same general principle: unit by unit, first make a list of all the cells containing naked multiples (i.e., pairs, triples, or quads), and then process the multiples that appear the correct number of times within the unit. If it sounds confusing, read on and it will become clear.

To avoid repeated explanations, let's start by saying that the implementation of each naked strategy consists of two functions, one applying the strategy to a specific unit and one executing the unit function for each unit (i.e., row, column, and box) of the Sudoku. You have already encountered this structure in Chapter 4, and will find it again on several occasions. If you look at the three general functions (Listings 5-1, 5-2, and 5-3), you will see that they are conceptually identical.

Listing 5-1. naked_pair.c

```
/* naked_pair.c
 *
 * Copyright (C) 2015  Giulio Zambon  - http://zambon.com.au/
 *
 */
#include <stdio.h>
#include <stdlib.h>
#include "def.h"
#include "naked_pair.h"
#include "naked_pair_unit.h"

int naked_pair() {
#ifdef LOG_IN_OUT
  printf("--- naked_pair >>>\n");
#endif
  int result = FALSE;
  for (int k = 0; k < 9  &&  !result; k++) {
    if (   naked_pair_unit("row", row[k])
        || naked_pair_unit("column", col[k])
        || naked_pair_unit("box", box[k])
        ) {
      result = TRUE;
      }
    }
```

```
#ifdef LOG_IN_OUT
  printf("<<< naked_pair ---\n");
#endif
  return result;
  }
```

Listing 5-2. naked_triple.c

```
/* naked_triple.c
 *
 * Copyright (C) 2015  Giulio Zambon  - http://zambon.com.au/
 *
 */
#include <stdio.h>
#include <stdlib.h>
#include "def.h"
#include "naked_triple.h"
#include "naked_triple_unit.h"

int naked_triple() {
#ifdef LOG_IN_OUT
  printf("--- naked_triple >>>\n");
#endif
  int result = FALSE;
  for (int k = 0; k < 9  &&  !result; k++) {
    if (   naked_triple_unit("row", row[k])
        || naked_triple_unit("column", col[k])
        || naked_triple_unit("box", box[k])
        ) {
      result = TRUE;
      }
    }
#ifdef LOG_IN_OUT
  printf("<<< naked_triple ---\n");
#endif
  return result;
  }
```

Listing 5-3. naked_quad.c

```
/* naked_quad.c
 *
 * Copyright (C) 2015  Giulio Zambon  - http://zambon.com.au/
 *
 */
#include <stdio.h>
#include <stdlib.h>
#include "def.h"
#include "naked_quad.h"
#include "naked_quad_unit.h"
```

```c
int naked_quad() {
#ifdef LOG_IN_OUT
  printf("--- naked_quad >>>\n");
#endif
  int result = FALSE;
  for (int k = 0; k < 9  &&  !result; k++) {
    if (  naked_quad_unit("row", row[k])
        || naked_quad_unit("column", col[k])
        || naked_quad_unit("box", box[k])
        ) {
      result = TRUE;
      }
    }
#ifdef LOG_IN_OUT
  printf("<<< naked_quad ---\n");
#endif
  return result;
  }
```

You could create a single function executing the appropriate unit function, as shown in Listing 5-4 (warning: it was never tested and the C module is not included in the sources attached to this book).

Listing 5-4. naked.c (Not Tested)

```c
/* naked.c
 *
 * Copyright (C) 2015  Giulio Zambon  - http://zambon.com.au/
 *
 */
#include <stdio.h>
#include <stdlib.h>
#include "def.h"
#include "naked.h"
#include "naked_pair_unit.h"
#include "naked_triple_unit.h"
#include "naked_quad_unit.h"

int naked(int multiplicity) {
#ifdef LOG_IN_OUT
  printf("--- naked(%d) >>>\n", multiplicity);
#endif
  typedef int (*naked_f_ptr_t)(char*, char[9][2]);
  naked_f_ptr_t naked_all[] = {
      NULL,
      NULL,
      naked_pair_unit,
      naked_triple_unit,
      naked_quad_unit
      };
```

```
  int result = FALSE;
  for (int k = 0; k < 9  &&  !result; k++) {
    if (   naked_all[multiplicity]("row", row[k])
        || naked_all[multiplicity]("column", col[k])
        || naked_all[multiplicity]("box", box[k])
        ) {
      result = TRUE;
      }
    }
#ifdef LOG_IN_OUT
  printf("<<< naked(%d) ---\n", multiplicity);
#endif
  return result;
  }
```

Then, naked(multiplicity) would replace naked_pair(), naked_triple(), and naked_quad(). It is true that if you did so you would eliminate some duplication in the code, but each strategy function needs to conform to the standard prototype defined in def.h:

```
typedef int (*f_ptr_t)(void);
```

Therefore, you would need to create the following shell functions:

```
int naked_pair()   { return naked(2); }
int naked_triple() { return naked(3); }
int naked_quad()   { return naked(4); }
```

All in all, the duplication of code is not substantial and the implementation is simpler. But in Chapter 9, you will see how to implement all "lines" strategies by means of a generic function because in that case, had you kept the strategies separate, you would have had to duplicate a substantial amount of code.

naked_pair_unit()

This function consists of two main parts: the first one prepares a list of the cells that contain naked pairs (see Listing 5-5), and the second one processes the list (see Listing 5-6).

Listing 5-5. naked_pair_unit.c–Part 1

```
/* naked_pair_unit.c
 *
 * Copyright (C) 2015  Giulio Zambon  - http://zambon.com.au/
 *
 */
#include <stdio.h>
#include <stdlib.h>
#include "cleanup_around.h"
#include "def.h"
#include "naked_pair_unit.h"
#include "remove_candidate.h"

int naked_pair_unit(char *what, char unit[9][2]) {
#ifdef LOG_IN_OUT
  printf("--- naked_pair_unit (%s) >>>\n", what);
#endif
```

```
int result = FALSE;
int i1[9] = {0};
int i2[9] = {0};
int kRow[9] = {0};
int kCol[9] = {0};
int kk[9] = {0};
int n_pair = 0;

// Make a list of the cells with naked pairs.
for (int k = 0; k < 9; k++) {
  int kR = unit[k][0];
  int kC = unit[k][1];
  char *elem = grid[kR][kC];
  if (elem[0] == 2) {
    kRow[n_pair] = kR;
    kCol[n_pair] = kC;
    kk[n_pair] = k;
    for (int i = 1;
         i <= 9 && i2[n_pair] == 0;
         i++
         ) {
      if (elem[i] == TRUE) {
        if (i1[n_pair] == 0) {
          i1[n_pair] = i;
          }
        else {
          i2[n_pair] = i;
          }
        } // if (elem[i]..
      } // for (int i..
    n_pair++;
    } // if (elem[0]..
  } // for (int k..
```

In each unit, there can only be two naked pairs with the same candidates. That is, if "a" and "b" are two different numbers, you can only find up to two "ab" pairs in each unit. Therefore, you can store the information associated with all naked pairs of a unit in the following vectors:

```
int i1[9] = {0};
int i2[9] = {0};
int kRow[9] = {0};
int kCol[9] = {0};
int kk[9] = {0};
```

where

i1 is one of the numbers of the naked pair.
i2 is the other number of the naked pair.
kRow is the row ID of the cell with the naked pair.
kCol is the col ID of the cell with the naked pair.
kk is the position of the cell within the unit.

Notice that all vectors consist of nine elements, because there are nine cells in a unit. I am pretty sure (although I have not demonstrated it) that it is impossible to construct a unit with a naked pair in each cell, but even if that were the case, you can afford to overdimension the vectors. As I always say: better safe than sorry!

For example, see what happens when naked_pair_unit() makes a list of naked pairs for the box shown in Figure 5-1.

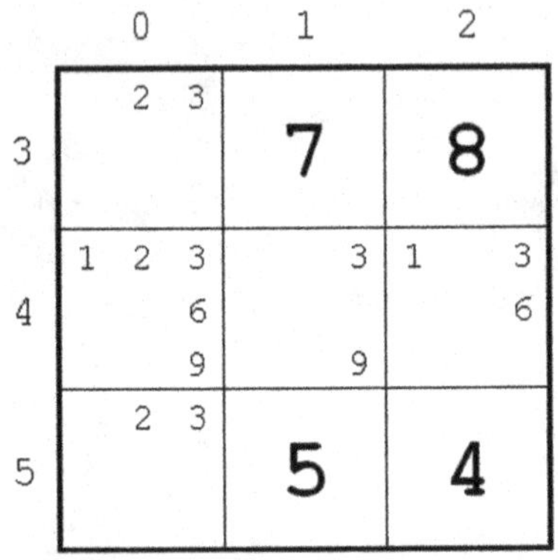

Figure 5-1. *Box with naked pairs*

At the beginning, the variable n_pair is zero. When naked_pair_unit() checks (3,0), it does the following:

```
kRow[0] = 3;
kCol[0] = 0;
kk[0] = 0;
i1[0] = 2;
i2[0] = 3;
```

It then increments n_pair to 1. When it reaches (4,1), it updates the vectors

```
kRow[1] = 4;
kCol[1] = 1;
kk[1] = 4;
i1[1] = 3;
i2[1] = 9;
```

and increments n_pair to 2.

It then does a further update of the vectors when it reaches (5,0)

```
kRow[2] = 5;
kCol[2] = 0;
kk[2] = 6;
i1[2] = 2;
i2[2] = 3;
```

and increments n_pair to 3.

The information in kk seems redundant, because it is always possible to determine which element of a unit a cell occupies. But this requires you to know what type of unit you are working on. Rather than using the information in the parameter what or add a further parameter with a numeric identification of the unit type, it is simpler to record the position in kk and be done with the matter.

Listing 5-6. naked_pair_unit.c–Part 2

```
  if (n_pair > 1) {
    for (int k1 = 0; k1 < n_pair - 1; k1++) {
      for (int k2 = k1 + 1; k2 < n_pair; k2++) {
        if (i1[k1] == i1[k2] && i2[k1] == i2[k2]) {
          int printed = FALSE;
          for (int k = 0; k < 9; k++) {
            if (k != kk[k1] && k != kk[k2]) {
              int kR = unit[k][0];
              int kC = unit[k][1];
              char *elem = grid[kR][kC];
              int i_remove[2];
              int n_remove = 0;
              if (elem[i1[k1]] == TRUE) {
                i_remove[n_remove] = i1[k1];
                n_remove++;
                result = TRUE;
                }
              if (elem[i2[k1]] == TRUE) {
                i_remove[n_remove] = i2[k1];
                n_remove++;
                result = TRUE;
                }
#ifdef LOG_NAKED_PAIR
              if (n_remove > 0 && !printed && !silent) {
                printf("naked_pair_unit: (%d,%d) and"
                    " (%d,%d) in the same %s"
                    " only contain %d and %d\n",
                    kRow[k1], kCol[k1], kRow[k2],
                    kCol[k2], what, i1[k1], i2[k1]
                    );
                printed = TRUE;
                }
#endif
                for (int ki = 0; ki < n_remove; ki++) {
                  remove_candidate(
                          "naked_pair_unit",
                          i_remove[ki], kR, kC
                          );
                  if (grid[kR][kC][0] == 1) {
                    cleanup_around(kR, kC);
                    }
                  }
```

```
          } // if (k..
        } // for (int k..
      } // if (i1[k1]..
    } // for (int k2..
  } // for (int k1..
} // if (n_pair..
```

```
#ifdef LOG_IN_OUT
  printf("<<< naked_pair_unit (%s) ---\n", what);
#endif
  return result;
  }
```

The two for-loops at the beginning of Listing 5-6 assign to k1 and k2 all possible combinations of two numbers in the interval 0 to n_pair (excluding n_pair). In the example, the possible combinations are [0 1], [0 2], and [1 2], because n_pair is 3.

The combination [0 1] causes the check if (i1[k1] == i1[k2] && i2[k1] == i2[k2]) to fail, because i1[0] == i1[1] is not true. But the check succeeds with the combination [0 2]. This tells you that you have found a naked pair and that you can remove from all other cells of the unit the candidates for the two numbers that form the naked pair.

The two statements

```
for (int k = 0; k < 9; k++) {
  if (k != kk[k1] && k != kk[k2]) {
```

go through all the cells of the unit while skipping those with the naked pair, but you have a problem: you want to log that you have found the naked pair, but only once per pair, and only if candidates are actually removed from at least one cell as a result of finding the naked pair. To understand why this causes a problem, consider what you need to do when k reaches the value of 3.

Cell 3 of the unit has the coordinates (4,0) and that cell contains both numbers of the pair (i.e., 2 and 3). Therefore, you want to log the removal of both 2 and 3 from that cell. But in other Sudokus, it could be that only one of the two numbers is present (i.e., either 2 or 3). To cater for that eventuality, it appears that you would need to log twice: when you check for the first number and when you check for the second one. But it wouldn't be nice to have essentially the same block of statements twice, once for the first number and once for the second. To avoid it, you can store the numbers you can remove in a small vector of two elements and use it for both the logging and the removal.

After defining the vector i_remove[2] and the counter n_remove, when you remove the candidate for a number, you store its value in i_remove and count it in n_remove. Then, after checking a cell for both numbers of the pair, you can easily decide whether to log the naked pair or not. Refer to the code highlighted in bold.

Also, to ensure that the discovery of a naked pair is only displayed once regardless of how many candidates can be removed, you can wrap the logging statements in an if(!printed) conditional statement. You initialize the variable printed to FALSE and then set it to TRUE immediately after printing.

naked_triple_unit()

Not surprisingly, the implementation of this strategy is very similar to the implementation of naked_pair() (see Listing 5-7).

Listing 5-7. naked_triple_unit.c

```c
/* naked_triple_unit.c
 *
 * Copyright (C) 2015  Giulio Zambon  - http://zambon.com.au/
 *
 */
#include <stdio.h>
#include <stdlib.h>
#include "cleanup_around.h"
#include "def.h"
#include "naked_triple_unit.h"
#include "remove_candidate.h"

int naked_triple_unit(char *what, char unit[9][2]) {
#ifdef LOG_IN_OUT
  printf("--- naked_triple_unit (%s) >>>\n", what);
#endif
  int result = FALSE;
  int i1[9] = {0};
  int i2[9] = {0};
  int i3[9] = {0};
  int kRow[9] = {0};
  int kCol[9] = {0};
  int kk[9] = {0};
  int n_triple = 0;

  // Make a list of the cells with naked triples.
  for (int k = 0; k < 9; k++) {
    int kR = unit[k][0];
    int kC = unit[k][1];
    char *elem = grid[kR][kC];
    if (elem[0] == 3) {
      kRow[n_triple] = kR;
      kCol[n_triple] = kC;
      kk[n_triple] = k;
      for (int i = 1;
          i <= 9 && i3[n_triple] == 0;
          i++
          ) {
        if (elem[i] == TRUE) {
          if (i1[n_triple] == 0) {
            i1[n_triple] = i;
            }
```

```
        else if (i2[n_triple] == 0) {
          i2[n_triple] = i;
          }
        else {
          i3[n_triple] = i;
          }
        } // if (elem[i]..
      } // for (int i..
    n_triple++;
    } // if (elem[0]..
  } // for (int k..

  if (n_triple > 2) {
    for (int k1 = 0; k1 < n_triple - 2; k1++) {
      for (int k2 = k1 + 1; k2 < n_triple - 1; k2++) {
        for (int k3 = k2 + 1; k3 < n_triple; k3++) {
          if (    i1[k1] == i1[k2] && i1[k1] == i1[k3]
              && i2[k1] == i2[k2] && i2[k1] == i2[k3]
              && i3[k1] == i3[k2] && i3[k1] == i3[k3]
              ) {
            int printed = FALSE;
            for (int k = 0; k < 9; k++) {
              if (    k != kk[k1]
                  && k != kk[k2]
                  && k != kk[k3]
                  ) {
                int kR = unit[k][0];
                int kC = unit[k][1];
                char *elem = grid[kR][kC];
                int i_remove[3];
                int n_remove = 0;
                if (elem[i1[k1]] == TRUE) {
                  i_remove[n_remove] = i1[k1];
                  n_remove++;
                  result = TRUE;
                  }
                if (elem[i2[k1]] == TRUE) {
                  i_remove[n_remove] = i2[k1];
                  n_remove++;
                  result = TRUE;
                  }
                if (elem[i3[k1]] == TRUE) {
                  i_remove[n_remove] = i3[k1];
                  n_remove++;
                  result = TRUE;
                  }
#ifdef LOG_NAKED_TRIPLE
                if (    n_remove > 0
                    && !printed
                    && !silent
                    ) {
```

```
                    printf("naked_triple_unit: (%d,%d) "
                           ", (%d,%d), and contain "
                           "(%d,%d) in the same %s only"
                           " contain %d, %d, and %d\n",
                           kRow[k1], kCol[k1], kRow[k2],
                           kCol[k2], kRow[k3], kCol[k3],
                           what, i1[k1], i2[k1], i3[k1]
                           );
                    printed = TRUE;
                    }
#endif
                for (int ki = 0;
                    ki < n_remove;
                    ki++
                    ) {
                    remove_candidate(
                       "naked_triple_unit",
                       i_remove[ki], kR, kC
                       );
                    if (grid[kR][kC][0] == 1) {
                      cleanup_around(kR, kC);
                      }
                    }
                  } // if (k..
                } // for (int k..
              } // if (i1[k1]..
            } // for (int k3..
          } // for (int k2..
        } // for (int k1..
      } // if (n_triple..

#ifdef LOG_IN_OUT
  printf("<<< naked_triple_unit (%s) ---\n", what);
#endif
  return result;
  }
```

In fact, to obtain naked_triple_unit.c from naked_pair_unit.c, you only need to make a global replacement of "pair" with "triple" and then do the following modifications (highlighted in bold in Listing 5-7):

1. Insert int i3[9] = {0}; after int i2[9] = {0};
2. Change if (elem[0] == 2) to if (elem[0] == 3)
3. In for (int i = 1; i <= 9 && i2[n_triple] == 0; i++) change i2 to i3.
4. Expand

```
   else {
     i2[n_triple] = i;
     }
```

to

```
  else if (i2[n_triple] == 0) {
    i2[n_triple] = i;
    }
  else {
    i3[n_triple] = i;
    }
```

5. Expand

```
  if (n_triple > 1) {
    for (int k1 = 0; k1 < n_triple - 1; k1++) {
      for (int k2 = k1 + 1; k2 < n_triple; k2++) {
        if (i1[k1] == i1[k2] && i2[k1] == i2[k2]) {
```

to

```
  if (n_triple > 2) {
    for (int k1 = 0; k1 < n_triple - 2; k1++) {
      for (int k2 = k1 + 1;
           k2 < n_triple - 1;
           k2++
          ) {
        for (int k3 = k2 + 1;
             k3 < n_triple;
             k3++
            ) {
          if (    i1[k1] == i1[k2]
              && i1[k1] == i1[k3]
              && i2[k1] == i2[k2]
              && i2[k1] == i2[k3]
              && i3[k1] == i3[k2]
              && i3[k1] == i3[k3]
```

6. Insert

```
  if (elem[i3[k1]] == TRUE) {
    i_remove[n_remove] = i3[k1];
    n_remove++;
    result = TRUE;
    }
```

after the identical check on elem[i2[k1]].

7. Update the log entry to show three cells instead of two.

The only change worth commenting on is the if in modification 5. Its purpose is to check that the three triplets are identical. When you used an if to compare pairs, you only needed to check that the first number of pair one was the same as the first number of pair two and that the second number of pair one was the same as the second number of pair two. With three triplets, you have to check that each one of the three numbers (stored in i1, i2, and i3) is identical to the corresponding number in the other two triplets (which are identified by k1, k2, and k3). That's why two comparisons become six.

naked_quad_unit()

After reading the previous section, it should be clear to you that naked_quad_unit() (see Listing 5-8) can be easily obtained from naked_triplet_unit(). Notice that the loops in the second part of the function have now become four, and the if includes 12 comparisons. If you wanted to develop a naked_quint_unit(), the loops would become five, and the if would include 20 comparisons.

Listing 5-8. naked_quad_unit.c

```c
/* naked_quad_unit.c
 *
 * Copyright (C) 2015  Giulio Zambon  - http://zambon.com.au/
 *
 */
#include <stdio.h>
#include <stdlib.h>
#include "cleanup_around.h"
#include "def.h"
#include "naked_quad_unit.h"
#include "remove_candidate.h"

int naked_quad_unit(char *what, char unit[9][2]) {
#ifdef LOG_IN_OUT
  printf("--- naked_quad_unit (%s) >>>\n", what);
#endif
  int result = FALSE;
  int i1[9] = {0};
  int i2[9] = {0};
  int i3[9] = {0};
  int i4[9] = {0};
  int kRow[9] = {0};
  int kCol[9] = {0};
  int kk[9] = {0};
  int n_quad = 0;

  // Make a list of the cells with naked quads.
  for (int k = 0; k < 9; k++) {
    int kR = unit[k][0];
    int kC = unit[k][1];
    char *elem = grid[kR][kC];
    if (elem[0] == 4) {
      kRow[n_quad] = kR;
      kCol[n_quad] = kC;
      kk[n_quad] = k;
      for (int i = 1;
          i <= 9 && i4[n_quad] == 0;
          i++
          ) {
        if (elem[i] == TRUE) {
          if (i1[n_quad] == 0) {
            i1[n_quad] = i;
            }
```

```
          else if (i2[n_quad] == 0) {
            i2[n_quad] = i;
            }
          else if (i3[n_quad] == 0) {
            i3[n_quad] = i;
            }
          else {
            i4[n_quad] = i;
            }
          } // if (elem[i]..
        } // for (int i..
      n_quad++;
      } // if (elem[0]..
    } // for (int k..

  if (n_quad > 3) {
    for (int k1 = 0; k1 < n_quad - 3; k1++) {
      for (int k2 = k1 + 1; k2 < n_quad - 2; k2++) {
        for (int k3 = k2 + 1; k3 < n_quad - 1; k3++) {
          for (int k4 = k3 + 1; k4 < n_quad; k4++) {
            if (    i1[k1] == i1[k2]
                 && i1[k1] == i1[k3]
                 && i1[k1] == i1[k4]
                 && i2[k1] == i2[k2]
                 && i2[k1] == i2[k3]
                 && i2[k1] == i2[k4]
                 && i3[k1] == i3[k2]
                 && i3[k1] == i3[k3]
                 && i3[k1] == i3[k4]
                 && i4[k1] == i4[k2]
                 && i4[k1] == i4[k3]
                 && i4[k1] == i4[k4]
               ) {
              int printed = FALSE;
              for (int k = 0; k < 9; k++) {
                if (    k != kk[k1] && k != kk[k2]
                     && k != kk[k3] && k != kk[k4]
                   ) {
                  int kR = unit[k][0];
                  int kC = unit[k][1];
                  char *elem = grid[kR][kC];
                  int i_remove[4];
                  int n_remove = 0;
                  if (elem[i1[k1]] == TRUE) {
                    i_remove[n_remove] = i1[k1];
                    n_remove++;
                    result = TRUE;
                    }
```

```
                  if (elem[i2[k1]] == TRUE) {
                    i_remove[n_remove] = i2[k1];
                    n_remove++;
                    result = TRUE;
                    }
                  if (elem[i3[k1]] == TRUE) {
                    i_remove[n_remove] = i3[k1];
                    n_remove++;
                    result = TRUE;
                    }
                  if (elem[i4[k1]] == TRUE) {
                    i_remove[n_remove] = i4[k1];
                    n_remove++;
                    result = TRUE;
                    }
#ifdef LOG_NAKED_QUAD
                  if (    n_remove > 0
                      && !printed
                      && !silent
                      ) {
                    printf("naked_quad_unit: (%d,%d) "
                          ", (%d,%d), (%d,%d), and "
                          "(%d,%d)" in the same %s "
                          "only contain %d, %d, %d, "
                          "and %d\n", kRow[k1],
                          kCol[k1], kRow[k2],
                          kCol[k2], kRow[k3],
                          kCol[k3], kRow[k4],
                          kCol[k4], what, i1[k1],
                          i2[k1], i3[k1], i4[k1]
                          );
                    printed = TRUE;
                    }
#endif
                  for (int ki = 0;
                      ki < n_remove;
                      ki++
                      ) {
                    remove_candidate(
                          "naked_quad_unit",
                          i_remove[ki],
                          kR, kC
                          );
                    if (grid[kR][kC][0] == 1) {
                      cleanup_around(kR, kC);
                      }
                    }
```

```
                } // if (k..
              } // for (int k..
            } // if (i1[k1]..
          } // for (int k4..
        } // for (int k3..
      } // for (int k2..
    } // for (int k1..
  } // if (n_quad..

#ifdef LOG_IN_OUT
  printf("<<< naked_quad_unit (%s) ---\n", what);
#endif
  return result;
  }
```

Now, could you develop a single function to handle all naked strategies? Perhaps, but it would make almost unreadable a function that is already quite hefty. The function would always have four for-loops and a six-condition if, with the difference that one of them would be "switched off" for the triples and two of them for the pairs.

Summary

This chapter told you how to implement the naked strategies. The next chapter is very similar to this one and will describe the "hidden" strategies: hidden pair at level 1 and hidden triple at level 2.

CHAPTER 6

■ ■ ■

Implementing "Hidden" Strategies

The two "hidden" strategies, hidden pair and hidden triple, have the same general design: first, they build lists of the cells containing each candidate number; then, they analyze the lists to see whether pairs or triples are hidden inside the lists.

As it is done for the naked strategies described in Chapter 5, you implement each hidden strategy with two functions, one applying the strategy to a unit and one executing the unit function for each row, column, and box of the Sudoku. Again, as with the naked strategies, you will find that the two general functions for pairs and triples (Listings 6-1 and 6-2) are almost identical.

Listing 6-1. hidden_pair.c

```c
/* hidden_pair.c
 *
 * Copyright (C) 2015  Giulio Zambon  - http://zambon.com.au/
 *
 */
#include <stdio.h>
#include <stdlib.h>
#include "def.h"
#include "hidden_pair.h"
#include "hidden_pair_unit.h"

int hidden_pair() {
#ifdef LOG_IN_OUT
  printf("--- hidden_pair >>>\n");
#endif
  int result = FALSE;
  for (int k = 0; k < 9 && !result; k++) {
    if (   hidden_pair_unit("row", row[k])
        || hidden_pair_unit("column", col[k])
        || hidden_pair_unit("box", box[k])
        ) {
      result = TRUE;
      }
    }
#ifdef LOG_IN_OUT
  printf("<<< hidden_pair ---\n");
#endif
  return result;
  }
```

Listing 6-2. hidden_triple.c

```c
/* hidden_triple.c
 *
 * Copyright (C) 2015  Giulio Zambon  - http://zambon.com.au/
 *
 */
#include <stdio.h>
#include <stdlib.h>
#include "def.h"
#include "hidden_triple.h"
#include "hidden_triple_unit.h"

int hidden_triple() {
#ifdef LOG_IN_OUT
  printf("--- hidden_triple >>>\n");
#endif
  int result = FALSE;
  for (int k = 0; k < 9  &&  !result; k++) {
    if (   hidden_triple_unit("row", row[k])
        || hidden_triple_unit("column", col[k])
        || hidden_triple_unit("box", box[k])
        ) {
      result = TRUE;
      }
    }
#ifdef LOG_IN_OUT
  printf("<<< hidden_triple ---\n");
#endif
  return result;
  }
```

hidden_pair_unit()

The first part of hidden_pair_unit() (see Listing 6-3) builds lists of cell coordinates for each candidate number.

Listing 6-3. hidden_pair_unit.c–Part 1

```c
/* hidden_pair_unit.c
 *
 * Copyright (C) 2015  Giulio Zambon  - http://zambon.com.au/
 *
 */
#include <stdio.h>
#include <stdlib.h>
#include "cleanup_around.h"
#include "def.h"
#include "hidden_pair_unit.h"
#include "remove_candidate.h"
```

```
int hidden_pair_unit(char *what, char unit[9][2]) {
#ifdef LOG_IN_OUT
  printf("--- hidden_pair_unit (%s) >>>\n", what);
#endif
  int result = FALSE;

  int n[10] = {0};
  int coords[10][2][2];
  for (int j1 = 0; j1 < 9; j1++) {
    int kR = unit[j1][ROW];
    int kC = unit[j1][COL];
    char *elem = grid[kR][kC];
    if (elem[0] > 1) {
      for (int i = 1; i <= 9; i++) {
        if (elem[i] != FALSE) {
          if (n[i] < 2) {
            coords[i][n[i]][ROW] = kR;
            coords[i][n[i]][COL] = kC;
          }
          n[i]++;
        } // if (elem[i]..
      } // for (int i..
    } // if (elem[0]..
  } // for (int j1..
```

The array `coords` stores the row and column IDs of the cells that contain each candidate, while the vector `n` counts the cells. To make it clear, refer to the example in Figure 6-1.

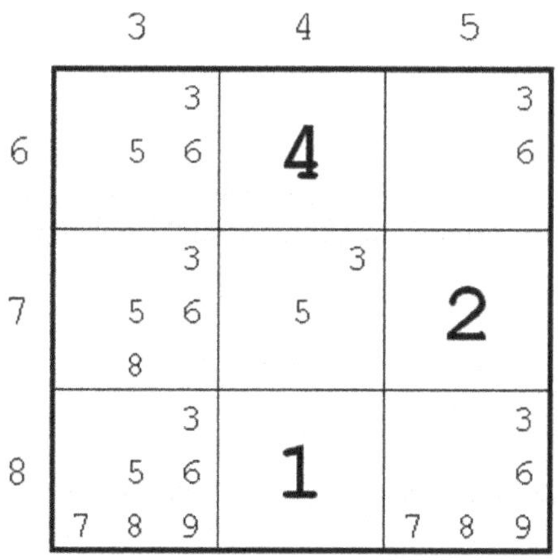

Figure 6-1. *Box with hidden pairs*

The first cell you process is $(6,3)$. It results in the following assignments:

```
coords[3][0][0] = 6;
coords[3][0][1] = 3;
n[3] = 1;
coords[5][0][0] = 6;
coords[5][0][1] = 3;
n[5] = 1;
coords[6][0][0] = 6;
coords[6][0][1] = 3;
n[6] = 1;
```

That is, the coordinates of $(6,3)$ are saved for all three candidates it contains. $(6,4)$ is skipped, and $(6,5)$ results in the following assignments:

```
coords[3][1][0] = 6;
coords[3][1][1] = 5;
n[3] = 2;
coords[6][1][0] = 6;
coords[6][1][1] = 5;
n[6] = 2;
```

Now, when you process $(7,3)$, things go differently.

```
n[3] = 3;
coords[5][1][0] = 7;
coords[5][1][1] = 3;
n[5] = 2;
n[6] = 3;
coords[8][0][0] = 7;
coords[8][0][1] = 3;
n[8] = 1;
```

coords only has space for the coordinates of two cells, and the candidates for 3 and 6 have already appeared twice before. Therefore, although you increment the counters of cells containing candidates for 3 and 6, you do not save the coordinates of the cells.

This happens again when you process $(7,4)$.

```
n[3] = 4;
n[5] = 3;
```

You skip $(7,5)$, and while processing $(8,3)$, you make the following assignments:

```
n[3] = 5;
n[5] = 4;
n[6] = 4;
coords[7][0][0] = 8;
coords[7][0][1] = 3;
n[7] = 1;
coords[8][1][0] = 8;
coords[8][1][1] = 3;
n[8] = 2;
```

```
coords[9][0][0] = 8;
coords[9][0][1] = 3;
n[9] = 1;
```

You skip $(8,4)$ and then complete the unit by processing $(8,5)$.

```
n[3] = 6;
n[6] = 5;
coords[7][1][0] = 8;
coords[7][1][1] = 5;
n[7] = 2;
n[8] = 3;
coords[9][1][0] = 8;
coords[9][1][1] = 5;
n[9] = 2;
```

Figure 6-2 summarizes the end result of the assignments.

digit	1	2	3	4	5	6	7	8	9
n	0	0	6	0	4	4	2	3	2
coords									
0			(6,3)		(6,3)	(6,3)	(8,3)	(7,3)	(8,3)
1			(6,5)		(7,3)	(6,5)	(8,5)	(8,3)	(8,5)

Figure 6-2. *Listing cells per candidate number*

Although the table shows the coordinates of two cells for all unsolved numbers, only 7 and 9 appear in two cells because only for them n equals 2 . Further, as they appear in the same two cells, they form two pairs. If they were the only two candidates in those two cells, they would be naked pairs, but as you know that $(8,3)$ and $(8,5)$ also contain other candidates, they are hidden pairs.

Incidentally, in this list, n cannot ever be 1 because by the time the Solver attempts to use hidden pair, unique has already removed all candidates that appear only once.

Now, you have just to see how hidden_pair_unit() arrives to the same conclusions and what happens when it does. For this, you have to refer to Listing 6-4.

Listing 6-4. hidden_pair_unit.c–Part 2

```
for (int i = 1; i <= 9; i++) {
  if (n[i] == 2) {
    int log_printed = FALSE;
    for (int ii = i+1; ii <= 9; ii++) {
      if (n[ii] == 2
          && coords[i][0][ROW] == coords[ii][0][ROW]
          && coords[i][0][COL] == coords[ii][0][COL]
          && coords[i][1][ROW] == coords[ii][1][ROW]
          && coords[i][1][COL] == coords[ii][1][COL]
          ) {
        for (int kCell = 0; kCell < 2; kCell++) {
          int kR = coords[i][kCell][ROW];
          int kC = coords[i][kCell][COL];
          char *elem = grid[kR][kC];
```

```
                  if (elem[0] > 2) {
                      result = TRUE;
#ifdef LOG_HIDDEN_PAIR
                      if (log_printed == FALSE && !silent) {
                          printf("hidden_pair_unit: %d and %d"
                                  " are only in (%d,%d) and "
                                  "(%d,%d) of the same %s\n",
                                  i, ii, coords[i][0][0],
                                  coords[i][0][1],
                                  coords[i][1][0],
                                  coords[i][1][1], what
                                  );
                          log_printed = TRUE;
                      }
#endif
                      for (int iii = 1; iii <= 9; iii++) {
                          if (    elem[iii] != FALSE
                              && i != iii
                              && ii != iii
                              ) {
                              remove_candidate("hidden_pair_unit",
                                          iii, kR, kC
                                          );
                          }
                      }
                  } // if (elem[0]..
              } // for (int kCell..
          } // if (n[ii]..
        } // for (int ii..
      } // if (n[i]..
    } // for (int i..

#ifdef LOG_IN_OUT
  printf("<<< hidden_pair_unit (%s) ---\n", what);
#endif
  return result;
  }
```

The outermost for-loop, with control variable i, goes through the numbers, and the if immediately inside the loop limits the processing to the candidate numbers that appear in exactly two cells. The for-loop with control variable ii ensures that i and ii together form all theoretically possible pairs, but, again, you only consider the iis that appear in exactly two cells. The second if does something more, though: it checks that the coordinates of the cells in which i and ii appear have identical coordinates. As a result, if the second if succeeds, you know that you have found a double pair of candidates.

The only thing that is left to do is to see whether the two cells containing your pairs also contain additional candidates, which you will then be able to remove (if they don't, you have found a naked pair, rather than a hidden one). You do this by checking whether the elem[0] of each one of the two cells (indexed by the value of kCell) exceeds 2.

In the case of the example in Figure 6-1, it turns out that we can eliminate the candidates for 3, 5, 6, and 8 from (8,3) and the candidates for 3, 6, and 8 in (8,5). The log entries are very satisfying.

```
hidden_pair_unit: 7 and 9 are only in (8,3) and (8,5) of the same box
hidden_pair_unit: removed 3 from (8,3)
hidden_pair_unit: removed 5 from (8,3)
hidden_pair_unit: removed 6 from (8,3)
hidden_pair_unit: removed 8 from (8,3)
hidden_pair_unit: removed 3 from (8,5)
hidden_pair_unit: removed 6 from (8,5)
hidden_pair_unit: removed 8 from (8,5)
```

You have certainly noticed that, whenever you need to access the Sudoku grid, you use a variable called elem (which stands for "element"). There is actually no compelling reason for doing so. For example, you could replace the three statements in bold in Listing 6-4 with the following two:

```
if (grid[kR][kC][0] > 2) {
...
if (grid[kR][kC][iii] != FALSE && i != iii && ii != iii) {
```

But elem makes the code more readable. The same consideration applies to kR and kC, which are not absolutely necessary. Some programmers might actually find that by "hiding" grid[kR][kC] behind elem, you actually make the code *less* readable. Ultimately, it is just a matter of taste.

hidden_triple_unit()

The only significant difference between hidden_triple_unit() and hidden_pair_unit() is that in hidden_triple_unit() (see Listing 6-5) you need to look for three triplets of candidates instead of two pairs.

Listing 6-5. hidden_triple_unit.c

```
/* hidden_triple_unit.c
 *
 * Copyright (C) 2015  Giulio Zambon  - http://zambon.com.au/
 *
 */
#include <stdio.h>
#include <stdlib.h>
#include "def.h"
#include "hidden_triple_unit.h"
#include "remove_candidate.h"

int hidden_triple_unit(char *what, char unit[9][2]) {
#ifdef LOG_IN_OUT
  printf("--- hidden_triple_unit (%s) >>>\n", what);
#endif
```

```
int result = FALSE;
int n[10] = {0};
int coords[10][3][2];
for (int j1 = 0; j1 < 9; j1++) {
  int kR = unit[j1][ROW];
  int kC = unit[j1][COL];
  char *elem = grid[kR][kC];
  if (elem[0] > 1) {
    for (int i = 1; i <= 9; i++) {
      if (elem[i] != FALSE) {
        if (n[i] < 3) {
          coords[i][n[i]][ROW] = kR;
          coords[i][n[i]][COL] = kC;
        }
        n[i]++;
      } // if (elem[i]..
    } // for (int i..
  } // if (elem[0]..
} // for (int j1..

for (int i1 = 1; i1 <= 9; i1++) {
  if (n[i1] == 3) {
    int log_printed = FALSE;
    for (int i2 = i1+1; i2 <= 9; i2++) {
      if (
          n[i2] == 3
       && coords[i1][0][ROW] == coords[i2][0][ROW]
       && coords[i1][0][COL] == coords[i2][0][COL]
       && coords[i1][1][ROW] == coords[i2][1][ROW]
       && coords[i1][1][COL] == coords[i2][1][COL]
       && coords[i1][2][ROW] == coords[i2][2][ROW]
       && coords[i1][2][COL] == coords[i2][2][COL]
        ) {
        for (int i3 = i2+1; i3 <= 9; i3++) {
          if (
            n[i3] == 3
         && coords[i1][0][ROW] == coords[i3][0][ROW]
         && coords[i1][0][COL] == coords[i3][0][COL]
         && coords[i1][1][ROW] == coords[i3][1][ROW]
         && coords[i1][1][COL] == coords[i3][1][COL]
         && coords[i1][2][ROW] == coords[i3][2][ROW]
         && coords[i1][2][COL] == coords[i3][2][COL]
              ) {
            for (int kCell = 0;
                kCell < 3;
                kCell++
                ) {
              int kRow = coords[i1][kCell][ROW];
              int kCol = coords[i1][kCell][COL];
              char *elem = grid[kRow][kCol];
```

```c
                if (elem[0] > 3) {
                    result = TRUE;
#ifdef LOG_HIDDEN_TRIPLE
                    if (    log_printed == FALSE
                        && !silent
                        ) {
                        printf("hidden_triple_unit: %d, "
                            "%d, and %d are only in "
                            "(%d,%d), (%d,%d), and "
                            "(%d,%d) of the same"
                            "%s\n", i1, i2, i3,
                            coords[i1][0][0],
                            coords[i1][0][1],
                            coords[i1][1][0],
                            coords[i1][1][1],
                            coords[i1][2][0],
                            coords[i1][2][1], what
                            );
                        log_printed = TRUE;
                        }
#endif
                    for (int ki = 1; ki <= 9; ki++) {
                        if (    elem[ki]
                            && ki != i1
                            && ki != i2
                            && ki != i3
                            ) {
                            remove_candidate(
                                    "hidden_triple_unit",
                                    ki,
                                    kRow, kCol
                                    );
                        }
                    }
                } // if (elem[0]..
            } // for (int kCell..
        } // if (n[i3]..
        } // for (int i3..
    } // if (n[i2]..
    } // for (int i2..
    } // if (n[i1]..
    } // for (int i1..

#ifdef LOG_IN_OUT
  printf("<<< hidden_triple_unit (%s) ---\n", what);
#endif
  return result;
  }
```

The first loop, where you list the cells for each number, is almost identical to the corresponding loop of hidden_pair_unit(). The only difference is that you save the coordinates of the first three cells instead of the first two.

In the second part of the function, the difference is that you have to look for all possible triples of numbers instead of all possible pairs. As a result, you need to replace the two for-loops controlled by i and ii with three loops controlled by i1, i2, and i3. This also implies that, instead of comparing the coordinates of two cells for two numbers ([i][0] with [ii][0] and [i][1] with [ii][1]), you have to compare the coordinates of three cells for three numbers ([i1][0] with [i2][0] and [i3][0]; [i1][1] with [i2][1] and [i3][1]; and [i1][2] with [i2][2] and [i3][2]).

Also, obviously, you need to expand the log entries accordingly.

Summary

In this chapter you learned how to implement the hidden strategies; in Chapter 7 you will learn another level 1 strategy: box-line.

CHAPTER 7

▓ ▓ ▓

Implementing "Box-Line"

As with most strategies, you implement "box-line" with two functions: one general that conforms to the type f_ptr_t as defined in def.h and one to handle an individual unit. The general function, box_line() (see Listing 7-1), executes box_line_unit() (see Listings 7-2 and 7-3) for each possible row and column of the Sudoku.

box_line()

box_line() is pretty obvious, but notice that it passes a flag to box_line_unit()to distinguish between rows and columns. It is actually not strictly necessary, but it makes the log entries clearer.

Listing 7-1. box_line.c

```c
/* box_line.c
 *
 * Copyright (C) 2015  Giulio Zambon  - http://zambon.com.au/
 *
 */
#include <stdio.h>
#include <stdlib.h>
#include "box_line.h"
#include "box_line_unit.h"
#include "def.h"

int box_line() {
#ifdef LOG_IN_OUT
  printf("--- box_line >>>\n");
#endif
  int result = FALSE;
  for (int k = 0; k < 9  &&  !result; k++) {
    if (box_line_unit(ROW, row[k])  ||  box_line_unit(COL, col[k])) {
      result = TRUE;
      }
    }
#ifdef LOG_IN_OUT
  printf("<<< box_line ---\n");
#endif
  return result;
  }
```

box_line_unit()

box_line_unit(), again, like with many other strategies, consists of two for-loops: one to collect information (see Listing 7-2) and one to do the analysis (see Listing 7-3).

Listing 7-2. box_line_unit.c–Part 1

```
/* box_line_unit.c
 *
 * Copyright (C) 2015  Giulio Zambon  - http://zambon.com.au/
 *
 */
#include <stdio.h>
#include <stdlib.h>
#include "box_line_unit.h"
#include "cleanup_around.h"
#include "def.h"
#include "remove_candidate.h"

int box_line_unit(int row_col, char line[9][2]) {
#ifdef LOG_IN_OUT
  printf("--- box_line_unit (%s) >>>\n", unit_names[row_col]);
#endif
  int result = FALSE;
  int b[10]; for (int i = 0; i < 10; i++) { b[i] = -1; }
  int rc[10];
  for (int j1 = 0; j1 < 9; j1++) {
    int kR = line[j1][ROW];
    int kC = line[j1][COL];
    char *elem = grid[kR][kC];
    if (elem[0] > 1) {
      for (int i = 1; i <= 9; i++) {
        if (elem[i] != FALSE) {
          int kB = kR/3*3 + kC/3;
          if (b[i] == -1) {
            b[i] = kB;
            rc[i] = (row_col == ROW) ? kR : kC;
          }
          else if (b[i] != kB) {
            b[i] = -2;
          }
        } // if (elem[i]..
      } // for (int i..
    } // if (elem[0]..
  } // for (int j1..
```

You collect the information in two vectors that have one element per number candidate: b, initialized to -1, stores the box ID in which each candidate is found. rc stores the cell index of the candidate within the line—that is, the column ID if the unit is a row or the row ID if the unit is a column. As usual, to follow the algorithm, look at the example in Figure 7-1.

Figure 7-1. *An example for box-line*

	0	1	2	3	4	5	6	7	8
0	9	2	1	3 8	3 6 8	4	5	7	3 6
1	7	3 6	5	2	1 3 6	9	8	4	1 3 6
2	3 6	8	4	5	7	1 3 6	2	1 3 6	9
3	2	7	9	4	1 3 6	1 3 6	1 6	8	5
4	5	4	6	1 3 8	1 2 3 8 9	1 2 3	7	1 2 3 9	1 2 3
5	8	1	3	7	2 6 9	5	4	2 6 9	2 6
6	4	3 6	2	1 3	1 3 5	7	9	1 5 6	8
7	1	9	7	6	2 5	8	3	2 5	4
8	3 6	5	8	9	4	1 2 3 6	1 6	1 2 6	7

If you consider row 3, you will see that all candidates for 3 are in box 4. Therefore, as row 3 must include the number 3, it means that all three other candidates for 3 in box 4 (i.e., in the cells (4,3), (4,4), and (4,5)) can be removed.

When the big for-loop in Listing 7-2 executes, it goes through all the cells of row 3. After ignoring the first four cells because they are solved, it reaches (3,4). Then, after checking for each number candidate that the corresponding element of b is still set to -1, it makes the following assignments, two for each candidate found in cell (3,4):

```
b[1] = 4;    // the box ID
rc[1] = 4;   // the column ID
b[3] = 4;
rc[3] = 4;
b[6] = 4;
rc[6] = 4;
```

When (3,5) is processed, the two vectors remain unchanged because, although the elements of b corresponding to the three numbers are no longer set to -1, they contain the same box ID of the previously processed cell (3,4).

But when you process (3,6), the box ID is 5—that is, different from that stored in b[1] and b[6] for the numbers 1 and 6 found in (3,6). Therefore, b[1] and b[6] are set to -2.

You ignore (3,7) and (3,8) because they are already solved.

At the end of the scan, the two vectors for row 3 look as follows:

```
     0    1    2   3    4    5    6   7    8    9
b:  -1   -2   -1   4   -1   -1   -2  -1   -1   -1
rc: -1    4   -1   4   -1   -1    4  -1   -1   -1
```

You can see that only the element of b associated with number 3 is non-negative. A similar thing happens when box_line() scans column 8.

```
     0    1    2    3    4    5    6   7    8    9
b:  -1   -2    5   -2   -1   -1   -2  -1   -1   -1
rc: -1    1    4    0   -1   -1    0  -1   -1   -1
```

In this case, the non-negative element of b is that associated with number 2. Note that there can be more than one number in a line that has a non-negative element in b. For example, if no candidate for 3 had been present in (4,8), b[3] would have remained set to 2 instead of being overwritten with a -2. But this scan does not take place because box_line() returns after the previous scan results in the removal of 3s in (4,3), (4,4), and (4,5).

Listing 7-3. box_line_unit.c–Part 2

```
for (int i = 1; i <= 9; i++) {
  if (b[i] >= 0) {
    int log_printed = FALSE;
    int kB = b[i];
    int kL = rc[i];
    for (int kE = 0; kE < 9; kE++) {
      int kR = box[kB][kE][ROW];
      int kC = box[kB][kE][COL];
      int kRC = (row_col == ROW) ? kR : kC;
      if (kRC != kL) {
        char *elem = grid[kR][kC];
        if (elem[i] != FALSE) {
          result = TRUE;
#ifdef LOG_BOX_LINE
          if (!log_printed && !silent) {
            printf("box_line_unit: all candidates "
                "for %d of %s %d are in box %d\n"
                , i, unit_names[row_col], kL, kB
                );
            log_printed = TRUE;
          }
#endif
          remove_candidate("box_line_unit",
                    i, kR, kC
                    );
```

```
        if (grid[kR][kC][0] == 1) {
          cleanup_around(kR, kC);
          }
        } // if (elem[i]..
      } // if (kRC..
    } // for (int kE..
  } // if (b[i]..
} // for (int i..

#ifdef LOG_IN_OUT
  printf("<<< box_line_unit (%s) ---\n",
       unit_names[row_col]
       );
#endif
  return result;
  }
```

When the big for-loop in Listing 7-3 executes, you ignore all elements of b with the exception of those greater than or equal to zero. You then go through all the elements of the box with ID given by b[i] and remove all the candidates for i that have a column ID (or a row ID) different from that saved in rc[i].

In the example, the execution of box_line() results in the following log entries:

```
box_line_unit: all candidates for 3 of row 3 are in box 4
box_line_unit: removed 3 from (4,3)
box_line_unit: removed 3 from (4,4)
box_line_unit: removed 3 from (4,5)
```

followed by:

```
box_line_unit: all candidates for 2 of column 8 are in box 5
box_line_unit: removed 2 from (4,7)
box_line_unit: removed 2 from (5,7)
```

when box_line() successfully executes a second time after the unique, naked pair, and hidden pair strategies fail to remove any candidate.

Summary

This chapter explained how you can implement box-line. Chapter 8 describes the implementation of a similar strategy: pointing line, which is the last of the level 1 strategies.

CHAPTER 8

Implementing "Pointing Line"

As I explained in Chapter 2, pointing line is similar to box-line in that they both look at the intersection of a line with a box. Therefore, it is not surprising that the implementations of the two strategies are quite similar.

The general function, pointing_line() (see Listing 8-1), executes pointing_line_box() (see Listing 8-2) for each possible box of the Sudoku.

pointing_line()

The function is so simple that I'm going to show it without any further comment.

Listing 8-1. pointing_line.c

```
/* pointing_line.c
 *
 * Copyright (C) 2015  Giulio Zambon  - http://zambon.com.au/
 *
 */
#include <stdio.h>
#include <stdlib.h>
#include "def.h"
#include "pointing_line.h"
#include "pointing_line_box.h"

int pointing_line() {
#ifdef LOG_IN_OUT
  printf("--- pointing_line >>>\n");
#endif
  int result = FALSE;
  for (int k = 0; k < 9  &&  !result; k++) {
    result |= pointing_line_box(k, box[k]);
    }
#ifdef LOG_IN_OUT
  printf("<<< pointing_line ---\n");
#endif
  return result;
  }
```

pointing_line_box()

This function turns out to be simpler than box_line_unit() (compare Listing 8-2 with Listings 7-2 and 7-3).

Listing 8-2. pointing_line_box.c

```
/* pointing_line_box.c
 *
 * Copyright (C) 2015  Giulio Zambon  - http://zambon.com.au/
 *
 */
#include <stdio.h>
#include <stdlib.h>
#include "cleanup_around.h"
#include "def.h"
#include "pointing_line_box.h"
#include "remove_candidate.h"

int pointing_line_box(int squid, char box[9][2]) {
#ifdef LOG_IN_OUT
  printf("--- pointing_line_box >>>\n");
#endif
  int result = FALSE;
  int rc[10][2];
  for (int i = 0; i < 10; i++) {
    for (int k = 0; k < 2; k++) {
      rc[i][k] = -1;
      }
    }
  for (int k = 0; k < 9; k++) {
    int kR = box[k][ROW];
    int kC = box[k][COL];
    char *elem = grid[kR][kC];
    if (elem[0] > 1) {
      for (int i = 1; i <= 9; i++) {
        if (elem[i]) {
          for (int krc = 0; krc < 2; krc++) {
            if (rc[i][krc] == -1) {
              rc[i][krc] = box[k][krc];
              }
            else if (box[k][krc] != rc[i][krc]) {
              rc[i][krc] = -2;
              }
            } // for (int krc..
          } // if (elem[i]..
        } // for (int i..
      } // if (elem[0]..
    } // for (int k..
```

```
   int log_printed = FALSE;
   int kRC[2] = {0};
   for (int i = 1; i <= 9; i++) {
     for (int krc = 0; krc < 2; krc++) {
       if (rc[i][krc] >= 0) {
         kRC[krc] = rc[i][krc];
         for (int kk = 0; kk < 9; kk++) {
           kRC[1-krc] = kk;
           int kR = kRC[ROW];
           int kC = kRC[COL];
           if (squid != kR/3*3+kC/3) {
             char *elem = grid[kR][kC];
             if (elem[i]) {
               result = TRUE;
#ifdef LOG_POINTING_LINE
               if (!log_printed && !silent) {
                 printf("pointing_line_box: all"
                        " candidates for %d of box %d"
                        " are in ", i, squid
                        );
                 if (krc == ROW) {
                   printf("row %d\n", kR);
                   }
                 else {
                   printf("column %d\n", kC);
                   }
                 log_printed = TRUE;
                 }
#endif
               remove_candidate("pointing_line_box",
                                i, kR, kC
                                );
               if (grid[kR][kC][0] == 1) {
                 cleanup_around(kR, kC);
                 }
               } // if (elem[i]..
             } // if (squid..
           } // for (int kk..
         } // if (rc[i][k]..
       } // for (int k..
     } // for (int i..

#ifdef LOG_IN_OUT
  printf("<<< pointing_line_box ---\n");
#endif
  return result;
  }
```

The first big for-loop, as usual, collects information. This time it is about the elements of a box. The array rc, initialized to -1, stores the row ID and the column ID of the candidates. Figure 8-1 shows an example that can help you understand how to use the array.

	0	1	2	3	4	5	6	7	8
0	5			9					6
1		2		4		8	9	7	
2			9				2		
3		5		3	1	4		9	
4	1	9			8			6	3
5		3		6		9		1	
6	2		5	9	4		6		
7	9	4		8		6		2	
8	7				2				9

Figure 8-1. An example for pointing-line

The first for-loop looks for numbers whose candidates, within the box being scanned, are aligned on a row or on a column. You might not find any, but if you do, you don't know in advance whether they belong to a single row or to a single column. The only thing you can be sure of is that it can be either a row or a column but not both of them. If you are not convinced of that, consider that to be aligned along both a row and a column, a bunch of cells must be reduced to a single one, and you are not interested in numbers that have already been solved.

Follow what happens when you scan box 4 with pointing_line_box(). As you ignore all the cells that have been solved, the first cell you process has coordinates (4,3). All the elements of the array are still set to -1. Therefore, you make the following assignments (remember that ROW == 0 and COL == 1):

```
rc[2][ROW] = 4;
rc[2][COL] = 3;
rc[5][ROW] = 4;
rc[5][COL] = 3;
rc[7][ROW] = 4;
rc[7][COL] = 3;
```

When you process (4,5), you make the following assignments:

```
rc[2][COL] = -2;
rc[5][COL] = -2;
rc[7][COL] = -2;
```

That is, you set the columns to -2 because (4,5) belongs to column 5 while the column stored in the array is 3. Then, when you process (5,4), you do the following:

```
rc[5][ROW] = -2;
rc[7][ROW] = -2;
```

This is because the current row is 5 while the row stored in rc is 4. At the end of the loop, the array contains the following values:

```
              0    1    2    3    4    5    6    7    8    9
rc[*][ROW]:  -1   -1    4   -1   -1   -2   -1   -2   -1   -1
rc[*][COL]:  -1   -1   -2   -1   -1   -2   -1   -2   -1   -1
```

As you can see, the only non-negative value is rc[2][ROW], which is equal to 4. It means that while examining the current box (i.e., box 4), all the candidates for 2 are in row 4 (given by the value of rc[2] [ROW])—that is, in the three cells that constitute the intersection of box 4 with row 4 (i.e., (4,3), (4,4), and (4,5), but (4,4) can be ignored because it is already solved). As one of them must be the solution, you can remove all other candidates for 2 from the rest of row 4. In the example, this means the 2 in (4,2).

The control variable krc allows you to use the same code to process rows and columns. In the second part of pointing_line_box(), where it analyzes the result of the first part, the use of krc is a bit more tricky, because you must be able to access both coordinates at the same time. The solution is to define the little vector kRC and apply the following trick (oops! I mean algorithm):

```
1   int kRC[2] = {0};
2   for (int krc = 0; krc < 2; krc++) {
3     if (rc[i][krc] >= 0) {
4       kRC[krc] = rc[i][krc];
5       for (int kk = 0; kk < 9; k++) {
6         kRC[1-krc] = kk;
7         int kR = kRC[ROW];
8         int kC = kRC[COL];
9         ...
```

In line 4, you assign to kRC[krc] the row or column ID that was found to be non-negative. If you are looking at a row, krc is 0. Therefore, the statement in line 4 sets kRC[0] (i.e., kRC[ROW]). The control variable kk of the for-loop in line 5 represents column IDs, and the assignment in line 6 is equivalent to kRC[COL] = kk, because 1-krc is equal to 1.

If, on the other hand, you are looking at a column, krc is 1 and line 4 sets kRC[1] (i.e., kRC[COL]). Then, kk represents row IDs, and the assignment in line 6 is equivalent to kRC[ROW] = kk, because 1-krc is equal to 0.

In conclusion, regardless of whether you are dealing with a row or a column, you set kR and kC in lines 7 and 8 correctly.

The rest of the analysis should be clear: if the cell you are looking at does *not* belong to the same box (i.e., if squid != kR/3*3+kC/3), you can remove from it any candidate for the number i. The following are the resulting log entries:

```
pointing_line_box: all candidates for 2 of box 4 are in row 4
pointing_line_box: removed 2 from (4,2)
```

Summary

Now that you have learned how to implement pointing-line, the last of the level 1 strategies, it is time to learn the "lines" strategies. Chapter 9 describes all three strategies in that group: "lines-2" at level 2 and "lines-3" and "lines-4" at level 3.

CHAPTER 9

■ ■ ■

Implementing "Lines" Strategies

As I already said in Chapter 2, the lines strategies rely on parallel rows and columns. You can implement all lines strategies with three small functions named `lines_2()`, `lines_3()`, and `lines_4()` (see the respective Listings 9-1, 9-2, and 9-3) that set up the arguments for and then execute a generalized function named `lines()` (see Listing 9-4).

lines_2()

The idea is to form, one by one, all possible combinations of two line IDs and then pass them to `lines()` for processing. The number of possible line pairs is ($C_{9,2}$ means: number of combinations of nine objects taken two at a time).

$$C_{9,2} = 9*8 / 2! = 36$$

Listing 9-1. lines_2.c

```c
/* lines_2.c
 *
 * Copyright (C) 2015  Giulio Zambon  - http://zambon.com.au/
 *
 */
#include <stdio.h>
#include <stdlib.h>
#include "def.h"
#include "lines.h"
#include "lines_2.h"

int lines_2() {
#ifdef LOG_IN_OUT
  printf("--- lines_2 >>>\n");
#endif
  int result = FALSE;
  char comb[2];
```

```
  for (int kRC = 0; kRC < 2 && !result; kRC++) {
    for (int k1 = 0; k1 < 8 && !result; k1++) {
      for (int k2 = k1+1; k2 < 9 && !result; k2++) {
        comb[0] = k1;
        comb[1] = k2;
        for (int i = 1; i <= 9 && !result; i++) {
          result |= lines(kRC, comb, 2, i);
          }
        } // for (int k2..
      } // for (int k1..
    } // for int kRC..
#ifdef LOG_IN_OUT
  printf("<<< lines_2 ---\n");
#endif
  return result;
  }
```

To build the combinations of line IDs, you need two for-loops: the outermost one runs from 0 to 7, while the innermost one runs from 1 to 8. Inside the innermost loop, the two variables k1 and k2 then go through the pairs of values [0 1], [0 2], ... [0 8], [1 2], ... [1 8], ... [7 8], which you pass to lines() in the small vector comb.

If you had placed the for-loop controlled by kRC inside the k1 and k2 loops, you would have halved the number of times the assignments that you need to make to comb[0] and comb[1]. But the idea of trying first the rows and then the columns is *nicer* than alternating between rows and columns. This has nothing to do with logic, but, hey, how long does it take for a modern computer to make 72 additional assignments?

If you are thinking that you could have passed k1 and k2 directly to lines(), think again: for lines_4(), you will need four line IDs. You could have defined four IDs, but the idea of passing one dummy parameter to lines() when applying lines_3() and two dummy parameters when applying lines_2() is not appealing.

lines_3()

The only difference between lines_3() and lines_2() is that you build combinations of three line IDs instead of pairs. The number of possible line triplets is

$$C_{9,3} = 9*8*7 / 3! = 84$$

Listing 9-2. lines_3.c

```
/* lines_3.c
 *
 * Copyright (C) 2015  Giulio Zambon  - http://zambon.com.au/
 *
 */
#include <stdio.h>
#include <stdlib.h>
#include "def.h"
#include "lines.h"
#include "lines_3.h"
```

```
int lines_3() {
#ifdef LOG_IN_OUT
  printf("--- lines_3 >>>\n");
#endif
  int result = FALSE;
  char comb[3];
  for (int kRC = 0; kRC < 2 && !result; kRC++) {
    for (int k1 = 0; k1 < 7 && !result; k1++) {
      for (int k2 = k1+1; k2 < 8 && !result; k2++) {
        for (int k3 = k2+1; k3 < 9 && !result; k3++) {
          comb[0] = k1;
          comb[1] = k2;
          comb[2] = k3;
          for (int i = 1; i <= 9 && !result; i++) {
            result |= lines(kRC, comb, 3, i);
            }
          } // for (int k3..
        } // for (int k2..
      } // for (int k1..
    } // for int kRC..
#ifdef LOG_IN_OUT
  printf("<<< lines_3 ---\n");
#endif
  return result;
  }
```

lines_4()

The only difference between lines_4() and the previous two functions is that you build combinations of four line IDs instead of triplets or pairs. The number of possible line quadruplets is

$$C_{9,4} = 9*8*7*6 \; / \; 4! \; = 126$$

Listing 9-3. lines_4.c

```
/* lines_4.c
 *
 * Copyright (C) 2015  Giulio Zambon  - http://zambon.com.au/
 *
 */
#include <stdio.h>
#include <stdlib.h>
#include "def.h"
#include "lines.h"
#include "lines_4.h"
```

```c
int lines_4() {
#ifdef LOG_IN_OUT
  printf("--- lines_4 >>>\n");
#endif
  int result = FALSE;
  char comb[4];
  for (int kRC = 0; kRC < 2 && !result; kRC++) {
    for (int k1 = 0; k1 < 6 && !result; k1++) {
      for (int k2 = k1+1; k2 < 7 && !result; k2++) {
        for (int k3 = k2+1; k3 < 8 && !result; k3++) {
          for (int k4 = k3+1;
               k4 < 9 && !result;
               k4++
               ) {
            comb[0] = k1;
            comb[1] = k2;
            comb[2] = k3;
            comb[3] = k4;
            for (int i = 1; i <= 9 && !result; i++) {
              result |= lines(kRC, comb, 4, i);
              }
            } // for (int k4..
          } // for (int k3..
        } // for (int k2..
      } // for (int k1..
    } // for int kRC..
#ifdef LOG_IN_OUT
  printf("<<< lines_4 ---\n");
#endif
  return result;
  }
```

lines()

This is where you implement the logic of the lines strategies (see Listing 9-4).

Listing 9-4. lines.c

```c
/* lines.c
 *
 * Copyright (C) 2015  Giulio Zambon  - http://zambon.com.au/
 *
 */
#include <stdio.h>
#include <stdlib.h>
#include <string.h>
#include "cleanup_around.h"
#include "def.h"
#include "lines.h"
#include "remove_candidate.h"
```

```
int lines(int kRC, char *comb, int n, int i) {
#ifdef LOG_IN_OUT
  printf("--- lines (%s) [", unit_names[kRC]);
  for (int k = 0; k < n; k++) printf("%d", comb[k]);
  printf("] %d >>>\n", i);
#endif

  int result = FALSE;
  int list[9] = {0};
  int n_list = 0;
  int abort = FALSE;
  for (int k = 0; k < n && !abort; k++) {
    int kk[2];
    kk[0] = comb[k];
    for (int j = 0; j < 9 && !abort; j++) {
      kk[1] = j;
      int kR = kk[kRC];
      int kC = kk[1-kRC];
      char *elem = grid[kR][kC];
      if (elem[i]) {
        if (elem[0] == 1) {
          abort = TRUE;
          }
        else {
          if (!list[j]) n_list++;
          list[j] = TRUE;
          }
        } // if (elem[i]..
      } // for (int j..
    } // for (int k..

  if (!abort && n_list == n) {
    int log_printed = FALSE;
    for (int jj = 0; jj < 9; jj++) {
      if (list[jj]) {
        int kk[2];
        kk[1] = jj;
        for (int k = 0; k < 9; k++) {
          if (memchr(comb, k, n) == NULL) {
            kk[0] = k;
            int kR = kk[kRC];
            int kC = kk[1-kRC];
            char *elem = grid[kR][kC];
            if (elem[i]) {
              result = TRUE;
```

```
#ifdef LOG_LINES
            if (!log_printed && !silent) {
                printf("lines(%d): the %ss", n,
                        unit_names[kRC]
                        );
                for (int k1 = 0; k1 < n; k1++) {
                    printf(" %d", comb[k1]);
                }
                printf(" let us eliminate %d from the"
                        %ss", i, unit_names[1-kRC]
                        );
                for (int k1 = 0; k1 < 9; k1++) {
                    if (list[k1]) printf(" %d", k1);
                }
                printf("\n");
                log_printed = TRUE;
            }
#endif
            remove_candidate("lines", i, kR, kC);
            if (grid[kR][kC][0] == 1) {
                cleanup_around(kR, kC);
            }
            } // if (elem[i]..
        } // if (memchr(..
      } // for (int k..
    } // if (list[jj]..
  } // for (int jj..
} // if (!abort..
#ifdef LOG_IN_OUT
  printf("<<< lines (%s) [", unit_names[kRC]);
  for (int k = 0; k < n; k++) printf("%d", comb[k]);
  printf("] %d ---\n", i);
#endif
  return result;
}
```

There are n line IDs stored in comb. They can be row IDs or column IDs, depending on the value of kRC (0 for rows, 1 for columns). To see whether the lines strategies apply, you have to count and identify the cross-lines (columns if kRC == ROW and rows if kRC == COL) containing candidates for i. As the lines strategies only apply to cells that are not solved, if you find that i solves any of the cells you check, you must abort the execution of lines().

To understand how the algorithm works, look at the example in Figure 9-1.

An Example

As usual, the first part of the function collects information and the second part processes it. Let's see what happens in the first part of lines() when comb contains [0 8], kRC == COL, and i == 4 (and n == 2 because this is an example for lines_2()).

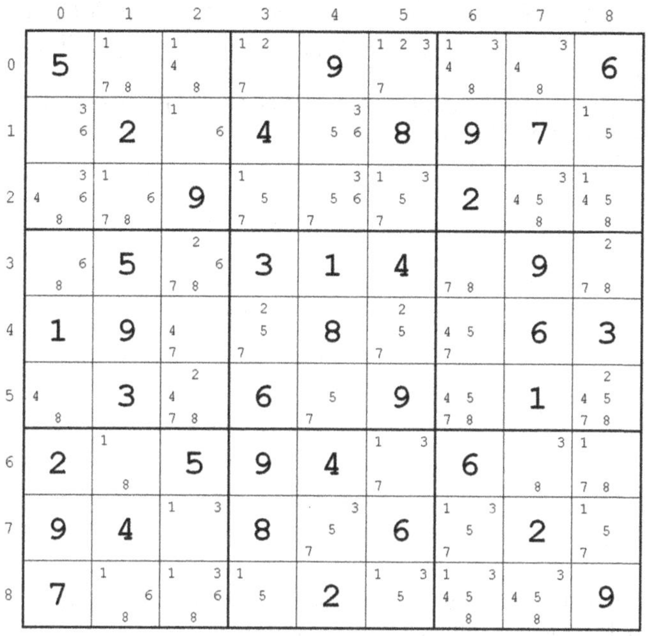

Figure 9-1. *An example for lines-2*

The control variable k of the outermost loop selects one column after the other, while the second loop, with control variable j goes through all the cells of the column. By using kRC to index the small vector kk, you determine the coordinates of the current cell (kR,kC).

If the cell contains a candidate for i (when elem[i] != 0) together with other candidates (when elem[0] != 1), you increment the cell counter n_list and set to TRUE the element of list that corresponds to the cell. As both n_list and list are defined and initialized to zero before entering the first loop, they bring together the results of scanning both columns of the combination. This is why you only increment n_list, which counts the cross-lines, the first time you encounter a new cross-line. To fully understand how the algorithm works, follow how you update the two variables as the scanning of the two columns proceeds.

The first column you scan is column 0 (you scan a column because in the example kRC is set to COL, and the column ID is 0 because comb is set to [0 8]) looking for a 4 (because in the example i is set to 4). The first cell containing a candidate for 4 is (2,0), which results in the following assignments:

```
n_list = 1;
list[2] = TRUE;
```

The next cell of column 0 with a candidate for 4 is (5,0), and the corresponding assignments are

```
n_list = 2;
list[5] = TRUE;
```

You then begin scanning column 8 (the column ID is the second one in comb, which is set to [0 8]). As a candidate for 4 only appears in row 2 and 5, you leave both n_list and list unchanged.

The second part of lines() starts with a check on n_list. With the combination of columns [0 8] for the number 4, n_list, at 2, matches n. This means that the strategy lines-2 applies. You only need to check whether it results in the actual removal of candidates.

As a counterexample, if you had been looking at, say, the column combination [0 7] instead of [0 8], when scanning column 7, you would have set n_list and list as follows:

```
n_list = 3;
list[0] = TRUE;
```

when processing (0,7) and

```
n_list = 4;
list[0] = TRUE;
```

when processing (2,7) and

```
n_list = 5;
list[8] = TRUE;
```

when processing (8,7).

Contrary to what happened with the combination [0 8], in this case you would have immediately returned unsuccessfully, because n_list would have been different from n (5 instead of 2).

To see whether you can remove candidates for i within the cross-lines (which, in the example, are rows) with IDs saved in list, you go through list (with the jj-loop) and only scan the cross-lines for which list[jj] is TRUE. You stored the cross-line IDs into list precisely to be able to go through them quickly.

While you are scanning the cross-lines, you obviously don't want to remove candidates that belong to the lines (which in the example are columns) of the combination. To ensure that you skip those cells, you use the character-search function memchr() of the standard string library. You can do that because comb is a vector of characters instead of integers, and you did it precisely to be able to use memchr(). With an array of integers, you would have needed to replace

```
if (memchr(comb, k, n) == NULL)
```

with

```
if (k != comb[0] && k != comb[1])
```

but then, the number of lines n would have been hard-coded to 2. To handle lines_3() and lines_4() you would have needed something like

```
int go_on = FALSE;
switch (n) {
  case 4: go_on = (k != comb[3]);
  case 3: go_on &= (k != comb[2]);
  case 2: go_on &= (k != comb[0] && k != comb[1]);
          break;
  default:
    printf("*** lines: programming error (%d)\n", n);
    break;
  }
if (go_on) { ...
```

but it would have not been very elegant.

A note of warning before moving on: this implementation of lines() produces unpredictable results when operating on a Sudoku grid that is in some way inconsistent. If, for example, some candidates should have been removed after solving a cell but have not, lines() goes, so to speak, bananas. But you have to make the assumption that the grid is consistent and clean when you apply this strategy; otherwise, to be safe, you would need to make the code so complicated to be almost unreadable.

Following are the log entries for the example you have analyzed:

```
lines(2): the columns 0 8 let us eliminate 4 from the rows 2 5
lines: removed 4 from (2,7)
lines: removed 4 from (5,2)
lines: removed 4 from (5,6)
```

Summary

This chapter described the implementation of the lines strategy. In Chapter 10, you will learn how to implement the last of the level 2 strategies: "Y-wing."

■ ■ ■

Implementing "Y-wing"

The Y-wing strategy is quite complex, which is reflected in the complexity of its implementation.

Key to the implementation of Y-wing (and of XY-chain, as you will see in Chapter 11) are two arrays defined for convenience in their own separate modules (see Listing 10-1).

Listing 10-1. pairs_data.c

```
/* pairs_data.c
 *
 * Copyright (C) 2015  Giulio Zambon  - http://zambon.com.au/
 *
 */
#include "pairs_data.h"

char n_x_pairs[10][10] = {{0}};
char *x_pairs[10][10][3] = {{{0}}};
```

n_x_pairs counts the number of pairs for every possible combination of two candidate numbers and x_pairs stores the coordinates of the cells that contain the pairs, whereby x_pairs's third index is used to identify the coordinates (see def.h in Listing 3-1).

```
#define ROW 0
#define COL 1
#define BOX 2
```

Note that x_pairs is a table of pointers because there can be more than one pair with the same combination of numbers.

The top-level strategy function is y_wing() (see Listing 10-2). Its purpose is to provide a standard f_ptr_t interface (see again def.h) to the function pairs_find(), which is shared between Y-wing and XY-chain.

pairs_find() (see Listings 10-3, 10-4, 10-5, and 10-6) then executes y_wing_digit() (see Listing 10-7) for each candidate number.

To determine what area of the Sudoku grid is affected by two distinct cells, y_wing_digit() makes use of the utility function intersection() (see Listing 10-8), which in turn executes footprint() (see Listing 10-9).

This certainly sounds confusing, and the only way of explaining how the various functions interact is to study them one at a time, beginning with the top one.

Listing 10-2. y_wing.c

```
/* y_wing.c
 *
 * Copyright (C) 2015   Giulio Zambon   - http://zambon.com.au/
 *
 */
#include <stdio.h>
#include <stdlib.h>
#include "def.h"
#include "pairs_find.h"
#include "y_wing.h"

int y_wing() {
#ifdef LOG_IN_OUT
  printf("--- y_wing >>>\n");
#endif
  int result = pairs_find(DEF_Y_WING);
#ifdef LOG_IN_OUT
  printf("<<< y_wing ---\n");
#endif
  return result;
  }
```

As you can see, y_wing() is trivial. All the work takes place within pairs_find(). In Chapter 11, you will see that the only difference between y_wing() and xy_chain() is the change of the pairs_find() parameter from DEF_Y_WING to DEF_XY_CHAIN. This is possible because Y-wing and XY-chain are in fact the same strategy, but you apply the former to three cells while the latter requires four or more cells. It makes sense to consider them separately because human players find Y-wing much easier to apply than XY-chain.

pairs_find()

The purpose of pairs_find() is to identify all naked pairs present in the Sudoku grid. As C does not support dynamic arrays, pairs_find() needs three steps before it can execute the y_wing_digit(): first, it counts the pairs so that it can calculate how much memory space is necessary to store the list of pairs; then, it allocates from the heap the memory it needs; and finally, it fills in the list of pairs.

Listing 10-3 shows how the initial counting is done.

Listing 10-3. pairs_find.c–Part 1: Initial Counting

```
/* pairs_find.c
 *
 * Copyright (C) 2015   Giulio Zambon   - http://zambon.com.au/
 *
 */
#include <stdio.h>
#include <stdlib.h>
#include "def.h"
#include "pairs_data.h"
#include "pairs_find.h"
#include "xy_chain_digit.h"
#include "y_wing_digit.h"
```

```c
int pairs_find(int chain_type) {
#ifdef LOG_IN_OUT
  printf("--- pairs_find (%d) >>>\n", chain_type);
#endif

  int result = FALSE;

  for (int k = 0; k <= 9; k++) {
    for (int j = 0; j <= 9; j++) {
      n_x_pairs[k][j] = 0;
      }
    }

  for (int k = 0; k < 9; k++) {
    for (int j = 0; j < 9; j++) {
      char *elem = grid[k][j];
      if (elem[0] == 2) {
        int nn[2] = {0, 0};
        int n = 0;
        for (int i = 1; j <= 9 && n < 2; i++) {
          if (elem[i] == TRUE) {
            nn[n] = i;
            n++;
            }
          }
        n_x_pairs[nn[0]][nn[1]]++;
        n_x_pairs[nn[0]][0]++;
        n_x_pairs[nn[1]][nn[0]]++;
        n_x_pairs[nn[1]][0]++;
        n_x_pairs[0][0]++;
        } // if (elem[0]..
      } // for (int j..
    } // for (int k..
```

Before doing anything else, pairs_find() resets the array of counters (n_x_pairs). An initialization is not sufficient because n_x_pairs and x_pairs are globally defined. Therefore, they keep their values between successive executions of pairs_find().

The two for-loops scan the whole grid one cell at a time, and the check on elem[0] ensures that only the naked pairs are processed. You use the little vector nn to store the numbers of the current pair. Notice that the two lines in bold make the array symmetric. That is, n_x_pairs[i1][i2] == n_x_pairs[i2][i1]. This is not strictly necessary, but it makes it possible to access the same value using either member of the pair first, thereby making the usage of the array easier. Also note that the 0-th elements of rows and columns of the array store the totals.

Once you know the number of pairs, you can allocate the memory necessary to store their coordinates, as shown in Listing 10-4.

Listing 10-4. pairs_find.c–Part 2: Memory Allocation

```c
char *data_block = (char*)malloc(
                n_x_pairs[0][0] * sizeof(char*) * 3
                );
if (data_block != NULL) {
  char *offset = data_block;
  for (int i1 = 1; i1 <= 9; i1++) {
    for (int i2 = 1; i2 <= 9; i2++) {
      for (int kkk = 0; kkk < 3; kkk++) {
        x_pairs[i1][i2][kkk] = offset;
        offset += n_x_pairs[i1][i2];
        }
      } // for (int i2..
    } // for (int i1..
  } // if (data_block..
else {
  printf("*** pairs_find: malloc failure\n");
  exit(EXIT_FAILURE);
}
```

n_x_pairs[0][0] contains the total number of pairs. As the array x_pairs stores three pointers for each pair (one for row IDs, one for column IDs, and one for box IDs), data_block must have space for at least n_x_pairs[0][0]*sizeof(char*)*3 bytes. Once you make the space available to pairs_find(), you set up the 300 elements of x_pairs to point to locations within data_block with exactly the space needed to save the pair coordinates.

This is a delicate operation, because a mistake in the calculation of the offsets will result in unpredictable errors and crashes.

In any case, once you have set up x_pairs, you need to fill it in. For this, refer to Listing 10-5.

Listing 10-5. pairs_find.c–Part 3: x_pairs

```c
for (int i1 = 1; i1 <= 9; i1++) {
  for (int i2 = 1; i2 <= 9; i2++) {
    n_x_pairs[i1][i2] = 0;
    }
  }
for (int k = 0; k < 9; k++) {
  for (int j = 0; j < 9; j++) {
    char *elem = grid[k][j];
    if (elem[0] == 2) {
      int nn[2] = {0, 0};
      int n = 0;
      for (int i = 1; j <= 9 && n < 2; i++) {
        if (elem[i] == TRUE) {
          nn[n] = i;
          n++;
          }
        } // for (int i..
      int i1 = nn[0];
      int i2 = nn[1];
      int n = n_x_pairs[i1][i2];
```

```
        n_x_pairs[i1][i2]++;
        n_x_pairs[i2][i1]++;
        x_pairs[i1][i2][ROW][n] = (char)k;
        x_pairs[i1][i2][COL][n] = (char)j;
        x_pairs[i1][i2][BOX][n] = (char)(k/3*3+j/3);
        x_pairs[i2][i1][ROW][n] = (char)k;
        x_pairs[i2][i1][COL][n] = (char)j;
        x_pairs[i2][i1][BOX][n] = (char)(k/3*3+j/3);
        } // if (elem[0]..
      } // for (int j..
    } // for (int k..
```

To fill in x_pairs, you recount the pairs and, while doing so, also save their coordinates. But notice that the for-loop to reset n_x_pairs does not clear the first elements of the array (i.e., those with one or both indices equal to zero). This is because, while you need the counters associated with individual numbers to progressively fill x_pairs, you don't need the totals. Therefore, there is no point in clearing them only to have to add them up again.

The box IDs are not strictly necessary, because you can always calculate them from row ID and column ID, but they are convenient to have around and generally make the strategy code more readable.

Finally, with n_x_pairs and x_pairs ready, you can execute y_wing_digit() (see Listing 10-6).

Listing 10-6. pairs_find.c–Part 4: Execute Y-wing

```
typedef int (*chain_funct_ptr_t)(int);
chain_funct_ptr_t chain_functs[] = {
    y_wing_digit, xy_chain_digit
    };
for (int i = 1; i <= 9 && !result; i++) {
  if (n_x_pairs[i][0] >= 2) {
    result |= chain_functs[chain_type](i);
    }
  } // for (int i..

free(data_block);

#ifdef LOG_IN_OUT
  printf("<<< pairs_find (%d) ---\n", chain_type);
#endif
  return result;
  }
```

Looking at the code, it becomes clear why you introduced pairs_find() at all: the identification of naked pairs is necessary for more than one strategy. Therefore, it makes sense to extract the common code into a separate function. In section "intersection()", you will see that the same happens with that function.

Notice that the for-loop that tries all numbers is aborted as soon as a strategy is successful. This is because any removal alters the Sudoku grid. Therefore, after a removal, n_x_pairs and x_pairs no longer reflect its current status.

This last part of pairs_find() has also another very important function: to free the memory block allocated with malloc(). It is always necessary to release all allocated memory, and the best place to do so is before exiting the function that allocated it.

y_wing_digit()

This function is where you implement Y-wing. As it requires several nested loops, it is not possible to break it down into parts that you can study separately. You will have to swallow it in a single big gulp (see Listing 10-7).

Listing 10-7. y_wing_digit.c

```c
/* y_wing_digit.c
 *
 * Copyright (C) 2015  Giulio Zambon  - http://zambon.com.au/
 *
 */
#include <stdio.h>
#include <stdlib.h>
#include "cleanup_around.h"
#include "def.h"
#include "intersection.h"
#include "pairs_data.h"
#include "remove_candidate.h"
#include "y_wing_digit.h"

int y_wing_digit(int i0) {
#ifdef LOG_IN_OUT
  printf("--- y_wing_digit (%d) >>>\n", i0);
#endif

#define A 0
#define B 1
#define C 2

  int success = FALSE;

  // +-------+
  // | i0+i1 |
  // +-------+-------+
  // | i1+i2 | i2+i0 |
  // +-------+-------+
  int coords[3][3];     // [cell][unit]
  for (int i1 = 1; i1 <= 9; i1++) {
    for (int i1k = 0; i1k < n_x_pairs[i0][i1]; i1k++) {

      // If we arrive here, i0 is paired with i1, and
      // i1k goes through all the pairs of i0 with i1
      coords[A][ROW] = x_pairs[i0][i1][ROW][i1k];
      coords[A][COL] = x_pairs[i0][i1][COL][i1k];
      coords[A][BOX] = x_pairs[i0][i1][BOX][i1k];
```

```c
for (int i2 = 1; i2 <= 9; i2++) {
  if (i2 != i0) {
    for (int i2k = 0; i2k < n_x_pairs[i1][i2]; i2k++) {

      // If we arrive here, i1 is paired with i2, and
      // i2k goes through all the pairs of i1 with i2
      coords[B][ROW] = x_pairs[i1][i2][ROW][i2k];
      coords[B][COL] = x_pairs[i1][i2][COL][i2k];
      coords[B][BOX] = x_pairs[i1][i2][BOX][i2k];

      if (i2 > i1 &&
          (   coords[A][ROW] == coords[B][ROW]
           || coords[A][COL] == coords[B][COL]
           || coords[A][BOX] == coords[B][BOX]
          )
         ) {
        for (int i3k = 0; i3k < n_x_pairs[i2][i0]; i3k++) {

          // If we arrive here, i2 is paired with i0, and
          // i3k goes through all the pairs of i2 made with i0
          coords[C][ROW] = x_pairs[i2][i0][ROW][i3k];
          coords[C][COL] = x_pairs[i2][i0][COL][i3k];
          coords[C][BOX] = x_pairs[i2][i0][BOX][i3k];

          if (   coords[C][ROW] != coords[A][ROW]
              && coords[C][COL] != coords[A][COL]
              && coords[C][BOX] != coords[A][BOX]
              && (   coords[C][ROW] == coords[B][ROW]
                  || coords[C][COL] == coords[B][COL]
                  || coords[C][BOX] == coords[B][BOX]
                 )
             ) {
            int printed = FALSE;
            void *mem_block = malloc(MAX_INTER_N*sizeof(struct rc_struct));
            if (mem_block == NULL) {
              printf("*** y_wing_digit (%d): malloc failure\n", i0);
              exit(EXIT_FAILURE);
            }
            rc_p_t inter = intersection(coords[A][ROW], coords[A][COL],
                coords[C][ROW], coords[C][COL], mem_block
                );
            rc_p_t p = inter;
            rc_p_t pp = p;
            while (p != NULL) {
              int kR = pp->row;
              int kC = pp->col;
              char *elem = grid[kR][kC];
              if (elem[i0]) {
                success = TRUE;
```

```c
#ifdef LOG_Y_WING
                      if (!printed && !silent) {
                        printf("y_wing_digit: (%d,%d):%d%d (%d,%d):%d%d "
                               "(%d,%d):%d%d\n",
                               coords[A][ROW], coords[A][COL], i0, i1,
                               coords[B][ROW], coords[B][COL], i1, i2,
                               coords[C][ROW], coords[C][COL], i2, i0
                               );
                        printf("y_wing_digit: intersection of (%d,%d) and "
                               "(%d,%d):", coords[A][ROW], coords[A][COL],
                               coords[C][ROW], coords[C][COL]
                               );
                        rc_p_t p1 = inter;
                        rc_p_t pp1 = p1;
                        do {
                          if (     pp1->row != coords[B][ROW]
                              || pp1->col != coords[B][COL]
                              ) {
                            printf(" (%d,%d)", pp1->row, pp1->col);
                            }
                          p1 = pp1->next;
                          pp1 = p1;
                          } while (p1 != NULL);
                        printf("\n");
                        printed = TRUE;
                        } // if (!printed..
#endif
                      remove_candidate("y_wing_digit", i0, kR, kC);
                      if (grid[kR][kC][0] == 1) {
                        cleanup_around(kR, kC);
                        }
                      } // if (elem[i0]..
                    p = pp->next;
                    pp = p;
                    }

              free(mem_block);
              } // if (coords[C][ROW]..
          } // for (int i3k..
        } // if (i2 > i1..
      } // for (int i2k..
    } // if (i2 != i0..
  } // for (int i2..
 } // for (int i1k..
 } // for (int i1..

#ifdef LOG_IN_OUT
  printf("<<< y_wing_digit (%d) ---\n", i0);
#endif
  return success;
  }
```

Y-wing requires a mini-chain of three cells containing naked pairs of candidate numbers. If you identify the numbers with i0, i1, and i2, the three cells must contain the pairs [i0 i1], [i1 i2], and [i2 i0]. A, B, and C identify the three cells.

The array coords stores the coordinates of the three cells, so that, for example, coords[A][ROW] refers to the row ID of the cell containing the pair [i0 i1], and coords[C][COL] refers to the column ID of the cell containing the pair [i2 i0].

The first for-loop selects i1 and the second for-loop selects the [i0 i1] pair (i.e., cell A). After selecting the first cell, you use the third for-loop to select i2 and the fourth one to select the [i1 i2] pair (i.e., cell B). Notice that you only accept i2 if it is different from i0, because the strategy requires three distinct numbers.

At this point, y_wing_digit() checks that i2 is greater than i1. This is to avoid processing the same chain twice from its two ends. For example, if you process the chain [4 1], [1 6], and [6 4], you don't want to process [4 6], [6 1], and [1 4] as well. In the same if-statement, you also check that the first two cells share at least one unit. That is, A and B must be in the same row, in the same column, or in the same box. They can obviously share row and box (or column and box), but at this stage, you only need to check that their "footprints" overlap, without going into more details.

The fifth (and last) big for-loop selects the [i2 i0] pair (i.e., cell C).

Before proceeding, you check that the second and third cells share at least one unit. This ensures that you are looking at a chain of three cells. In the same if-statement, you also check that the third cell doesn't share any unit with the first one. The reason is that when that happens, the i0s of the first and third cells are mutually exclusive without going through the chain, which makes the Y-wing strategy no longer applicable. If this check is successful, it means that Y-wing applies. What remains to be seen is whether the cells (or cell) that can "see" both A and C contain any i0 to remove. In other words, you have pulled your net, but you don't know yet whether you have caught anything.

To see whether you have caught i0s that you can remove, you first need to identify all the cells that can see both A and C. You do this by executing intersection(). You will see how that function works in the next section, but for now you only need to know that it accepts row and column IDs of the two cells and returns a pointer to the list you need.

As y_wing_digit() doesn't know how many cells are going to be in the list, it allocates enough space to contain the largest possible list.

```
void *mem_block = malloc(MAX_INTER_N*sizeof(struct rc_struct));
```

with both MAX_INTER_N and rc_struct defined in def.h as follows:

```
#define MAX_INTER_N 13
typedef struct rc_struct *rc_p_t;
typedef struct rc_struct {
  int row;
  int col;
  rc_p_t next;
  } rc_struct;
```

If you remove the code that prints the log entry, you reduce the rest of the Y-wing strategy to the following:

```
rc_p_t inter = intersection(coords[A][ROW],
                            coords[A][COL],
                            coords[C][ROW],
                            coords[C][COL], mem_block
                            );
```

```
rc_p_t p = inter;
rc_p_t pp = p;
while (p != NULL) {
  int kR = pp->row;
  int kC = pp->col;
  char *elem = grid[kR][kC];
  if (elem[i0]) {
    success = TRUE;
    remove_candidate("y_wing_digit", i0, kR, kC);
    if (grid[kR][kC][0] == 1) {
      cleanup_around(kR, kC);
      }
    } // if (elem[i0]..
  p = pp->next;
  pp = p;
  }
```

It is a while-loop that crawls through the linked list of cells seen by both ends of the chain, checks whether each one of them contains a candidates for i0, and removes it. Note that although B can see both A and C, it contains the naked pair [i1 i2]. Therefore, it cannot contain i0.

Notice that y_wing_digit() wouldn't need to check the return value of intersection(). This is because A and C are always visible, at the very least, by B. Therefore, the intersection cannot ever be empty and the while-loop could be replaced with a do-loop. Still, it is a good programming practice to be a bit defensive....

The only things that y_wing_digit() needs to do before returning is release the memory block with free(mem_block).

intersection()

The purpose of this function is to find all the cells that can "see" two given cells, whereby a cell can see another cell if it belongs to the same row, column, or box. It does so by executing footprint() for each one of the two cells, where the footprint of a cell is intended as the list of cells that it can see. Then, it is just a matter of determining which cells appear in both footprint lists.

Listing 10-8. intersection.c

```
/* intersection.c
 *
 * Copyright (C) 2015  Giulio Zambon  - http://zambon.com.au/
 *
 */
#include <stdio.h>
#include <stdlib.h>
#include "def.h"
#include "footprint.h"
#include "intersection.h"

rc_p_t intersection(int r1, int c1, int r2, int c2, void *mem) {
#ifdef LOG_IN_OUT
  printf("--- intersection (%d,%d) (%d,%d) >>>\n",
         r1, c1, r2, c2
         );
#endif
```

```c
int cells_found = FALSE;
rc_p_t retval = (rc_p_t)mem;
rc_p_t foot1;
rc_p_t foot2;

// Allocate the memory for the two footprints
void *mem_foots = malloc(
                (FOOT_N * sizeof(rc_struct_t)) << 1
                );
if (mem_foots != NULL) {
  rc_p_t mem1 = (rc_p_t)mem_foots;
  rc_p_t mem2 = (rc_p_t)(
            mem_foots + FOOT_N * sizeof(rc_struct_t)
            );

  // Obtain the two footprints
  foot1 = footprint(r1, c1, mem1);
  foot2 = footprint(r2, c2, mem2);
  }
else {
  printf("*** intersection (%d,%d) (%d,%d): malloc"
        " failure\n", r1, c1, r2, c2
        );
  exit(EXIT_FAILURE);
  }

// Build the list of cells common to the two
// footprints
rc_p_t p = retval;
rc_p_t p1 = foot1;
rc_p_t p_prev = NULL;
rc_p_t p_temp;
do {
  rc_p_t p2 = foot2;
  do {
    if (p2->row == p1->row && p2->col == p1->col) {
      cells_found = TRUE;
      p->row = p1->row;
      p->col = p1->col;
      p_prev = p;
      p_temp = p + 1;
      p->next = p_temp;
      p = p_temp;
      }
    p_temp = p2->next;
    p2 = p_temp;
    } while (p2 != NULL);
  p_temp = p1->next;
  p1 = p_temp;
  } while (p1 != NULL);
```

```
// Terminate the chain by clearing the 'next'
// pointer of the last cell
p_prev->next = NULL;

  free(mem_foots);

#ifdef LOG_IN_OUT
  printf("<<< intersection(%d,%d) (%d,%d) ---\n",
         r1, c1, r2, c2
         );
#endif
  return (cells_found) ? retval : NULL;
  }
```

FOOT_N is defined in footprint.h to be 20.

Rather than trying to identify in which way the two footprints overlap, intersection() uses the brute-force approach of comparing the coordinates of each cell of the first footprint with the coordinates of each cell of the second footprint. This is safer and easier to understand.

You could have allocated the mem block within intersection(), but it is a bad practice to allocate memory in a function and release it somewhere else. It makes it more difficult to track the blocks of memory that you have allocated and sometimes leads to blocks not being released, which in turn causes what is normally called "a memory leak." For the same reason, you allocate the working memory needed by the double execution of footprint() (i.e., mem_foots) within intersection().

footprint()

This function's task is to build a linked list of the 20 cells that can "see" a given cell. footprint() does it by scanning the whole grid by rows. The key if-statements in Listing 10-9 are highlighted in bold.

Listing 10-9. footprint.c

```
/* footprint.c
 *
 * Copyright (C) 2015  Giulio Zambon  - http://zambon.com.au/
 *
 */
#include <stdio.h>
#include <stdlib.h>
#include "def.h"
#include "footprint.h"

rc_p_t footprint(int row, int col, void *mem) {
#ifdef LOG_IN_OUT
  printf("--- footprint >>>\n");
#endif

  rc_p_t rc = (rc_p_t)mem;
  int box = row/3*3+col/3;
```

```
rc_p_t p = rc;
rc_p_t next;
for (int k = 0; k < 9; k++) {
  for (int j = 0; j < 9; j++) {
    if (k != row || j != col) {
      if (k == row || j == col || k/3*3+j/3 == box) {
        p->row = k;
        p->col = j;
        next = p + 1;
        p->next = next;
        p = next;
      } // if (k == row..
    } // if (k..
  } // for (int j..
} // for (int k..

// Terminate the chain by clearing the 'next' pointer of the last cell
p = rc + (FOOT_N - 1);
p->next = NULL;

#ifdef LOG_IN_OUT
  printf("<<< footprint ---\n");
#endif
  return rc;
}
```

The first if skips the cell of which footprint is to be determined. The second if selects the cells that share with the requested cell the row ID, the column ID, or the box ID.

An Example

Now that you know all the functions involved, go through an example to see how the algorithm works in practice (see Figure 10-1).

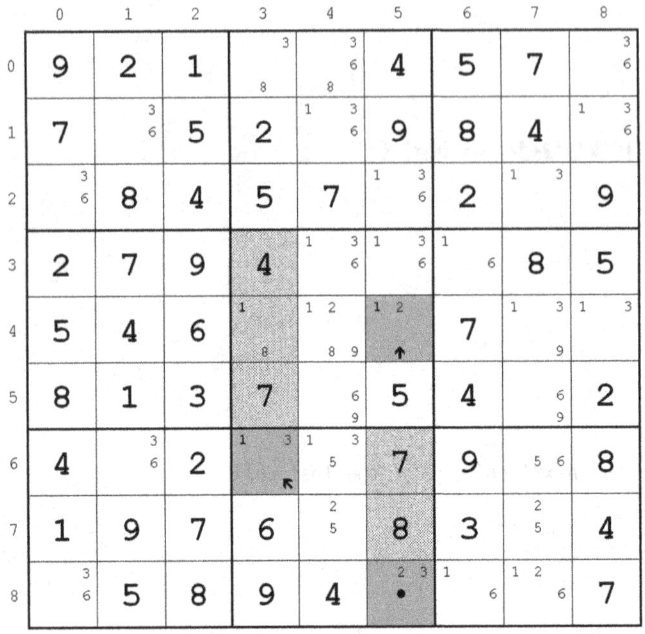

Figure 10-1. *An example for Y-wing*

You can apply Y-wing to the three cells $(4,5)$, $(8,5)$, and $(6,3)$ and remove the number 1 from the five cells highlighted in light gray. As four of them are already solved, Y-wing results in the removal of the 1 in $(4,3)$.

pairs_find() finds 19 naked pairs. You pick up the action of the program when pairs_find() executes y_wing_digit() for the number 1. i0 is therefore equal to 1.

The first for-loop of y_wing_digit() (with control variable i1) starts by selecting i1 = 1. Obviously, as the numbers in a pair must be different from each other, n_x_pairs[i0][i1] (i.e., n_x_pairs[1][1]) is zero, and the second for-loop (with control variable i1k) never starts. The first for-loop then tries i1 = 2. This time, the second for-loop finds a [1 2] pair in $(4,5)$. Therefore, it sets

```
coords[A][ROW] = x_pairs[i0][i1][ROW][i1k]; // where x_pairs[1][2][ROW][0] is 4
coords[A][COL] = x_pairs[i0][i1][COL][i1k]; // where x_pairs[1][2][COL][0] is 5
coords[A][BOX] = x_pairs[i0][i1][BOX][i1k]; // where x_pairs[1][2][BOX][0] is 4
```

The third for-loop (with control variable i2) tries i2 = 1, but the if-statement immediately inside the loop discards it. The next try is i2 = 2, but there cannot be pairs with identical i1 and i2. Therefore, the third loop exits before entering the fourth one (the loop with control variable i2k). Finally, the third loop tries i2 = 3 and finds a [2 3] pair in $(8,5)$, and the fourth loop sets the following:

```
coords[B][ROW] = x_pairs[i1][i2][ROW][i2k]; // where x_pairs[2][3][ROW][0] is 8
coords[B][COL] = x_pairs[i1][i2][COL][i2k]; // where x_pairs[2][3][COL][0] is 5
coords[B][BOX] = x_pairs[i1][i2][BOX][i2k]; // where x_pairs[2][3][BOX][0] is 7
```

i2 is greater than i1 and the two cells A and B have the same column. Therefore, the if-statement inside the fourth for-loop succeeds.

The fifth for-loop (with control variable i3k), which looks for pairs containing i2 and i0 (i.e., 3 and 1), finds one in (2,7), but the complex if-statement inside the fifth for-loop fails. Its purpose is to ensure that C and A share no unit (which is the case) and that C shares at least one unit with B, and this fails, because C is (2,7) and B is (8,5). The second [3 1] pair in the list is located in (4,8) and it fails because it is in the same row of A, which is (4,5). Finally, the third [3 1] pair, which is located in (6,3) satisfies all if-conditions. As a result, y_wing_digit() executes intersection() with the cells (4,5) and (6,3).

intersection() returns the following list of cells: (3,3), (4,3), (5,3), (6,5), and (7,5). Of these, only (4,3) is unsolved and contains a candidate for 1, and y_wing_digit() removes it.

The log entry is as follows:

```
y_wing_digit: (4,5):12 (8,5):23 (6,3):31
y_wing_digit: intersection of (4,5) and (6,3): (3,3) (4,3) (5,3) (6,5) (7,5)
y_wing_digit: removed 1 from (4,3)
cleanup_unit [row of (4,3)]: removed 8 from (4,4)
cleanup_unit [column of (4,3)]: removed 8 from (0,3)
cleanup_unit [row of (0,3)]: removed 3 from (0,4)
cleanup_unit [row of (0,3)]: removed 3 from (0,8)
cleanup_unit [row of (0,8)]: removed 6 from (0,4)
cleanup_unit [column of (0,8)]: removed 6 from (1,8)
cleanup_unit [column of (0,3)]: removed 3 from (6,3)
cleanup_unit [row of (6,3)]: removed 1 from (6,4)
cleanup_unit [box of (0,3)]: removed 3 from (1,4)
cleanup_unit [box of (0,3)]: removed 3 from (2,5)
```

Summary

In this chapter, you learned about the implementation of Y-wing, which will form the basis for the implementation of XY-chain, the level 3 strategy you will learn about in Chapter 11 and, together with line-4, one of the most difficult.

CHAPTER 11

■ ■ ■

Implementing "XY-chain"

This strategy is an extension of Y-wing. Therefore, it is not surprising that the two strategies share a significant amount of code.

The top-level strategy function is xy_chain() (see Listing 11-1). Like y_wing(), its purpose is to provide a standard f_ptr_t interface (see def.h in Listing 3-1) to the function pairs_find() (see Listings 10-3, 10-4, 10-5, and 10-6). pairs_find() executes xy_chain_digit() (see Listing 11-2) for each candidate number, which in turn uses xy_chain_step() (see Listing 11-4) to follow the chain of cells that is at the core of the XY-chain strategy. To determine what area of the Sudoku grid is affected by two distinct cells, xy_chain_step() executes the utility function intersection() (see Listing 10-8), which calls footprint() (see Listing 10-9).

Listing 11-1. xy_chain.c

```c
/* xy_chain.c
 *
 * Copyright (C) 2015  Giulio Zambon  - http://zambon.com.au/
 *
 */
#include <stdio.h>
#include <stdlib.h>
#include "def.h"
#include "pairs_find.h"
#include "xy_chain.h"

int xy_chain() {
#ifdef LOG_IN_OUT
  printf("--- xy_chain >>>\n");
#endif
  int result = pairs_find(DEF_XY_CHAIN);
#ifdef LOG_IN_OUT
  printf("<<< xy_chain ---\n");
#endif
  return result;
  }
```

xy_chain_digit()

The purpose of xy_chain_digit() is to start chains that begin with a particular number.

Listing 11-2. xy_chain_digit.c

```
/* xy_chain_digit.c
 *
 * Copyright (C) 2015  Giulio Zambon  - http://zambon.com.au/
 *
 */
#include <stdio.h>
#include <stdlib.h>
#include "def.h"
#include "pairs_data.h"
#include "xy_chain_digit.h"
#include "xy_chain_step.h"

int xy_chain_digit(int i0) {
#ifdef LOG_IN_OUT
  printf("--- xy_chain_digit (%d) >>>\n", i0);
#endif

  int n_found = 0;
  for (int i1 = 1; i1 <= 9 && n_found == 0; i1++) {
    for (int i01 = 0; i01 < n_x_pairs[i0][i1] && n_found == 0; i01++) {

      // Flag x_pairs[i0][i1][ROW][i01] and x_pairs[i0][i1][COL][i01]
      // to avoid using the same cell more than once within the chain
      int kR01 = x_pairs[i0][i1][ROW][i01];
      int kC01 = x_pairs[i0][i1][COL][i01];
      x_pairs[i0][i1][ROW][i01] += 10;
      x_pairs[i1][i0][ROW][i01] += 10;

      // Start the chain.
      {
        int kB01 = x_pairs[i0][i1][BOX][i01];
        chain_info_struct_t i0_info;
        chain_info_struct_t i1_info;
        i0_info.digit = i0;
        i1_info.digit = i1;
        i1_info.coords[ROW] = i0_info.coords[ROW] = kR01;
        i1_info.coords[COL] = i0_info.coords[COL] = kC01;
        i1_info.coords[BOX] = i0_info.coords[BOX] = kB01;
        i0_info.next = &i1_info;
        i1_info.next = NULL;
        n_found += xy_chain_step(&i0_info, 1);
      }
```

```
    // Restore the grid.
    x_pairs[i0][i1][ROW][i01] -= 10;
    x_pairs[i1][i0][ROW][i01] -= 10;
    } // for (int i01..
  } // for (int i1 = 1..

#ifdef LOG_IN_OUT
  printf("<<< xy_chain_digit (%d) ---\n", i0);
#endif
  return n_found > 0;
  }
```

As in y_wing_digit(), the first two for-loops go in sequence through all the cells containing a naked pair that includes i0 as a candidate. After selecting the cell from which the chain is to start, xy_chain_digit() flags it as already in use by adding 10 to its row ID. This is to avoid xy_chain_step() using it again when extending the chain. The choice of the value 10 makes possible a simple check: rows with ID < 9 are free, while rows with ID > 9 are already part of the chain. As x_pairs is symmetrical, it is necessary to flag both x_pairs[i0][i1] and x_pairs[i1][i0]. Obviously, xy_chain_digit() restores the original row IDs after processing a cell, so that the same cell can be used for other chains.

To start the chain, xy_chain_digit() builds the first two links, one for each number of the first pair (for the definition of the link type, see chain_info_struct in Listing 11-3) and passes it to xy_chain_step() (see Listing 11-4).

Listing 11-3. xy_chain_step.h

```
/* xy_chain_step.h
 *
 * XY-chain strategy: moving along the chain till the end.
 *
 * Returns the number of candidates removed.
 *
 * Copyright (C) 2015  Giulio Zambon  - http://zambon.com.au/
 *
 */
#ifndef XY_CHAIN_STEP
#define XY_CHAIN_STEP

typedef struct chain_info_struct *chain_info_struct_p;
typedef struct chain_info_struct {
  int number;
  int coords[3];
  chain_info_struct_p next;
  } chain_info_struct_t;

extern int chain_length;

int xy_chain_step(chain_info_struct_p info, int depth);

#endif
```

The structure chain_info_struct contains a number candidate, the coordinates of the cell where the candidate is located, and a pointer to a structure of the same type (i.e., to the next link of the chain).

xy_chain_step()

This is where all the work is done. This function is quite a whopper, but I have never been in favor of breaking up a large function into separate functions unless there is a "natural" way to do it. In this case, I believe that spreading the algorithm over more than one function would be unwieldy and confusing.

Listing 11-4. xy_chain_step.c

```c
/* xy_chain_step.c
 *
 * Copyright (C) 2015  Giulio Zambon  - http://zambon.com.au/
 *
 */
#include <stdio.h>
#include <stdlib.h>
#include "cleanup_around.h"
#include "def.h"
#include "intersection.h"
#include "pairs_data.h"
#include "remove_candidate.h"
#include "xy_chain_step.h"

#define MAX_DEPTH 8

int chain_length;

int xy_chain_step(chain_info_struct_p info, int depth) {
#ifdef LOG_IN_OUT
  printf("--- xy_chain_step (%d) >>>\n", depth);
#endif

  int n_found = 0;
  chain_info_struct_p next = info->next;
  chain_info_struct_p ix_info_p;
  do {
    ix_info_p = next;
    next = ix_info_p->next;
    } while (next != NULL);
  int i0 = info->digit;
  int ix = ix_info_p->digit;

  for (int iy = 1; iy <= 9 && n_found == 0; iy++) {
    for (int ixy = 0; ixy < n_x_pairs[ix][iy] && n_found == 0; ixy++) {

      int kRxy = x_pairs[ix][iy][ROW][ixy];
      if (kRxy < 9) {
        int kCxy = x_pairs[ix][iy][COL][ixy];
        int kBxy = x_pairs[ix][iy][BOX][ixy];
```

```
          if (    kRxy == ix_info_p->coords[ROW]
               || kCxy == ix_info_p->coords[COL]
               || kBxy == ix_info_p->coords[BOX]
             ) {
          int found_something_this_time = FALSE;
          if (iy == io && depth > 2) {
            int printed = FALSE;
            void *mem_block = malloc(MAX_INTER_N * sizeof(struct rc_struct));
            if (mem_block == NULL) {
              printf("*** xy_chain_step: malloc failure\n");
              exit(EXIT_FAILURE);
              }
            int kRO = info->coords[ROW];
            int kCO = info->coords[COL];
            rc_p_t inter = intersection(kRO, kCO, kRxy, kCxy, mem_block);

            // Check whether intersecting cells contain io as candidates.
            rc_p_t p = inter;
            rc_p_t pp = p;
            while (p != NULL) {
              int kR = pp->row;
              int kC = pp->col;
              if (kR < 9 && grid[kR][kC][io]) {
                found_something_this_time = TRUE;
                n_found++;
#ifdef LOG_XY_CHAIN
                if (!printed && !silent) {
                  printf("xy_chain_step: (%d,%d):%d", info->coords[ROW],
                      info->coords[COL], info->digit
                      );
                  next = info->next;
                  printf("%d", next->digit);
                  do {
                    chain_info_struct_p next1 = next->next;
                    if (next1 != NULL) {
                      printf(" (%d,%d):%d%d", next1->coords[ROW],
                          next1->coords[COL], next->digit, next1->digit
                          );
                      }
                    next = next1;
                    } while (next != NULL);
                  printf(" (%d,%d):%d%d\n", kRxy, kCxy, ix, iy);
                  printf("xy_chain_step: intersection of (%d,%d) and (%d,%d):",
                      kRO, kCO, kRxy, kCxy
                      );
                  rc_p_t p = inter;
                  rc_p_t pp = p;
                  do {
                    printf(" (%d,%d)", pp->row, pp->col);
                    p = pp->next;
                    pp = p;
```

125

```
                    } while (p != NULL);
                printf("\n");
                printed = TRUE;
                } // if (!printed..
#endif

            { // Scan the whole chain to determine its length
              // and update chain_length
              chain_info_struct_p info1 = info->next;
              chain_length = 1;
              do {
                chain_length++;
                chain_info_struct_p info2 = info1->next;
                info1 = info2;
                } while (info1 != NULL);
              }

            remove_candidate("xy_chain_step", i0, kR, kC);
            if (grid[kR][kC][0] == 1) {
              cleanup_around(kR, kC);
              }
            } // if (elem[i0]..
          p = pp->next;
          pp = p;
          }

      free(mem_block);
      } // if (iy..

    if (!found_something_this_time) {

      // The chain is to be extended
      x_pairs[ix][iy][ROW][ixy] += 10;
      x_pairs[iy][ix][ROW][ixy] += 10;
      chain_info_struct_t iy_info;
      iy_info.digit = iy;
      iy_info.coords[ROW] = kRxy;
      iy_info.coords[COL] = kCxy;
      iy_info.coords[BOX] = kBxy;
      iy_info.next = NULL;
      ix_info_p->next = &iy_info;

      // Keep following the chain
      if (depth < MAX_DEPTH) {
        n_found += xy_chain_step(info, depth + 1);
        }

      // Clean up behind you
      ix_info_p->next = NULL;
      x_pairs[ix][iy][ROW][ixy] -= 10;
      x_pairs[iy][ix][ROW][ixy] -= 10;
```

```
        } // if (!found_something_this_time..
      } // if (kRxy ==..
    } // if (kRxy <..
  } // for (int ixy..
} // for (int iy..
```

```
#ifdef LOG_IN_OUT
  printf("<<< xy_chain_step (%d) ---\n", depth);
#endif
  return n_found;
  }
```

xy_chain_step() goes through the current chain until it reaches its end and saves a pointer to the last link in ix_info_p. For convenience, it also stores the first and last numbers of the current chain, respectively, in i0 and ix. The first two for-loops go through all the pairs containing ix, whereby the if-statement immediately inside the second for-loop ensures that the cell is not one of those already included in the current chain. If the cell is still unused, xy_chain_step() saves its coordinates. At this point, xy_chain_step() has convenient access to the following information:

i0: the first number of the chain;

ix: the last number of the chain as it currently stands;

iy: a number paired with ix that could complete or extend the chain;

kRxy,kCxy,kSxy: the unit IDs of the cell with the [ix iy] pair.

The check

```
if (    kRxy == ix_info_p->coords[ROW]
    || kCxy == ix_info_p->coords[COL]
    || kSxy == ix_info_p->coords[BOX]
    ) {
```

ensures that the cell containing [ix iy] shares at least one unit with the last cell of the current chain—that is, that the new cell is linked to the previous one.

The next if-statement finds out whether the new number (i.e., iy) is identical to the initial one (i.e., i0) but also ensures that the current chain contains at least two cells. iy == i0 tells you that you have reached the end of the chain, but why should you check the length?

If you removed the check on the chain length, it could be that you complete the chain when depth == 2. That would mean that with the new cell, the chain would reach a length of 3. For example, the chain could consist of the cell (4,2) with the pair [3 1], (4,0) with [1 5], and (3,0) with [5 3]. It would be a Y-wing!

In fact, you could have ignored the Y-wing strategy and simply get it as a particular case of XY-chain, but many web sites talk about Y-wing. Also, the general XY-chain is more complicated to implement and more difficult to understand. Therefore, it makes sense to describe it and implement it separately.

So, you only need to change the 2 to 1 to get Y-wing handled by the XY-chain functions. In practice though, considering that Y-wing is a level 2 strategy, XY-chain is level 3, and you only attempt level 3 strategies when all level 2s have been unsuccessful, you would also need to disable Y-wing for XY-chain to take over. If you remove the check completely, it can happen that the chain only contains two cells. For example, (4,2) with [3 1] and (4,0) with [1 3]. But you already handle such occurrences with the naked pair strategy!

In any case, after the iy == i0 check, the chain is completed. However, you still need to see whether there are i0 candidates you can remove from the cells that can see both the initial cell of the chain and the cell with coordinates (kRxy,kCxy). After allocating a block of memory to store the list of cells, xy_chain_step() executes intersection(kR0, kC0, kRxy, kCxy, mem_block),where (kR0,kC0) are the coordinates of the initial cell.

You can easily follow the while-loop if you remove the part that prints the log entry.

If the iy == i0 check fails or if depth <= 2 or if the do-loop doesn't find any i0 candidate to be removed, found_something_this_time remains set to FALSE. It means that you can attempt to extend the chain. You accomplish this by appending to the chain the cell with the [ix iy] pair and executing xy_chain_step() recursively.

The fact that you extend the chain when you encounter an instance of i0 that doesn't result in the removal of candidates implies that pairs within the chain can contain i0 and you must not remove those cells from the chain. This explains why you have the condition that kR be less than 9 before checking whether grid[kR][kC][i0] is true. In any case, using a flagged row ID (i.e., an ID to which you added 10) to index the Sudoku grid would lead to unpredictable results.

You have probably noticed that xy_chain_step() only calls itself recursively up to eight times. The longer the chain, the higher the risk of running out of memory, and, in any case, it seems unreasonable to look for chains containing more than nine cells.

The following is an example of a log entry with the longest possible chain:

```
xy_chain_step: (4,2):13 (3,0):35 (3,6):58 (3,2):84 (5,1):49 (7,1):94 (7,5):47 (2,5):75
(2,1):51
xy_chain_step: intersection of (4,2) and (2,1): (0,2) (1,2) (2,2) (3,1) (4,1) (5,1)
xy_chain_step: removed 1 from (2,2)
```

As usual, let's look at an example in some detail.

An Example

Figure 11-1 shows a short chain for the number 9 that begins in (8,1) and ends in (0,0). It allows you to remove the candidates for 9 in (1,1), (6,0), and (8,1) because they are visible by the 9s at both ends of the chain.

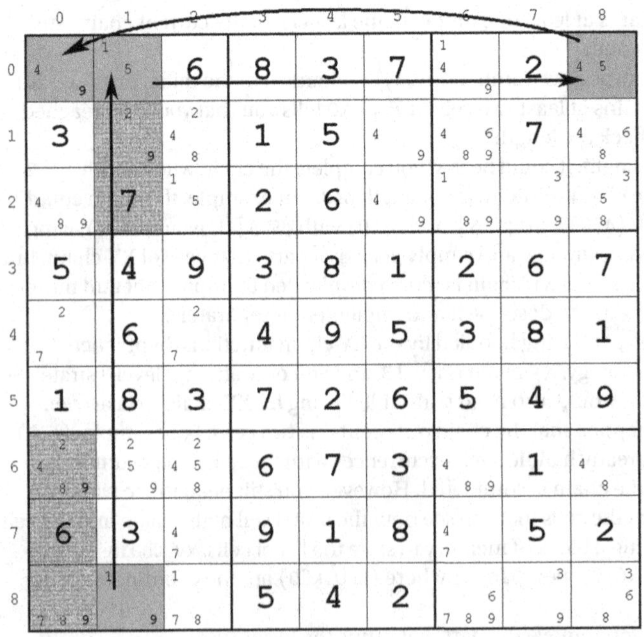

Figure 11-1. An example for XY-chain

If you add to pairs_find.c the code shown in Listing 11-5 (it is already in the source file but commented out), you obtain the list of pairs reproduced in Listing 11-6.

Listing 11-5. pairs_find( )–Displaying the List of Pairs

```
for (int i1 = 1; i1 <= 9; i1++) {
  if (n_x_pairs[i1][0] > 0) {
    printf("\ntotal #pairs for %d: %d\n", i1,
           n_x_pairs[i1][0]
           );
  }
  for (int i2 = 1; i2 <= 9; i2++) {
    if (n_x_pairs[i1][i2] > 0) {
      printf("%d %d [%d]:", i1, i2,
             n_x_pairs[i1][i2]
             );
      for (int kkk = 0;
           kkk < n_x_pairs[i1][i2];
           kkk++
           ) {
        printf(" (%d,%d)", x_pairs[i1][i2][0][kkk],
               x_pairs[i1][i2][1][kkk]
               );
      }
      printf("\n");
    }
  }
}
```

Listing 11-6. pairs_find( )–Example of List of Pairs

```
total #pairs for 1: 3
1 5 [2]: (0,1) (2,2)
1 9 [1]: (8,1)

total #pairs for 2: 3
2 7 [2]: (4,0) (4,2)
2 9 [1]: (1,1)

total #pairs for 3: 2
3 9 [2]: (2,7) (8,7)

total #pairs for 4: 7
4 5 [1]: (0,8)
4 7 [2]: (7,2) (7,6)
4 8 [1]: (6,8)
4 9 [3]: (0,0) (1,5) (2,5)

total #pairs for 5: 3
5 1 [2]: (0,1) (2,2)
5 4 [1]: (0,8)
```

```
total #pairs for 7: 4
7 2 [2]: (4,0) (4,2)
7 4 [2]: (7,2) (7,6)

total #pairs for 8: 1
8 4 [1]: (6,8)

total #pairs for 9: 7
9 1 [1]: (8,1)
9 2 [1]: (1,1)
9 3 [2]: (2,7) (8,7)
9 4 [3]: (0,0) (1,5) (2,5)
```

After trying the numbers from 1 to 8 without result, pairs_find() executes xy_chain_digit() for the number 9. xy_chain_digit() starts from the pair [9 1] in the cell (8,1), builds the linked chain {9,(8,1)} -> {1,(8,1)} -> NULL, and passes it to xy_chain_step() with depth set to 1.

Depth 1: xy_chain_step() tries with the first two for-loops to find a [1 iy] pair, and only succeeds when iy == 5. The [1 5] found is in (0,1). It adds the new cell to the chain to make {9,(8,1)} -> {1,(8,1)} -> {5,(0,1)} -> NULL and executes itself recursively with depth set to 2.

Depth 2: The first two for-loops of xy_chain_step(), looking for a [5 iy] pair, find at once the [5 1] pair in (0,1), which the previous execution of xy_chain_step() had changed to (10,1), and discards it because its row ID (i.e., kRxy) is greater than 9. It then finds another [5 1] pair in (2,2). This time, xy_chain_step() accepts the pair and adds it to the chain, to form {9,(8,1)} -> {1,(8,1)} -> {5,(0,1)} -> {1,(2,2)} -> NULL. After that, it calls itself recursively with depth set to 3.

Depth 3: The first two for-loops of xy_chain_step(), looking for a [1 iy] pair, find that all three pairs containing a 1 have been already taken (i.e., their cells have the row ID greater than 9). Therefore, it returns 0.

Depth 2: xy_chain_step() removes the last cell of the chain by executing

```
ix_info_p->next = NULL;
x_pairs[ix][iy][ROW][ixy] -= 10;
x_pairs[iy][ix][ROW][ixy] -= 10;
```

By doing so, it restores the chain to what it was when it started execution: {9,(8,1)} -> {1,(8,1)} -> {5,(0,1)} -> NULL. Back to the second for-loop statement, it turns out that both [5 1] pairs have been tried. The loop falls through and control passes to the first for-loop, which sets iy first to 2 and then to 3. In neither case can the second for-loop find a pair. But when the first for-loop sets iy to 4, the second loop finds a [5 4] pair in (0,8). As the new cell shares a unit with (0,1), xy_chain_step() adds it to the chain to form {9,(8,1)} -> {1,(8,1)} -> {5,(0,1)} -> {4,(0,8)} -> NULL and executes itself recursively with depth set to 3.

Depth 3: The first two for-loops of xy_chain_step(), looking for a [4 iy] pair, find the [5 4] in (0,8), but it has already been taken. Then, they find [4 7] in (7,2) and in (7,6), but they are discarded because they don't share any unit with (0,8). The next pair, [4 8] in (6,8) passes all the checks. Therefore xy_chain_step() adds it to the chain to form {9,(8,1)} -> {1,(8,1)} -> {5,(0,1)} -> {4,(0,8)} -> {8,(6,8)} -> NULL and executes itself recursively with depth set to 4.

Depth 4: The first two for-loops of xy_chain_step() discover that there is only one [8 iy] pair that, obviously, has already been taken. I say "obviously" because we execute xy_chain_step() only after finding a number in a pair. Now, if that number only appears in a single pair, that pair is what took us to xy_chain_step() in the first place, and must therefore already been taken. With nothing to do, xy_chain_step() returns 0.

Depth 3: xy_chain_step() restores the chain to {9,(8,1)} -> {1,(8,1)} -> {5,(0,1)} -> {4,(0,8)} -> NULL before looking for further [4 iy] pairs. It finds [4 9] in (0,0). As iy == i0 and depth > 2, xy_chain_step() executes intersection(8,1,0,0,mem_block), which returns the following list of cells: (0,1), (1,1), (2,1), (6,0), (7,0), and (8,0). Three of those cells contain candidates for 9 to be removed: (1,1), (6,0), and (8,0). The generated log entry is as follows:

```
xy_chain_step: (8,1):91 (0,1):15 (0,8):54 (0,0):49
xy_chain_step: intersection of (8,1) and (0,0): (0,1) (1,1) (2,1) (6,0) (7,0) (8,0)
xy_chain_step: removed 9 from (1,1)
cleanup_unit [row of (1,1)]: removed 2 from (1,2)
cleanup_unit [column of (1,1)]: removed 2 from (6,1)
xy_chain_step: removed 9 from (6,0)
xy_chain_step: removed 9 from (8,0)
```

xy_chain_step() restores the chain to {9,(8,1)} -> {1,(8,1)} -> {5,(0,1)} -> {4,(0,8)} -> NULL before looking for further pairs and numbers, but this time n_found == 3. Therefore, xy_chain_step() leaves the first two for-loops and returns 3. Actually, to be precise, the second for-loops exits because there are no further [4 9] pairs, and the first for-loop exits because 9 is the last number available. But the condition n_found == 0 is in both loops to terminate them when candidates are removed, regardless of the number or whether there are still available pairs.

Depth 2: xy_chain_step() restores the chain to {9,(8,1)} -> {1,(8,1)} -> {5,(0,1)} -> NULL and returns 3.

Depth 1: xy_chain_step() restores the chain to {9,(8,1)} -> {1,(8,1)} -> NULL and returns 3.

Depth 0: xy_chain_digit() removes the flags from the last two cells in x_pairs with

```
x_pairs[i0][i1][ROW][i01] -= 10;  // i.e., x_pairs[9][1][ROW][0] -= 10;
x_pairs[i1][i0][ROW][i01] -= 10;  // i.e., x_pairs[1][9][ROW][0] -= 10;
```

before returning TRUE.

pairs_find() exits the number-loop because 9 is the last number, but it would have done the same with any other number, because it only keeps going as long as result is FALSE. After exiting the loop, it frees the allocated memory and returns TRUE.

Summary

Once you have learned how to implement XY-chain, discussed in this chapter, Chapter 12 will present no problems. You will learn the last strategy that Solver implements: the level 3 "rectangle."

■ ■ ■

Implementing "Rectangle"

The rectangle strategy is the first level 3 strategy that is not an extension of easier ones. As I explained in Chapter 2, this strategy relies on sets of cells that form rectangular patterns. You implement it with the functions `rectangle()`, `rectangle_pattern()`, `rectangle_cell()`, and `rectangle_step()` (see Listings 12-1, 12-2, 12-3, and12-4, respectively).

rectangle()

To program the rectangle strategy, you need to check all possible rectangular patterns of cells and follow the chain around the four boxes that contain the corners of the patterns.

Only the following nine combinations of four boxes are possible: (0,1,4,3), (0,2,5,3), (0,1,7,6), (0,2,8,6), (1,2,5,4), (1,2,8,7), (3,4,7,6), (3,5,8,6), and (4,5,8,7), as you can see in Figure 12-1, which outlines the boxes with their IDs without showing the cells.

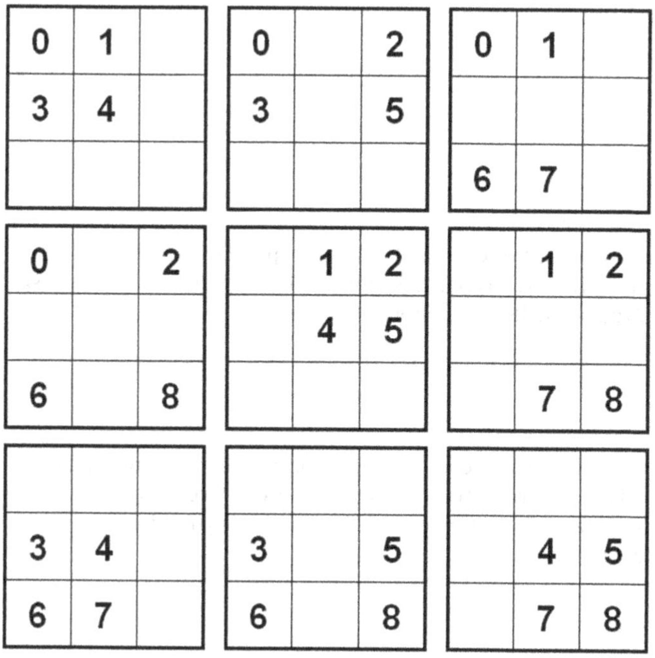

Figure 12-1. Patterns for the rectangle strategy

rectangle() loops through the nine combination and executes the function rectangle_pattern() for each one of them, as shown in Listing 12-1.

Listing 12-1. rectangle.c

```
/* rectangle.c
 *
 * Copyright (C) 2015  Giulio Zambon  - http://zambon.com.au/
 *
 */
#include <stdio.h>
#include <stdlib.h>
#include "def.h"
#include "rectangle.h"
#include "rectangle_cell.h"
#include "rectangle_pattern.h"

int rectangle() {
#ifdef LOG_IN_OUT
  printf("--- rectangle >>>\n");
#endif
  int result = FALSE;
  int pattern[9][4] = {
      {0,1,4,3}, {0,2,5,3}, {0,1,7,6},
      {0,2,8,6}, {1,2,5,4}, {1,2,8,7},
      {3,4,7,6}, {3,5,8,6}, {4,5,8,7}
      };
  for (int k = 0; k < 9  && !result; k++) {
    result = rectangle_pattern(pattern[k]);
    }
#ifdef LOG_IN_OUT
  printf("<<< rectangle ---\n");
#endif
  return result;
  }
```

Notice that you list the boxes of each combination clockwise and from the top-left corner. Neither the direction nor the box ID you choose to appear in the first position is important. What matters is that you list the IDs in sequence, so that you can follow a chain of cells going through the boxes.

rectangle_pattern()

When entering rectangle_pattern(), you set the four boxes containing the corner cells of our rectangle. But to proceed only makes sense if all boxes of the pattern contain at least one unsolved cell. To check whether this is the case is justified, considering that rectangle is a complex strategy that you try when simpler strategies have delivered what they could.

This is the purpose of the following piece of code, which you find at the beginning of the function (see Listing 12-2):

```c
int cells = TRUE;
for (int kB = 0; kB < 4 && cells; kB++) {
  cells = FALSE;
  int sID = pattern[kB];
  for (int kE = 0; kE < 9 && !cells; kE++) {
    int kR = box[sID][kE][ROW];
    int kC = box[sID][kE][COL];
    if (grid[kR][kC][0] > 1) cells = TRUE;
    }
  }
```

The outer for-loop goes through the four boxes of the pattern and the inner for-loop goes through the elements of each box. You set the variable cells to TRUE before entering the outer loop and to FALSE before entering the inner loop. The inner loop exits as soon as it finds an unsolved cell among the elements of a box, because there is no need to know whether the box contains more than one unsolved cell. The outer loop exits as soon as the scanning of a box fails to find an unsolved cell. In that case, rectangle_pattern() returns without attempting to apply the strategy.

Listing 12-2. rectangle_pattern.c

```c
/* rectangle_pattern.c
 *
 * Copyright (C) 2015  Giulio Zambon  - http://zambon.com.au/
 *
 */
#include <stdio.h>
#include <stdlib.h>
#include "def.h"
#include "rectangle_cell.h"
#include "rectangle_pattern.h"

int rectangle_pattern(int pattern[4]) {
#ifdef LOG_IN_OUT
  printf("--- rectangle_pattern (");
  for (int k = 0; k < 4; k++) {
    if (k > 0) printf(",");
    printf("%d", pattern[k]);
    }
  printf(") >>>\n");
#endif
  int result = FALSE;
  int cells = TRUE;
  for (int kB = 0; kB < 4 && cells; kB++) {
    cells = FALSE;
    int sID = pattern[kB];
    for (int kE = 0; kE < 9 && !cells; kE++) {
      int kR = box[sID][kE][ROW];
      int kC = box[sID][kE][COL];
      if (grid[kR][kC][0] > 1) cells = TRUE;
      }
    }
```

```
  if (cells) {
    for (int kB = 0; kB < 4  && !result; kB++) {
      int seq[4];
      for (int k = 0; k < 4; k++) {
        int kk = (kB + k) % 4;
        seq[k] = pattern[kk];
        }
      int sID = seq[0];
      for (int kE = 0; kE < 9  && !result; kE++) {
        int kR = box[sID][kE][ROW];
        int kC = box[sID][kE][COL];
        if (grid[kR][kC][0] > 1) result = rectangle_cell(seq, kR, kC);
        } // for (int kE..
      } // for (int kB..
    } // if (cells..

#ifdef LOG_IN_OUT
  printf("<<< rectangle_pattern (");
  for (int k = 0; k < 4; k++) {
    if (k > 0) printf(",");
    printf("%d", pattern[k]);
    }
  printf(") ---\n");
#endif
  return result;
  }
```

The rectangle strategy may result in the removal of a candidate in any of the unsolved cells of any of the four boxes. Therefore, the purpose of the second part of rectangle_pattern() is to attempt to apply the rectangle strategy starting from each possible cell of all four boxes. To identify the starting cells, it first selects the starting box with

```
for (int kB = 0; kB < 4; kB++)
```

Then, it builds a sequence of box IDs with the selected box appearing first. To do so, it takes advantage of the modulo operator:

```
int seq[4];
for (int k = 0; k < 4; k++) {
  int kk = (kB + k) % 4;
  seq[k] = pattern[kk];
  }
```

After the loop executes, the starting box ID always appears in seq[0], and the other three IDs complete the sequence in the correct order (arbitrarily chosen to be clockwise).

Once it has identified the starting box and prepared the sequence of boxes, rectangle_pattern() only needs to execute rectangle_cell() for each one of the unsolved cells of the starting box.

rectangle_cell()

The purpose of rectangle_cell() is to set up and start chains with each one of the candidates contained in a cell. This is what happens in the for-loop highlighted in bold in Listing 12-3.

Listing 12-3. rectangle_cell.c

```
/* rectangle_cell.c
 *
 * Copyright (C) 2015  Giulio Zambon  - http://zambon.com.au/
 *
 */
#include <stdio.h>
#include <stdlib.h>
#include "cleanup_around.h"
#include "def.h"
#include "rectangle_cell.h"
#include "rectangle_step.h"
#include "remove_candidate.h"

int rectangle_cell(int seq[4], int kR, int kC) {
#ifdef LOG_IN_OUT
  printf("--- rectangle_cell [");
  for (int k = 0; k < 4; k++) {
    if (k > 0) printf(",");
    printf("%d", seq[k]);
    }
  printf("] (%d,%d) >>>\n", kR, kC);
#endif
  int result = FALSE;

  char *elem = grid[kR][kC];
  for (int i = 1; i <= 9  &&  !result; i++) {
    if (elem[i]) {
      int res = rectangle_step(seq, 0, kR, kC, i, kR, kC);
      if (res == 0) {
#ifdef LOG_RECTANGLE
        if (!silent) {
          printf("rectangle_cell: %d in (%d,%d) leads to contradiction"
            " when chained through the boxes [%d,%d,%d,%d]\n",
            i, kR, kC, seq[0], seq[1], seq[2], seq[3]
            );
          }
#endif
        remove_candidate("rectangle_cell", i, kR, kC);
        if (grid[kR][kC][0] == 1) {
          cleanup_around(kR, kC);
          }
        result = TRUE;
        } // if (res..
      else if (res == -2) {
```

137

```
            result = TRUE;
            }
        } // if (elem[i]..
    } // for (int i..

#ifdef LOG_IN_OUT
  printf("<<< rectangle_cell [");
  for (int k = 0; k < 4; k++) {
    if (k > 0) printf(",");
    printf("%d", seq[k]);
    }
  printf("] (%d,%d) ---\n", kR, kC);
#endif
  return result;
  }
```

That is, if rectangle_step() (see Listing 12-4) returns zero, it means that the rectangle strategy detected an inconsistency and you can remove from the current starting cell of the current starting box (i.e., the cell with coordinates (kR,kC)) the candidate for the current number (i.e., the number i). As usual, when you remove a candidate, you also check whether this has resulted in a naked single and, if so, clean up around it.

rectangle_step()

This is where you do the hard work. The algorithm is complex and rectangle_step() also calls itself recursively to move from one box to the next. But let's see how it works (refer to Listing 12-4).

Listing 12-4. rectangle_step.c

```
/* rectangle_step.c
 *
 * Copyright (C) 2015  Giulio Zambon  - http://zambon.com.au/
 *
 */
#include <stdio.h>
#include <stdlib.h>
#include "cleanup_around.h"
#include "def.h"
#include "rectangle_cell.h"
#include "rectangle_step.h"
#include "remove_candidate.h"

int rectangle_step(int seq[4], int kBeq, int kR, int kC, int kN,
        int iR, int iC
        ) {
#ifdef LOG_IN_OUT
  printf("--- rectangle_step [");
  for (int k = kBeq; k < 4; k++) {
    printf("%d", seq[k]);
    if (k < 3) printf(",");
    }
```

```
    printf("] (%d,%d) %d >>>\n", kR, kC, kN);
#endif
    int result = 0;
    int kB = seq[kBeq+1];
    if (kBeq == 3) kB = seq[0];
    int n = 0;
    int rows[9] = {0, 0, 0, 0, 0, 0, 0, 0, 0};
    int cols[9] = {0, 0, 0, 0, 0, 0, 0, 0, 0};
    for (int kE = 0; kE < 9 && result >= 0; kE++) {
      int kkR = box[kB][kE][0];
      int kkC = box[kB][kE][1];
      char *elem = grid[kkR][kkC];
      if (elem[0] == 1) {
        if (elem[kN] != FALSE) {
          result = -1;
          }
        } // if (elem[0]..
      else if (elem[kN] != FALSE && kkR != kR && kkC != kC) {
        rows[n] = kkR;
        cols[n] = kkC;
        n++;
        } // if (elem[0].. else..
      } // for (int kE..

    if (n > 0 || kBeq == 3) {
      if (kBeq < 3) {
        for (int k = 0; k < n && result >= 0; k++) {
          int res = rectangle_step(seq, kBeq+1, rows[k], cols[k], kN, iR, iC);
          if (res < 0) {
            result = res;
            }
          else {
            result |= res;
            }
          } // for (int k..
        } // if (kBeq..
      else {
        for (int k = 0; k < n && result == 0; k++) {
          if (rows[k] == iR && cols[k] == iC) {
            result = 1;
            }
          } // for (int k..
        } // if (kBeq.. else..
      } // if (n > 0..
    else if (n == 0 && result != -1) {  // the pointing line strategy applies
      result = -2;
#ifdef LOG_POINTING_LINE
      if (!silent) {
```

```
        printf("rectangle_step: %d cannot solve (%d,%d) because all the %ds "
           "in box %d are aligned with it (pointing line strategy)\n",
           kN, kR, kC, kN, kB
           );
     }
#endif
    remove_candidate("rectangle_step", kN, kR, kC);
    if (grid[kR][kC][0] == 1) {
      cleanup_around(kR, kC);
      }
    } // if (n > 0.. else if (n..

#ifdef LOG_IN_OUT
  printf("<<< rectangle_step [");
  for (int k = kBeq; k < 4; k++) {
    printf("%d", seq[k]);
    if (k < 3) printf(",");
    }
  printf("] (%d,%d) %d return=%d ---\n", kR, kC, kN, result);
#endif
  return result;
  }
```

The parameters of rectangle_step() are

seq[4] Sequence of box IDs, with the starting box of the chain in first position.
kBeq   Current box within the chain, initially 0 and then 1, 2, and 3.
kR,kC   Coordinates of the current cell within the chain.
kN   Number you are looking for.
iR,iC   Coordinates of the chain's starting cell.

The following little algorithm ensures that the variable pointing to the next box is set to the starting box when the end of the chain is reached:

```
int kB = seq[kBeq+1];
if (kBeq == 3) kB = seq[0];
```

First, rectangle_step() makes a list of all the cells of the *next* box that include kN as a candidate but that are *not* aligned with the current cell (highlighted lines in Listing 12-4). If the candidate turns out to be the only one in a cell (i.e., if elem[0] == 1 and elem[kN] is true), it means that the current number is solved in the next box. Therefore, you can abort the application of the strategy for the current number (by setting result to -1). Note that when that happens, n remains set to 0, thereby causing rectangle_step() to skip the rest of the statements. If you follow the return from rectangle_step() to rectangle_cell(), you will see that rectangle_cell() goes to the next candidate when rectangle_step() returns a non-zero value.

The delicate bits are in the part that starts with the line

```
if (n > 0 || kBeq == 3) {
```

To understand the algorithm, you need to run through all possibilities listed in Table 12-1.

Table 12-1. *Possibilities Within* `rectangle_step()`

	n == 0	n > 0
kBeq < 3	case A	case B
kBeq == 3	case C	case D

The explanation, as you will see in a moment, is quite complicated. But don't despair: I will walk you through the example shown in Figure 12-2 step by step.

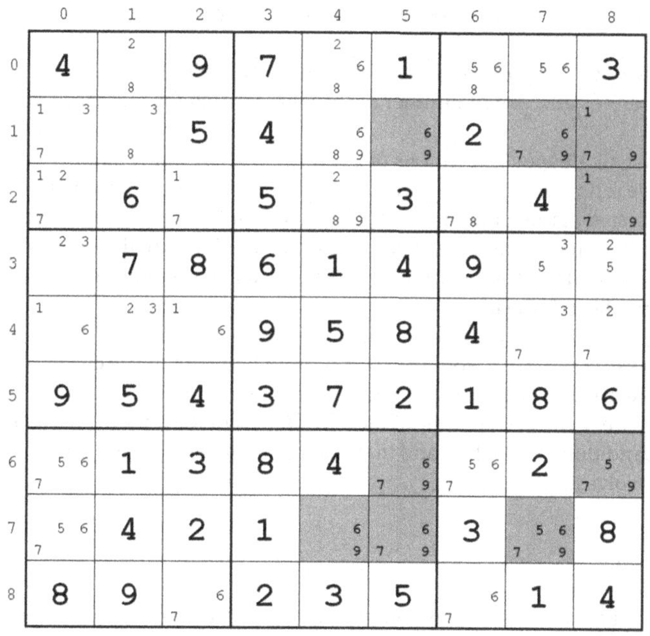

Figure 12-2. *An example for rectangle*

Case A: n == 0 and kBeq < 3

To understand what is happening, you need to consider the value of `result`.

It is -1 when the algorithm highlighted in Listing 12-4 has discovered that the current number has already solved one of the cells of the next box. When that happens, you don't need to do anything. `rectangle_cell()` will then try the next number (if the current one is less than 9).

If `result` is *not* -1, regardless of which box is current (i.e., for any value of kBeq), the fact that n is 0 tells you that the highlighted algorithm has found no nonaligned cell of the next box containing the current number as a candidate. In other words, all candidates for the current number in the next box are aligned with the current cell. *But wait a minute!* This is nothing other than the pointing-line strategy applied to the box containing the current cell. `rectangle_step()` can therefore remove the current number from the current cell. After that, it sets `return` to -2 to tell `rectangle_cell()` that it shouldn't attempt further numbers for the current cell because a candidate has been removed. This will in turn abort the rectangle strategy.

141

Note that the Solver's mechanism of attempting simpler strategies before the more complex ones excludes the possibility of encountering an application of pointing-line while attempting rectangle. But not covering the possibility would be like writing a switch statement without a default: unsafe programming.

Case B: n > 0 and kBeq < 3

The two if-statements with conditions (n > 0 || kBeq == 3) and (kBeq < 3) succeed.

The fact that n is non-zero means that the algorithm highlighted in Listing 12-4 has found a candidate for the current number in at least one unsolved cell of the next box when that cell is *not* aligned with the current one. These are the candidates you are looking for and that could potentially result in the removal of the candidate in the initial cell.

kBeq < 3 means that you haven't yet scanned all four boxes of the current pattern (otherwise, kBeq, which starts from 0, would be set to 3).

Therefore, you need to keep going with the scanning of boxes, and you do so by executing rectangle_step() recursively.

rectangle_step() can return a negative, zero, or positive value. A negative result (either -1 or -2), as you have already seen, is a request to abort either the current number or the whole rectangle. Therefore, you just pass it on.

If the value is 0 or positive, it means that all "deeper" executions of rectangle_step() have succeeded. The only difference between 0 and a positive return value is that with 0, rectangle_step() has found no additional candidates. But you are not interested in the number of candidates. You only want to determine whether there is at least one of such candidates. In that case, the chain across the four boxes of the pattern has an alternative path, and you know that n was already greater than 0 before recursively executing rectangle_step() (otherwise, you would not be in "case B").

To handle a non-negative result value, you only need to return from the current execution of rectangle_step() with result |= res; (result += res; would also do, although the "or" more closely reflects the logic of the algorithm). When the first rectangle_step() of the "recursion well" returns to rectangle_cell(), a 0 will mean that there are no nonaligned candidates in any box of the pattern. Without alternatives, the conflict between the two candidates in the first and in the last box will tell you that the candidate in the initial cell cannot possibly solve it.

Case C: n == 0 and kBeq == 3

The if-statement with condition (n > 0 || kBeq == 3) succeeds, but the second one with condition (kBeq < 3) fails.

Recall that n tells you how many unsolved cells containing the current candidate are present in the next box but not aligned with the current cell. Further, kBeq == 3 tells you that the next box is the initial one of the pattern—that is, the box that contains the initial candidate you are trying to remove with rectangle. If n is 0, as all candidates of the next (i.e., initial) box are aligned with the current cell, it follows that that initial candidate is aligned with the current cell as well. This is precisely the contradiction you are looking for: the choice of that candidate makes it impossible for it to be a solution.

With n == 0, you don't enter the for-loop at all and return 0, causing rectangle_cell() to remove the candidate from the initial cell.

Case D: n > 0 and kBeq == 3

This case takes you to the same for-loop as case C, in which k goes through all n cells indexed by rows[] and cols[]. But this time, as n > 0, at least one cell is present. If among those cells the loop finds the initial cell, with coordinates (iR,iC), as the list contains cells that are *not* aligned with the current one, it means that there is no conflict between the initial and final cells, and rectangle, for the current candidate of the initial cell, fails.

All you need to do is return to rectangle_cell() a value other than 0, so that it can try other candidates (if available).

An Example

In Figure 12-2, the cells relevant for the application of the rectangle strategy are those with a gray background. Suppose that the 9 of box 1 is in (1,5). Then, (1,7) and (1,8) cannot contain a 9, and the 9 of box 2 must be in (2,8). If 9 solves (2,8), (6,8) cannot contain a 9, and the 9 of box 8 must be in (7,7). But if 9 solves (7,7), the only candidate for 9 left in box 7 is in (6,5). As this conflicts with the initial assumption that 9 solves (1,5), you must conclude that (1,5) cannot contain a 9.

So far so good, but let's see how the program does it. We pick up its solution when it attempts to apply rectangle() to the sixth pattern (1, 2, 8, and 7), by executing rectangle_pattern().

rectangle_pattern() goes through all possible four sequences of boxes: (1,2,8,7), (2,8,7,1), (8,7,1,2), and (7,1,2,8). The one you are interested in is the first one. The first two cells, (0,4) and (1,4), do not result in any candidate removal. Then, rectangle_pattern() executes rectangle_cell() for the cell (1,5) (which, as you already know, will result in the removal of the 9).

The cell contains two candidates: 6 and 9. Let's look at candidate 6 to see how rectangle fails. rectangle_cell() initiates the chain by executing rectangle_step().

rectangle_step(): for 6, kBeq 0, chain: (1,5)

The input arguments are

```
seq[4] = {1,2,8,7}
kBeq   = 0
kR, kC = 1, 5
kN     = 6
iR, iC = 1, 5
```

Following is the list of cells of box 2 nonaligned with (1,5) and containing a 6:

```
n = 2
rows = {0, 0}
cols = {6, 7}
```

As n > 0 and kBeq < 3, rectangle_step() calls itself recursively.

rectangle_step(): for 6, kBeq 1, chain (1,5) (0,6)

The input arguments are seq[4] = {1,2,8,7}

```
kBeq   = 1
kR, kC = 0, 6
kN     = 6
iR, iC = 1, 5
```

In other words, you increment kBeq, which represents the depth of iteration, and set the coordinates (kR,kC) to (0,6), thereby identifying the first cell in the list for box 2. You will deal with (0,7) later.

Following is the list of cells of box 8 nonaligned with (0,6) and containing a 6:

```
n = 1
rows = {7}
cols = {7}
```

As n > 0 and kBeq < 3, rectangle_step() calls itself recursively.

rectangle_step(): for 6, kBeq 2, chain (1,5) (0,6) (7,7)

The input arguments are

```
seq[4] = {1,2,8,7}
kBeq   = 2
kR, kC = 7, 7
kN     = 6
iR, iC = 1, 5
```

Following is the list of cells of box 7 nonaligned with (7,7) and containing a 6:

```
n = 1
rows = {6}
cols = {5}
```

As n > 0 and kBeq < 3, rectangle_step() calls itself recursively.

rectangle_step(): for 6, kBeq 3, chain (1,5) (0,6) (7,7) (6,5)

The input arguments are

```
seq[4] = {1,2,8,7}
kBeq   = 3
kR, kC = 6, 5
kN     = 6
iR, iC = 1, 5
```

Following is the list of cells of box 1 non-aligned with $(6,5)$ and containing a 6:

```
n = 2
rows = {0, 1}
cols = {4, 4}
```

This time, n > 0 and kBeq == 3. Therefore `rectangle_step()` executes the following lines of code:

```
for (int k = 0; k < n && result == 0; k++) {
  if (rows[k] == iR && cols[k] == iC) {
    result = 1;
    }
  }
```

As (iR, iC) is $(1,5)$, while rows and cols contain $(0,4)$ and $(1,4)$, the for-loop doesn't find any match. As a result, rectangle_step() returns zero. The recursions with kBeq 2 and 1 also return zero, because the line

```
result |= res;
```

bitwise ORs the zero returned by the deeper iteration with the initial 0 of its own result.

When control returns to the iteration with kBeq 0, as the result of the iteration with kBeq1 returns 0, rectangle_step() calls itself recursively once more. This occurs thanks to the following two lines of code:

```
for (int k = 0; k < n && result >= 0; k++) {
    int res = rectangle_step(seq, kBeq+1, rows[k], cols[k], kN, iR, iC);
```

Remember that, for kBeq 0, n is 2, and $(rows[1], cols[1])$ is $(0,7)$.

rectangle_step(): for 6, kBeq 1, chain (1,5) (0,7)

The input arguments are

```
seq[4] = {1,2,8,7}
kBeq    = 1
kR, kC = 0, 7
kN      = 6
iR, iC = 1, 5
```

Following is the list of cells of box 8 nonaligned with $(0,7)$ and containing a 6:

```
n = 1
rows = {6}
cols = {6}
```

As n > 0 and kBeq < 3, rectangle_step() calls itself recursively.

rectangle_step(): for 6, kBeq 2, chain (1,5) (0,7) (6,6)

The input arguments are

```
seq[4] = {1,2,8,7}
kBeq   = 2
kR, kC = 6, 6
kN     = 6
iR, iC = 1, 5
```

Following is the list of cells of box 7 nonaligned with (6,6) and containing a 6:

```
n = 2
rows = {7, 7}
cols = {4, 5}
```

As n > 0 and kBeq < 3, rectangle_step() calls itself recursively.

rectangle_step(): for 6, kBeq 3, chain (1,5) (0,7) (6,6) (7,4)

The input arguments are

```
seq[4] = {1,2,8,7}
kBeq   = 3
kR, kC = 7, 4
kN     = 6
iR, iC = 1, 5
```

Following is the list of cells of box 1 nonaligned with (7,4) and containing a 6:

```
n = 1
rows = {1}
cols = {5}
```

This time, n > 0 and kBeq == 3. Therefore rectangle_step() executes once more the following lines of code:

```
for (int k = 0; k < n && result == 0; k++) {
  if (rows[k] == iR && cols[k] == iC) {
    result = 1;
    }
  }
```

There is a match, because (iR,iC), which is (1,5), is in the cell list. Therefore, rectangle_step() returns 1, as do the "upper" iterations for kBeq 2, 1, and 0.

When control returns to rectangle_cell(), the 1 returned by rectangle_step() causes the candidate for 6 to be ignored, and the function starts a chain for 9.

rectangle_step(): for 9

rectangle_step() goes for 9 through iterations that are very similar to those you have already seen for 6. The chain goes through $(1,5)$, $(2,8)$, $(7,7)$, and $(6,5)$, and, as $(6,5)$ is aligned with $(1,5)$, the loop

```
for (int k = 0; k < n && result == 0; k++) {
```

finds no match. As a result, all the iterations return zero and rectangle succeeds. The following are the corresponding log entries:

```
rectangle_cell: 9 in (1,5) leads to contradiction when chained through the boxes [1,2,8,7]
rectangle_cell: removed 9 from (1,5)
cleanup_unit [row of (1,5)]: removed 6 from (1,4)
cleanup_unit [row of (1,5)]: removed 6 from (1,7)
cleanup_unit [column of (1,5)]: removed 6 from (6,5)
cleanup_unit [column of (1,5)]: removed 6 from (7,5)
cleanup_unit [box of (1,5)]: removed 6 from (0,4)
```

Pointing-line within rectangle

In the example of Figure 12-2, after using rectangle to remove the 9 in $(1,5)$ and cleaning up the 6s, you obtain the partially solved puzzle shown in Figure 12-3.

	0	1	2	3	4	5	6	7	8
0	4	2,8	9	7	2,8	1	5,6,8	5,6	3
1	1,3,7	3,8	5	4	6,8,9	6	2	7,9	1,7,9
2	1,2,7	6	1,7	5	2,8,9	3	7,8	4	1,7,9
3	2,3	7	8	6	1	4	9	3,5	2,5
4	1,6	2,3,1	6	9	5	8	4	3,7	2,7
5	9	5	4	3	7	2	1	8	6
6	5,6,7	1	3	8	4	7,9	5,6,7	2	5,7,9
7	5,6,7	4	2	1	6,9	7,9	3	5,6,7,9	8
8	8	9	6,7	2	3	5	6,7	1	4

Figure 12-3. Pointing line within rectangle

If you disable the easier strategies when trying the example, you will see rectangle at work as a pointing-line surrogate. Here is the log.

```
rectangle_step: 6 cannot solve (7,7) because all the 6s in box 7 are aligned with it
(pointing-line strategy)
rectangle_step: removed 6 from (7,7)
```

Obviously, without disabling any strategy, you would solve (7,4) with unique because the 6 in (7,4) is the only one in box 7.

Summary

In this chapter, you have learned the last and most complicated to implement of the analytical strategies. In Chapter 13, dedicated to "backtracking," you will learn how to solve Sudoku puzzles with brute force.

CHAPTER 13

Implementing "Backtrack"

As I have already explained in Chapter 2, backtracking is a nice way of saying "guessing." When you exhaust all strategies you know, you can only pick a cell that you haven't yet solved and try out one of its candidates. If you reach a contradiction, you need to revert the Sudoku grid back to what it was before your arbitrary choice and try another candidate—hence the "back" of backtracking.

The Solver program with the analytical strategies illustrated in the previous chapters solved 99.85% of the 30,000 generated puzzles (see Chapters 14–16 for more details), but for the remaining 0.15%, backtracking was the only way of solving the puzzles. In 38 puzzles of 30,000, the Solver had to guess once. In six of the remaining puzzles, it had to guess twice.

Gordon Royle of the University of Western Australia maintains a web site dedicated to minimum Sudokus (`http://staffhome.ecm.uwa.edu.au/~00013890/sudokumin.php`)—that is, puzzles that contain exactly 17 clues. From the site you can download 49,151 minimum Sudokus (as of February 4, 2015) guaranteed to have unique solutions. Not surprisingly, many of them are quite difficult, and the Solver had to resort to backtracking in 1,918 cases. The most difficult of all (see Figure 13-1) needed eight guesses.

	0	1	2	3	4	5	6	7	8
0							2	6	
1		9		8					
2								5	
3	2		6						7
4				7					4
5			1						
6					2	6	1		
7	8	4							
8							3		

Figure 13-1. *The hardest Sudoku*

Among the list of minimum Sudokus, you will also find what could be the most difficult puzzle that can still be solved analytically, without guessing (see Figure 13-2). To find the solution, the Solver applied a sequence of 32 strategies (not in sequence and ignoring cleanup and naked single): 2 x naked pair, 3 x pointing line, 4 x unique-loop, 5 x box-line, 3 x pointing line, and 15 x XY-chain.

	0	1	2	3	4	5	6	7	8
0		2	6						
1				4			1		
2		9							
3	4						9		
4				7			5		
5					8	6			
6					5			7	2
7	9			3					
8								6	

Figure 13-2. *The hardest analytical Sudoku*

Listing 13-1 shows how you can implement the backtrack strategy.

Listing 13-1. backtrack.c-Not Optimized

```
/* backtrack.c
 *
 * Copyright (C) 2015  Giulio Zambon  - http://zambon.com.au/
 *
 */
#include <stdio.h>
#include <stdlib.h>
#include "backtrack.h"
#include "cleanup_around.h"
#include "count_solved.h"
#include "def.h"
#include "display_strats_in_clear.h"
#include "solve.h"

#define MAX_DEPTH 10
```

```
int backtrack(int depth) {
#ifdef LOG_IN_OUT
  printf("--- backtrack (%d) >>>\n", depth);
#endif

  int result = FALSE;
  char grid_backup[9][9][10];
  int done = FALSE;

  // Select the cell
  for (int k = 0; k < 9 && !done; k++) {
    for (int j = 0; j < 9 && !done; j++) {
      if (grid[k][j][0] > 1) {

        // Process the cell
        char *elem = grid[k][j];
        if (!silent) {
          for (int kd = 0; kd < depth; kd++) {
            printf("  ");
          }
          printf("backtrack (%d): (%d,%d) has candidates", depth, k, j);
          for (int i = 1; i <= 9; i++) {
            if (elem[i]) printf(" %d", i);
          }
          printf("\n");
        } // if (!silent..
        int n_candidates = elem[0];
        int n_failures = 0;
        for (int i = 1; i <= 9 && !done; i++) {
          if (elem[i]) {

            // Save the current state of the grid
            for (int k1 = 0; k1 < 9; k1++) {
              for (int j1 = 0; j1 < 9; j1++) {
                for (int i1 = 0; i1 <= 9; i1++) {
                  grid_backup[k1][j1][i1] = grid[k1][j1][i1];
                }
              } // for (int j1..
            } // for (int k1..

            // Force a solution
            for (int i1 = 1; i1 <= 9; i1++) {
              elem[i1] = FALSE;
            }
            elem[i] = TRUE;
            elem[0] = 1;
            int orig_silent = silent;
            silent = TRUE;
            cleanup_around(k, j);
```

```
// Attempt to solve the puzzle
solve();
silent = orig_silent;

// Check the result
int do_restore = FALSE;
if (problem_found) {
  problem_found = FALSE;
  do_restore = TRUE;
  n_failures++;
  if (!silent) {
    for (int kd = 0; kd < depth; kd++) ("   ");
    printf("backtrack (%d): %d unsuccessful\n", depth, i);
    }
  } // if (problem_found..
else {
  if (!silent) {
    for (int kd = 0; kd < depth; kd++) printf("   ");
    printf("backtrack (%d): %d successful (%d solved)\n",
           depth, i, count_solved()
           );
    for (int kd = 0; kd < depth; kd++) printf("   ");
    printf("backtrack (%d) strategies:", depth);
    display_strats_in_clear();
    printf("\n");
    }
  if (count_solved() == 81) {
    strats_used[n_strats_used] = 40+depth;
    n_strats_used++;
    done = TRUE;
    result = TRUE;
    }
  else {
    int success = (depth < MAX_DEPTH)
                  ? backtrack(depth + 1)
                  : TRUE
                  ;
    if (success) {
      done = TRUE;
      result = TRUE;
      }
    else {
      do_restore = TRUE;
      n_failures++;
      }
    }
  } // if (problem_found.. else..
```

```
                // If unsuccessful, restore the grid to
                // its original content
                if (do_restore) {
                  for (int k1 = 0; k1 < 9; k1++) {
                    for (int j1 = 0; j1 < 9; j1++) {
                      for (int i1 = 0; i1 <= 9; i1++) {
                        grid[k1][j1][i1] =
                                    grid_backup[k1][j1][i1];
                      }
                    } // for (int j1..
                  } // for (int k1..
                } // if (do_restore..
              } // if (elem[i]..
            } // for (int i..

          // When all candidates fail, go back
          if (n_failures == n_candidates) done = TRUE;
          } // if (grid[k][j][0]..
        } // for (int j..
      } // for (int k..

 #ifdef LOG_IN_OUT
   printf("<<< backtrack (%d) ---\n", depth);
 #endif
   return result;
   }
```

The first two for-loops and the if-statement immediately inside them scan the Sudoku grid from the top-left corner and select the first unsolved cell. Then, the for-loop with control variable i and the if-statement that follows try out the candidates one by one.

To try a candidate out, backtrack() performs three steps: set the current candidate (i.e., the one identified by i) to solve its cell; attempt to solve the altered puzzle by executing solve(); and check whether solve() succeeds in finding the solution. If not, it sets i to the next candidate and tries again. Obviously, you must save the grid before each attempt and restore it after each failed attempt.

display_strats_in_clear() is a small function described in the next section. The name says it all.

To find out whether solve() is successful, backtrack() checks that the global variable problem_found has remained set to FALSE and that the number of solved cells has become 81.

You only set problem_found to TRUE within remove_candidate() (see Listing 3-10). This occurs when remove_candidate() removes the last candidate from a cell. Clearly, if a cell cannot contain any candidate, it means that the puzzle is impossible. That is, it means that backtrack() has chosen the wrong i.

If problem_found remains FALSE but the number of solved cells is less than 81, it means that one guess is not enough, and backtrack() must execute itself recursively on the partially solved puzzle. This happens in the following lines of code:

```
int success = (depth < MAX_DEPTH)
             ? backtrack(depth + 1)
             : TRUE
             ;
if (success) {
  done = TRUE;
  result = TRUE;
  }
```

```
else {
  do_restore = TRUE;
  n_failures++;
  }
```

The limit of ten recursive calls is purely arbitrary. In fact, as I said at the beginning of this chapter about the hardest Sudoku, the highest value of depth I have ever seen is 8.

display_strats_in_clear()

This is a straightforward utility function used only by backtrack() that converts the strategy codes of strategies from levels 0–3 into strategy names in clear (see Listing 13-2).

Listing 13-2. display_strats_in_clear.c

```
/* display_strats_in_clear.c
 *
 * Copyright (C) 2015  Giulio Zambon  - http://zambon.com.au/
 *
 */
#include <stdio.h>
#include <stdlib.h>
#include "def.h"
#include "display_strats_in_clear.h"

void display_strats_in_clear() {
  for (int k = 0; k < n_strats_used; k++) {
    int level = strats_used[k] / 10;
    int k_strat = strats_used[k] - level * 10;
    printf(" '%s'", strat_all_names[level][k_strat]);
    }
  printf("\n");
  }
```

Optimization

You might feel that choosing to begin backtracking with the first cell that has more than one candidate is not the most efficient choice.

Why not choose a cell with only two candidates? Then, either one of them must be correct. This is true, but consider that the amount of information you get when choosing between two alternatives is definitely less than what you get when the alternatives are more. That is, choosing between two candidates of a pair is more likely to leave some parts of the puzzle unsolved, which would force you to do further backtracking. Moreover, there might not be any pair in the puzzle. Therefore, backtrack() would need to be able to look for cells with three candidates when it doesn't find any pair, for cells with four candidates if there are no cells with triples, and so on. This would make the function more complicated than it already is.

In view of the aforementioned considerations, you are probably better off when backtrack() starts from a cell with the maximum number of candidates. To do so, you need to replace or remove the lines of code highlighted in bold in Listing 13-1. The optimized version is shown in Listing 13-3, where the new lines are in bold.

Listing 13-3. backtrack.c-Optimized

```c
/* backtrack.c
 *
 * Copyright (C) 2015   Giulio Zambon  - http://zambon.com.au/
 *
 */
#include <stdio.h>
#include <stdlib.h>
#include "backtrack.h"
#include "cleanup_around.h"
#include "count_solved.h"
#include "def.h"
#include "display_strats_in_clear.h"
#include "solve.h"

#define MAX_DEPTH 10

int backtrack(int depth) {
#ifdef LOG_IN_OUT
  printf("--- backtrack (%d) >>>\n", depth);
#endif

  int result = FALSE;
  char grid_backup[9][9][10];

  // Select the cell
  int k;
  int j;
  {
    int max_i = -1;
    int row_max_i;
    int col_max_i;
    for (k = 0; k < 9 && max_i < 9; k++) {
      for (j = 0; j < 9 && max_i < 9; j++) {
        if (grid[k][j][0] > max_i) {
          max_i = grid[k][j][0];
          row_max_i = k;
          col_max_i = j;
          }
        }
      }
    k = row_max_i;
    j = col_max_i;
    }

  // Process the cell
  char *elem = grid[k][j];
  if (!silent) {
    for (int kd = 0; kd < depth; kd++) printf("  ");
    printf("backtrack (%d): (%d,%d) has candidates", depth, k, j);
```

```
    for (int i = 1; i <= 9; i++) {
      if (elem[i]) printf(" %d", i);
      }
  printf("\n");
  } // if (!silent..
for (int i = 1; i <= 9 && !result; i++) {
  if (elem[i]) {

    // Save the current state of the grid
    for (int k1 = 0; k1 < 9; k1++) {
      for (int j1 = 0; j1 < 9; j1++) {
        for (int i1 = 0; i1 <= 9; i1++) {
          grid_backup[k1][j1][i1] = grid[k1][j1][i1];
          }
        } // for (int j1..
      } // for (int k1..

    // Force a solution
    for (int i1 = 1; i1 <= 9; i1++) {
      elem[i1] = FALSE;
      }
    elem[i] = TRUE;
    elem[0] = 1;
    int orig_silent = silent;
    silent = TRUE;
    cleanup_around(k, j);

    // Attempt to solve the puzzle
    solve();
    silent = orig_silent;

    // Check the result
    if (problem_found) {
      problem_found = FALSE;
      if (!silent) {
        for (int kd = 0; kd < depth; kd++) ("  ");
        printf("backtrack (%d): %d unsuccessful\n", depth, i);
        }
      } // if (problem_found..
    else {
      if (!silent) {
        for (int kd = 0; kd < depth; kd++) {
          printf("  ");
          }
        printf("backtrack (%d): %d successful (%d solved)\n",
               depth, i, count_solved()
               );
        for (int kd = 0; kd < depth; kd++) printf("  ");
        printf("backtrack (%d) strategies:", depth);
        display_strats_in_clear();
        printf("\n");
        }
```

```
      if (count_solved() == 81) {
        strats_used[n_strats_used] = 40 + depth;
        n_strats_used++;
        result = TRUE;
        }
      else if (depth < MAX_DEPTH) {
        result = backtrack(depth + 1);
        }
      } // if (problem_found.. else..

    // If unsuccessful, restore the grid to its
    // original content
    if (!result) {
      for (int k1 = 0; k1 < 9; k1++) {
        for (int j1 = 0; j1 < 9; j1++) {
          for (int i1 = 0; i1 <= 9; i1++) {
            grid[k1][j1][i1] = grid_backup[k1][j1][i1];
            }
          } // for (int j1..
        } // for (int k1..
      } // if (do_restore..
    } // if (elem[i]..
  } // for (int i..

#ifdef LOG_IN_OUT
  printf("<<< backtrack (%d) ---\n", depth);
#endif
  return result;
  }
```

As you can see, the function has become simpler, with fewer loops and fewer control variables. It is also more efficient.

Notice that backtrack() doesn't solely rely on "brute force" to find a solution. Instead, it exploits solve(), which uses the analytical strategies. A 100% brute-force approach would try all possible numbers in a cell, all possible numbers in another cell, and so on, until a solution finally turned up. You could implement such a strategy very simply, but it would be very inefficient and would require a long time to find the solution. Moreover, it wouldn't give you any indication of the comparative difficulty of the puzzles.

An Example

As an example, I want to show you a Sudoku that required the Solver to backtrack five times (i.e., to a maximum depth of 4).

The partially solved puzzle, after the analytical strategies have done their bit, is shown in Figure 13-3, with 24 cells solved.

	0	1	2	3	4	5	6	7	8
0	**1**	2 5 6 8	2 4 6 8	4 5 8	4 5	**7** (3)	2 4 6	**9**	3 4 6
1	4 5 7	**3**	4 6	1 4 5 9	**2**	1 5 9	1 4 6 7	4 6 7	**8**
2	2 4 7 8	2 7 8	**9**	**6**	1 3 4	1 3 8	**5**	2 3 4 7	1 3 4
3	2 4 7 8	2 7 8	**5**	**3**	1 6 7	1 2 6	**9**	4 6 7 8	1 4 6
4	4 7 9	**1**	3 4	5 7 9	**8**	5 6 9	4 6 7	3 4 5 6 7	**2**
5	**6**	2 7 8 9	2 3 8	1 2 5 7 9	1 5 7 9	**4**	1 7 8	3 5 7 8	1 3 5
6	**3**	2 5 6 8 9	2 6 8	2 4 5 7 8 9	4 5 6 7 9	2 5 6 8 9	2 4 8	**1**	4 5 6 9
7	2 5 8 9	**4**	**1**	2 5 8 9	3 5 6 9	2 3 5 6 8 9	2 6 8	2 5 6 8	**7**
8	2 5 8 9	2 5 6 8 9	**7**	1 2 4 5 8 9	1 4 5 6 9	1 2 5 6 8 9	**3**	2 4 5 6 8	4 5 6 9

Figure 13-3. *A hard Sudoku—1*

Listing 13-4 shows the backtracking log.

Listing 13-4. A Backtracking Log

```
backtrack (0): (6,3) has candidates 2 4 5 7 8 9
backtrack (0): 2 successful (27 solved)
backtrack (0) strategies:none
  backtrack (1): (4,7) has candidates 3 4 5 6 7
  backtrack (1): 3 unsuccessful
  backtrack (1): 4 successful (30 solved)
  backtrack (1) strategies:none
    backtrack (2): (7,5) has candidates 3 5 6 8 9
    backtrack (2): 3 successful (31 solved)
    backtrack (2) strategies:none
      backtrack (3): (8,1) has candidates 2 5 6 8 9
      backtrack (3): 2 unsuccessful
      backtrack (3): 5 successful (34 solved)
      backtrack (3) strategies:none
        backtrack (4): (0,2) has candidates 2 4 6 8
        backtrack (4): 2 unsuccessful
        backtrack (4): 4 unsuccessful
        backtrack (4): 6 unsuccessful
        backtrack (4): 8 unsuccessful
      backtrack (3): 6 unsuccessful
      backtrack (3): 8 unsuccessful
      backtrack (3): 9 unsuccessful
```

```
      backtrack (2): 5 unsuccessful
      backtrack (2): 6 unsuccessful
      backtrack (2): 8 unsuccessful
      backtrack (2): 9 unsuccessful
    backtrack (1): 5 unsuccessful
    backtrack (1): 6 unsuccessful
    backtrack (1): 7 unsuccessful
  backtrack (0): 4 successful (26 solved)
  backtrack (0) strategies:none
    backtrack (1): (7,5) has candidates 2 3 5 6 8 9
    backtrack (1): 2 unsuccessful
    backtrack (1): 3 successful (27 solved)
    backtrack (1) strategies:none
      backtrack (2): (8,5) has candidates 1 2 5 6 8 9
      backtrack (2): 1 successful (36 solved)
      backtrack (2) strategies:none
        backtrack (3): (4,7) has candidates 3 4 5 6 7
        backtrack (3): 3 unsuccessful
        backtrack (3): 4 unsuccessful
        backtrack (3): 5 unsuccessful
        backtrack (3): 6 unsuccessful
        backtrack (3): 7 unsuccessful
      backtrack (2): 2 unsuccessful
      backtrack (2): 5 unsuccessful
      backtrack (2): 6 unsuccessful
      backtrack (2): 8 successful (32 solved)
      backtrack (2) strategies:none
        backtrack (3): (5,3) has candidates 1 2 5 7 9
        backtrack (3): 1 unsuccessful
        backtrack (3): 2 unsuccessful
        backtrack (3): 5 unsuccessful
        backtrack (3): 7 unsuccessful
        backtrack (3): 9 unsuccessful
      backtrack (2): 9 unsuccessful
    backtrack (1): 5 successful (81 solved)
    backtrack (1) strategies:none
  sudoku: the final grid contains 81 solved cells
```

Let's follow the first iterations. backtrack() chooses (6,3) to start doing its job because it is the first cell it finds with the maximum number of candidates (six). In an attempt to solve the cell, backtrack() sets it to 2, which is the lowest candidate in the cell (there is no reason to choose another candidate. The log reports that solve() removes some candidates by cleaning up around (6,3) but is not able to apply any other strategy (hence the strategy:none). This leaves the puzzle with 27 cells solved, as shown in Figure 13-4, where the updates are marked in gray.

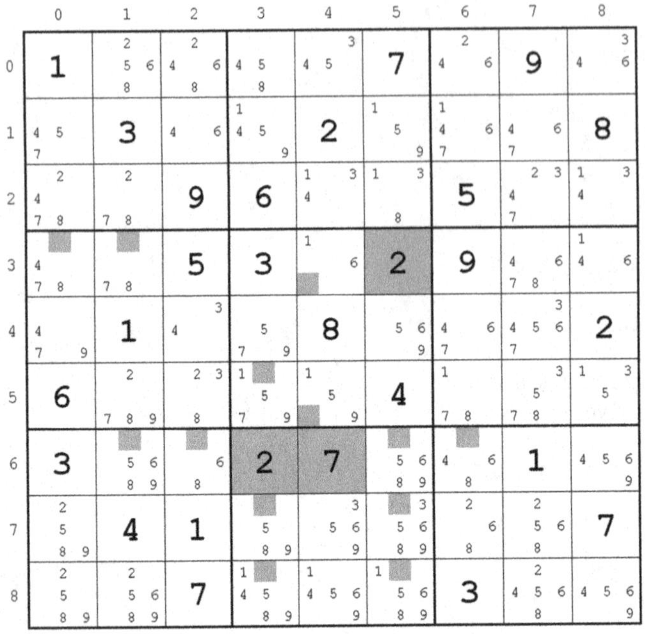

Figure 13-4. *A hard Sudoku—2*

As the number of solved cells is less than 81, backtrack() executes itself recursively. There are no more cells with six candidates, and the first one with five candidates is (4,7). The first possible number is 3, but it is unsuccessful. To see how this comes about, you can insert two lines into backtrack.c, which you will then remove after executing the Solver.

The first line is

```
if (depth == 1 && i == 3 && k == 4 && j == 7) silent = FALSE;
```

and you should insert it before the statement

```
solve();
```

It will cause the strategies to generate log entries during backtracking, which is not normally the case. The second line aborts the Solver

```
if (depth == 1 && i == 3 && k == 4 && j == 7) exit(0);
```

and should go immediately before the comment

```
// If unsuccessful, restore the grid to its original content
```

What you get is a log the relevant parts of which are shown in Listing 13-5. The two lines in bold are those also highlighted in Listing 13-4.

Listing 13-5. The Log of a Wrong Choice When Backtracking

```
backtrack (1): (4,7) has candidates 3 4 5 6 7
unique_unit: 2 in (2,7) is unique within the row
unique_unit: removed 4 from (2,7)
unique_unit: removed 7 from (2,7)
cleanup_unit [column of (2,7)]: removed 2 from (7,7)
cleanup_unit [column of (2,7)]: removed 2 from (8,7)
unique_unit: 2 in (5,1) is unique within the box
unique_unit: removed 7 from (5,1)
unique_unit: removed 8 from (5,1)
unique_unit: removed 9 from (5,1)
cleanup_unit [column of (5,1)]: removed 2 from (8,1)
unique_unit: 2 in (7,6) is unique within the column
unique_unit: removed 6 from (7,6)
unique_unit: removed 8 from (7,6)
cleanup_unit [row of (7,6)]: removed 2 from (7,0)
unique_unit: 2 in (8,0) is unique within the box
unique_unit: removed 5 from (8,0)
unique_unit: removed 9 from (8,0)
unique_unit: 9 in (4,0) is unique within the box
unique_unit: removed 7 from (4,0)
cleanup_unit [row of (4,0)]: removed 9 from (4,3)
cleanup_unit [row of (4,0)]: removed 9 from (4,5)
cleanup_unit [column of (4,0)]: removed 9 from (7,0)
cleanup_unit [row of (7,0)]: removed 5 from (7,3)
cleanup_unit [row of (7,0)]: removed 5 from (7,4)
cleanup_unit [row of (7,0)]: removed 5 from (7,5)
cleanup_unit [row of (7,0)]: removed 5 from (7,7)
cleanup_unit [column of (7,0)]: removed 5 from (1,0)
cleanup_unit [box of (7,0)]: removed 5 from (6,1)
cleanup_unit [box of (7,0)]: removed 5 from (8,1)
unique_unit: 8 in (5,6) is unique within the column
unique_unit: removed 1 from (5,6)
unique_unit: removed 7 from (5,6)
cleanup_unit [row of (5,6)]: removed 8 from (5,7)
cleanup_unit [box of (5,6)]: removed 8 from (3,7)
unique_unit: 5 in (0,1) is unique within the box
unique_unit: removed 8 from (0,1)
cleanup_unit [row of (0,1)]: removed 5 from (0,3)
cleanup_unit [row of (0,1)]: removed 5 from (0,4)
unique_unit: 1 in (1,6) is unique within the column
unique_unit: removed 4 from (1,6)
unique_unit: removed 7 from (1,6)
cleanup_unit [row of (1,6)]: removed 1 from (1,3)
cleanup_unit [row of (1,6)]: removed 1 from (1,5)
cleanup_unit [box of (1,6)]: removed 1 from (2,8)
unique_unit: 8 in (0,3) is unique within the row
unique_unit: removed 4 from (0,3)
```

```
cleanup_unit [column of (0,3)]: removed 8 from (7,3)
cleanup_unit [row of (7,3)]: removed 9 from (7,4)
cleanup_unit [row of (7,3)]: removed 9 from (7,5)
cleanup_unit [column of (7,3)]: removed 9 from (1,3)
cleanup_unit [column of (7,3)]: removed 9 from (5,3)
cleanup_unit [column of (7,3)]: removed 9 from (8,3)
cleanup_unit [box of (7,3)]: removed 9 from (6,5)
cleanup_unit [box of (7,3)]: removed 9 from (8,4)
cleanup_unit [box of (7,3)]: removed 9 from (8,5)
cleanup_unit [column of (0,3)]: removed 8 from (8,3)
cleanup_unit [box of (0,3)]: removed 8 from (2,5)
unique_unit: 9 in (1,5) is unique within the row
unique_unit: removed 5 from (1,5)
unique_unit: 5 in (1,3) is unique within the box
unique_unit: removed 4 from (1,3)
cleanup_unit [column of (1,3)]: removed 5 from (4,3)
cleanup_unit [row of (4,3)]: removed 7 from (4,6)
cleanup_unit [row of (4,6)]: removed 6 from (4,5)
cleanup_unit [column of (4,5)]: removed 5 from (6,5)
cleanup_unit [row of (6,5)]: removed 6 from (6,1)
cleanup_unit [row of (6,1)]: removed 9 from (6,8)
cleanup_unit [column of (6,1)]: removed 9 from (8,1)
cleanup_unit [row of (8,1)]: removed 6 from (8,4)
cleanup_unit [row of (8,1)]: removed 6 from (8,5)
cleanup_unit [row of (8,1)]: removed 6 from (8,7)
cleanup_unit [row of (8,1)]: removed 6 from (8,8)
cleanup_unit [row of (6,5)]: removed 6 from (6,6)
cleanup_unit [row of (6,6)]: removed 4 from (6,8)
cleanup_unit [column of (6,6)]: removed 4 from (0,6)
cleanup_unit [row of (0,6)]: removed 6 from (0,8)
cleanup_unit [column of (0,6)]: removed 6 from (4,6)
*** No candidates left in (4,6)
strategy: after 'unique-loop' the grid contains 53 solved cells
  backtrack (1): 3 unsuccessful
```

When remove_candidate() logs "no candidates left in (4,6)," it also sets the variable problem_found to TRUE. This causes backtrack() to log that 3 was unsuccessful and to try 4. This happens at depth 1. When depth 4 is reached, all four candidates of cell (0,2) fail. This means that the Sudoku is unsolvable and backtrack() must go back to depth 3 and try the next available candidate. When all candidates of depth 3, 2, and 1 also fail to provide a solution, backtrack() goes back to depth 0 and tries the second candidate (i.e., a 4) of cell (6,3). When backtrack() reaches depth 3, it discovers that all candidates in (4,7) fail. It keeps going up and down in depth until it manages to solve all 81 cells.

It turns out that the Solver only needs two guesses to solve the puzzle, as shown in Table 13-1.

Table 13-1. *The Solving Guesses*

Depth	cell	number
0	(6,3)	4
1	(7,5)	5

Summary

This chapter has told you how to solve analytically unsolvable puzzles. You now know how a computer program can solve all puzzles, even if it needs to resort to guessing. In Chapter 14, you will learn what to do when you have thousands (or more) of puzzles to solve.

CHAPTER 14

■ ■ ■

Solving Thousands of Puzzles

The Solver program accepts a Sudoku string as an argument. This is OK when you want to solve a few Sudokus, but it is completely inadequate when you want to obtain statistical data on solving puzzles. For that, you need to be able to solve thousands of puzzles one after the other. The obvious solution is to store Sudoku strings in a file and let the Solver load them one at a time. You do it by adding the following define to the beginning of sudoku_solver.c (see Listing 3-2, Listing 3-3, Listing 3-4, and Listing 3-5): #define USE_FILES. Then insert the code shown in Listing 14-1 immediately after checking the consistency of the strategy arrays (you can find the code for this book in the Source Code/Download area of the Apress web site (www.apress.com)).

Listing 14-1. sudoku_solver.c–Reading Puzzles from a File

```c
#ifdef USE_FILES

  char *infile = "puzzles.txt";
  char *outfile = "solutions.txt";
  FILE *fpr = fopen(infile, "r");
  FILE *fpw = fopen(outfile, "a");
  if (fpr == NULL) {
    printf("File \"%s\" failed to open\n", infile);
    }
  else if (fpw == NULL) {
    printf("File \"%s\" failed to open\n", outfile);
    }
  else {
    silent = TRUE;

    // Keep reading from file until you reach the EOF
    int n_lines = 0;
    int n_hints = 0;
    while (!feof(fpr) && n_hints >= 0) {
      char line[100];   // 90 would be enough, but...
      line[0] = '\0';
      (void)fgets(line, 99, fpr);
      if (line != NULL && strlen(line) > 80) {
        char sudoku_s[82];
        int seed;
        n_hints = -1;
        sscanf(line, "%s\t%d\t%d", sudoku_s, &seed, &n_hints);
```

```
        if (n_hints > 0) {
          fprintf(fpw, "%s\t%d\t%d", sudoku_s, seed, n_hints);
          init(sudoku_s);
          cleanup();
          solve();
          if (count_solved() < 81) {
            backtracking = TRUE;
            backtrack(0);
            backtracking = FALSE;
            }
          printf("%d\n", n_lines);
          fprintf(fpw, "\t%s\t%d\t%d",
            inconsistent_grid() ? "inconsistent" : "consistent",
            count_solved(),
            n_strats_used
            );
          for (int k = 0; k < n_strats_used; k++) {
            fprintf(fpw, "\t%d", strats_used[k]);
            }
          fprintf(fpw, "\n");
          n_lines++;
          } // if (n_hints..
        } // if (line..
      } // while (TRUE..
    } // if (fpr .. else ..
  if (fpr != NULL) fclose(fpr);
  if (fpw != NULL) fclose(fpw);

#else
```

Obviously, you also need to insert #endif before the return statement at the end of the module.

As you can see from the code, the Solver reads Sudoku strings from a file named puzzles.txt until it hits an EOF marker and writes lines of summary results in a file named solutions.txt.

You keep the code simple by doing the following: hard-code the file names rather than obtaining them from arguments; accept input lines with a fixed, TAB-separated format consisting of the Sudoku string, an identifier, and the number of clues in the puzzle; and, finally, perform only very basic checks on the validity of the input.

Before solving the puzzles, the Solver sets the silent flag to TRUE to suppress the log entries normally displayed. Instead, the Solver displays the puzzle identifier. By reducing the display to the bare minimum, you ensure that the execution proceeds as quickly as possible.

Following is an example of an output line:

```
20008001000190200045006102000400008906007000071000006004010700800000 9500070020034        116
          29        consistent    81     4      0     10     12     31
```

It starts with the information obtained from the input file (Sudoku string of the puzzle, identifier, and number of initial clues) and continues with either "consistent" or "inconsistent" (which you will never see with puzzles that the Generator program, described in Chapter 15, creates), the number of cells solved (not surprisingly, always 81, because backtrack() takes over when solve() fails), the number of strategies used (four in the example), and the list of strategies (0: unique; 10 = first strategy of level 1: naked pair, 12 = third of level 1 = box-line, and 31 = second of level 3 = XY-chain; backtrack, when used, is indicated with 40 + the maximum depth reached).

The Example of Minimum Sudokus

Minimum Sudokus are those with 17 clues. Nobody has mathematically proven that puzzles with 16 clues or less are impossible, but neither has anybody been able to find any of them. You can download the strings of 49,151 minimum Sudokus from `http://staffhome.ecm.uwa.edu.au/~00013890/sudokumin.php`.

To solve them as a block with the Solver, you need first to append to each line an identifier and the number of clues. You can do this easily by loading the list into a spreadsheet program, adding a column with a sequence number, and adding a second column with 17. Then, all you need to do is save the workbook as a tab-separated text file named `puzzles.txt`.

Figure 14-1 shows what you obtain when you plot the number of puzzles *vs.* the number of strategies needed to solve them.

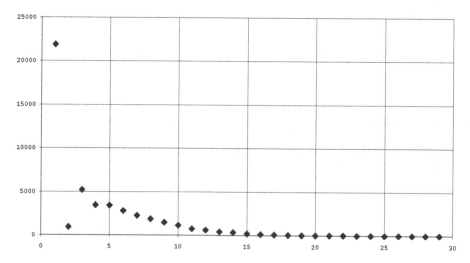

***Figure 14-1.** Number of puzzles vs. number of strategies*

As you can see from Figure 14-1, you can solve the vast majority of puzzles that don't require backtracking with five strategies or less. The actual figures are: 34,910 out of 47,233, or almost 3/4. Surprisingly, you can solve many fewer puzzles with two strategies (943) than with three (5,216). Note that this doesn't depend at all on the type of strategies, as the number includes them all with the exception of cleanup and naked single.

This anomaly could be due to the fact that unique-loop, as the only strategy of level 0 being logged, distorts the result, even if it is not clear at all why it should be so. Call it a hunch! To check whether this is the case, you only need to duplicate the same statistic but ignoring unique-loop. If you do so, you obtain the "good behaved" distribution shown in Figure 14-2, thereby confirming the special role of unique-loop among the strategies.

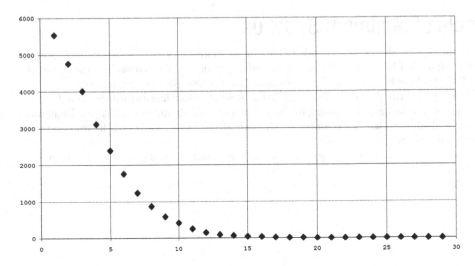

Figure 14-2. *Number of puzzles vs. number of strategies without unique-loop*

The number of puzzles rapidly decreases with the number of strategies needed to solve them. Any further analysis would be far beyond the scope of this book. I can tell you that the decrease is *fast!*

Figure 14-3 shows what you obtain when you plot the number of puzzles *vs.* the highest level of difficulty of the strategies needed to solve them.

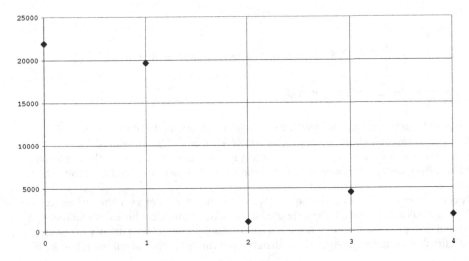

Figure 14-3. *Number of puzzles vs. highest level of difficulty of strategies*

Level 2 strategies occurred as the most difficult strategies to solve the puzzles fewer times than the strategies of any other level. But irregularities in the distribution of strategy types should not surprise you, because the classification of strategies is purely based on my perception of their difficulties for human solvers.

Table 14-1 shows how many times the Solver used any particular strategy.

Table 14-1. Strategy Usage to Solve Minimum Sudokus

Strategy	Level	Occurrences
unique-loop	0	87694
naked pair	1	42152
hidden pair	1	24085
box-line	1	24275
pointing-line	1	4266
naked triple	2	14
hidden triple	2	21
lines-2	2	484
naked quad	2	0
Y-wing	2	2346
rectangle	3	4539
XY-chain	3	3860
lines-3	3	111
lines-4	3	6
backtrack	4	1918

Naked quad never occurred, and lines-4, naked triple, and hidden triple were very rarely needed. The five most "useful" strategies turn out to be unique-loop, naked pair, box-line, hidden pair, and rectangle. But remember that this statistic applies to a very special category of puzzles: those with 17 clues. It could look substantially different with other selections of puzzles. In particular, it will be interesting to see what strategies are needed to solve the puzzles created with the Generator, described in Chapter 15.

Summary

In this chapter, you have learned how you can use the Solver to work on thousands of puzzles, and you've seen how a simple statistical analysis of the results can be intriguing. This concludes the part of this book dedicated to solving puzzles. In Chapter 15, you will start learning how to generate Sudokus, a challenge not to be underestimated.

CHAPTER 15

■ ■ ■

Generating Sudokus

To generate a valid Sudoku puzzle you have to go through the following two steps: generate a completed Sudoku and remove numbers from it in such a way that only one solution is possible with the clues that are left.

It sounds easy, but it isn't—especially the part involved in checking that the solution is unique.

The Sudoku generator I am going to describe to you is the fourth I have written. The first three generators were more cumbersome, used the strategies I developed for the Solver, and were seriously affected by some damning bad choices of mine.

Generating a Solved Sudoku

When I started working on the Generator, I already knew that I wanted to generate many Sudokus. For that reason, I built in file support from the very start. Listing 15-1 shows the global-definitions file, while Listing 15-2 shows the beginning of the Generator up to and including where it generates a solved Sudoku.

Listing 15-1. def.h—Global Definitions for the Generator

```
/* def.h
 *
 * Definitions and declarations
 *
 * Copyright (C) 2015  Giulio Zambon  - http://zambon.com.au/
 *
 */
#ifndef DEF
#define DEF

// General definitions
#define FALSE  0
#define TRUE   1

// Used in some strategies for clarity
#define ROW 0
#define COL 1
#define BOX 2
extern char *unit_names[3];
```

```
// grid declarations
extern char grid[9][9];
extern char row[9][9][2];
extern char col[9][9][2];
extern char box[9][9][2];
extern char solved[9][9];

// Flags
extern int silent;

// Patch because Windows doesn't recognize srandom() and random()
#ifdef __WIN32__
#define srandom srand
#define random rand
#endif

#endif
```

The side effect of using different random generators on the Mac and on the PC is that puzzles generated with the same random seed are different on the two systems. I don't think this is a problem. I executed many tests with srand() and rand() and am pretty confident that the statistical analyses of Chapter 16 remain perfectly valid, even if each individual puzzle is different.

Listing 15-2. sudoku_gen.c—Part 1: Generating a Solved Sudoku

```
/* sudoku_gen.c
 *
 * Copyright (C) 2015  Giulio Zambon  - http://zambon.com.au/
 *
 */
#include <stdio.h>
#include <stdlib.h>
#include <string.h>
#include <time.h>
#include "brute_comp.h"
#include "count_solved.h"
#include "def.h"
#include "display.h"
#include "display_string.h"
#include "fill.h"
#include "inconsistent_grid.h"
#include "inconsistent_unit.h"
#include "init.h"
#include "in_box.h"
#include "list_solved.h"
#include "multi_html.h"
#include "save_html.h"

#define LOG_TO_FILE___NO
#define FILE_NAME "puzzles.txt"
```

```
#define SAVE_HTML_PUZZLE
#define SAVE_HTML_SOLUTION

// N_GRIDS is defined in multi_html.h.
// When N_GRIDS is between 2 and 5, it triggers the creation of multi-grid
// puzzles. With any other value, the Generator creates a classic Sudoku.
#define DO_MULTI_GRID (N_GRIDS >= 2  &&  N_GRIDS <= 5)

// Parameters
#define N_SET_QUADS 5
#define N_SET_PAIRS 10
#define N_SET_CELLS 0
#define ADDITIONAL_CELLS TRUE
#define FIRST_SEED 123456
#define N_SEEDS 1

// Global variables
char *unit_names[3] = {"row", "column", "box"};
char grid[9][9];
char row[9][9][2];
char col[9][9][2];
char box[9][9][2];
char puzzle[9][9];
int silent = FALSE;

// Variables and functions local to this module
char solved[9][9];
int r_1[81];
int c_1[81];
int k_cell;
int remove_quads(int k_puz);
int remove_pairs(int k_puz);
void make_clue_list(void);
int remove_clues(int k_puz);
void remove_more_clues(int k_puz);
int check_uniqueness(void);

// The following table identifies the box of grid 0 that overlaps with other
// grids when creating multi-grid Sudokus.
// The first box refers to puzzle0 and second one to the other puzzle:
//
// N_GRIDS  kPuz=1  kPuz=2  kPuz=3  kPuz=4
//    2     b0-b8
//    3     b0-b8   b8-b0
//    4     b0-b8   b8-b0   b2-b6
//    5     b0-b8   b8-b0   b2-b6   b6-b2
//
// Puzzle:     0   1   2   3   4
int box0[] = {-1,  0,  8,  2,  6};
```

```
//========================================================================= main
int main(int argc, char *argv[]) {
  printf("*** sudoku_gen ***\n");
  char mess[32];
  int n_seeds = N_SEEDS;
  int k_try = 0;

#if DO_MULTI_GRID
  // When creating multi-grid puzzles, set n_seed to the number of
  // puzzles that are needed and prepare to write the puzzles to file
  n_seeds = N_GRIDS;
#endif

  // Open a file to log the results
  FILE *fp = NULL;
#ifdef LOG_TO_FILE
  fp = fopen(FILE_NAME, "a");
  if (fp == NULL) {
    printf("Unable to open the file '%s' for reading\n", FILE_NAME);
    return EXIT_FAILURE;                                                  //==>
    }
#endif

  // Try all the seeds in the given range
  unsigned long start_time = clock();

  for (int k_seed = 0; k_seed < n_seeds; k_seed++) {
    int seed = FIRST_SEED + k_seed;
    srand(seed);
    int brute_result;
    int n;

    // Keep repeating the generation until you find a unique solution
    char puzzle_string[82];
    char solution_string[82];
    do {

      // Generate a solved Sudoku
      do { init(); } while (fill());

      // Save the solved Sudoku
      for (int k = 0; k < 9; k++) {
        for (int j = 0; j < 9; j++) {
          solved[k][j] = grid[k][j];
          puzzle[k][j] = grid[k][j];
          }
        }
```

At first sight, the definitions that precede the beginning of the executable code look similar to those of the Solver. I will talk about the parameters as you need them, but consider the definition of the Sudoku grid. When generating a Sudoku, unlike when solving one, there is no need to keep track of the candidates. Consequently, the grid array has one dimension less, and the unsolved cells are simply set to 0.

Also notice that, beside grid[9][9], there are also a puzzle[9][9] and a solved[9][9]. That is where the Generator stores a puzzle and its reference solution, against which it must then match all subsequent attempted solutions of the same puzzle, in order to ensure uniqueness.

As you can see, you use FIRST_SEED and N_SEEDS together with the control variable k_seed of the subsequent for-loop to seed a different pseudorandom sequence for each puzzle you want to generate. A valid seed is any value between 0 and 2,147,483,647, for each one of which the Generator most likely produces a different puzzle. You cannot be sure that different seeds result in different puzzles, but after creating thousands of puzzles, I haven't yet encountered a case in which that is not true.

The functions declared below the comment "Variables and functions local to this module" are pieces of code of the main program that I carved out into separate functions to make the code easier to understand, although the main program only executes them once. I will explain the variables and the functions when you get to the point of removing clues.

Also the use of the variables n and brute_result will become clear as we progress through this chapter.

Listing 15-2 doesn't show the while-condition associated with the do-loop, but the explanatory comment before the do will have to suffice for the time being. Let's proceed one step at a time.

The first interesting bit is in the statement

```
do { init(); } while (fill());
```

This is where you do all the generation work. To understand it, you need to look at init() and fill() (Listings 15-3 and 15-4, respectively).

init() for the Generator

Listing 15-3. init.c for the Generator

```
/* init.c
 *
 * Copyright (C) 2015  Giulio Zambon  - http://zambon.com.au/
 *
 */
#include <stdio.h>
#include <stdlib.h>
#include "def.h"
#include "init.h"

void init() {

  // Initialize the sudoku arrays
  for (int k = 0; k < 9; k++) {
    for (int j = 0; j < 9; j++) {
      grid[k][j] = 0;
      row[k][j][0] = k;
      row[k][j][1] = j;
      col[j][k][0] = k;
      col[j][k][1] = j;
      box[k/3*3+j/3][k%3*3+j%3][0] = k;
      box[k/3*3+j/3][k%3*3+j%3][1] = j;
      }
    }
  }
```

init() for the Generator is simpler than its counterpart for the Solver described in Chapter 3 because the Sudoku grid for the Generator doesn't keep track of cell candidates and also because there is no input string to process. So, you only need to initialize the four arrays grid[ ][ ], row[ ][ ][ ], col[ ][ ][ ], and box[ ][ ][ ].

fill()

Listing 15-4. fill.c

```
/* fill.c
 *
 * Copyright (C) 2015  Giulio Zambon  - http://zambon.com.au/
 *
 */
#include <stdio.h>
#include <stdlib.h>
#include "def.h"
#include "display.h"
#include "fill.h"
#include "fill_digit.h"

int fill(void) {
  int problem_found = FALSE;
  int i;
  int kkount = 0;
  for (i = 1; i <= 9 && kkount < 729; i++) {
    int kount = 0;
    do {
      kount++;
      problem_found = fill_digit((char)i);
      if (!silent) printf("fill %d [%d %d]: %s\n",
          i, kount, kkount, (problem_found) ? "failed" : "succeeded"
          );
    } while (problem_found && kount < 9);

    if (problem_found) {
      for (int k = 0; k < 9; k++) {
        for (int j = 0; j < 9; j++) {
          if (grid[k][j] == i || grid[k][j] == i-1) grid[k][j] = 0;
        }
      }
      i -= 2;
    } // if (problem_found..
    kkount++;
  }
  return problem_found || kkount >= 729;
}
```

fill() uses fill_digit() to fill in the Sudoku grid one number at a time, from 1 to 9. As you will see in the next section, fill_digit() relies on the random generator to choose among the available cells. Due to the fact that in a 9x9 matrix there are many more impossible combinations than valid Sudokus, fill_digit()

often fails. When this happens, fill() clears the current number and resumes the attempt from the previous one. It subtracts -2 from the current number because i is automatically incremented at the end of the for-loop. This results in re-entering the code inside the for-loop with an i decremented by 1.

But this cannot go on forever. Therefore, after going through the loop 729 times, fill() gives up and returns with a failure indication. Then, the do-loop in the main program cleans up the Sudoku grid by executing init() and then restarts fill(). Why 729? It is 9 times 81 (i.e. 9 cubed). It seems a good value. The actual requirement is that the number of attempts is significantly greater than 81, so that fill() doesn't give up too easily.

If you start the Generator with silent set to FALSE, the following is an example of what fills() logs onto the standard output:

```
fill 1 [1 0]: succeeded
fill 2 [1 1]: succeeded
fill 3 [1 2]: succeeded
fill 4 [1 3]: succeeded
fill 5 [1 4]: succeeded
fill 6 [1 5]: succeeded
fill 7 [1 6]: failed
fill 7 [2 6]: failed
fill 7 [3 6]: succeeded
fill 8 [1 7]: failed
fill 8 [2 7]: failed
fill 8 [3 7]: failed
fill 8 [4 7]: failed
fill 8 [5 7]: succeeded
fill 9 [1 8]: succeeded
```

And here is another example with some backtracking.

```
fill 1 [1 0]: succeeded
fill 2 [1 1]: succeeded
fill 3 [1 2]: succeeded
fill 4 [1 3]: succeeded
fill 5 [1 4]: failed
fill 5 [2 4]: succeeded
fill 6 [1 5]: failed
fill 6 [2 5]: failed
fill 6 [3 5]: succeeded
fill 7 [1 6]: failed
fill 7 [2 6]: failed
fill 7 [3 6]: failed
fill 7 [4 6]: failed
fill 7 [5 6]: failed
fill 7 [6 6]: failed
fill 7 [7 6]: failed
fill 7 [8 6]: failed
fill 7 [9 6]: failed
fill 6 [1 7]: failed
fill 6 [2 7]: failed
fill 6 [3 7]: failed
fill 6 [4 7]: failed
```

```
fill 6 [5 7]: succeeded
fill 7 [1 8]: failed
fill 7 [2 8]: failed
fill 7 [3 8]: failed
fill 7 [4 8]: succeeded
fill 8 [1 9]: succeeded
fill 9 [1 10]: succeeded
```

Both examples resulted in a solved Sudoku, as confirmed by the fact that the last entry in the log states that fill() succeeded in placing the 9s. But now have a look at fill_digit() (see Listing 15-5), which includes an interesting algorithm.

fill_digit()

Listing 15-5. fill_digit.c

```c
/* fill_digit.c
 *
 * Copyright (C) 2015  Giulio Zambon   - http://zambon.com.au/
 *
 */
#include <stdio.h>
#include <stdlib.h>
#include "def.h"
#include "fill_digit.h"

int fill_digit(char i) {
  const int other_box[9][2][2] = {  // [this box][row/column][..]
              {/* 0 */ {-1     }, {-1     }},
              {/* 1 */ { 0, -1}, {-1     }},
              {/* 2 */ { 0,  1}, {-1     }},
              {/* 3 */ {-1     }, { 0, -1}},
              {/* 4 */ { 3, -1}, { 1, -1}},
              {/* 5 */ { 3,  4}, { 2, -1}},
              {/* 6 */ {-1     }, { 0,  3}},
              {/* 7 */ { 6, -1}, { 1,  4}},
              {/* 8 */ { 6,  7}, { 2,  5}},
            };
  int solved_cells[2][9] = {{-1, -1, -1, -1, -1, -1, -1, -1, -1}};

  int problem_found = FALSE;
  int n_cells;
  int cell[9][2];
  for (int kB = 0; kB < 9 && !problem_found; kB++) {
    problem_found = TRUE;
    n_cells = 0;
    for (int k = 0; k < 9; k++) {
      int kR = box[kB][k][ROW];
      int kC = box[kB][k][COL];
      if (grid[kR][kC] == 0) {
```

```
      int rc[2];
      rc[ROW] = kR;
      rc[COL] = kC;
      int conflict = FALSE;
      for (int kRC = 0; kRC < 2 && !conflict; kRC++) {
        int kkS = other_box[kB][kRC][0];
        if (kkS >= 0) {
          if (rc[kRC] == solved_cells[kRC][kkS]) {
            conflict = TRUE;
            }
          else {
            kkS = other_box[kB][kRC][1];
            if (kkS >= 0 && rc[kRC] == solved_cells[kRC][kkS]) {
              conflict = TRUE;
              }
            }
          } // if (kkS..
        } // for (int kRC..

      if (!conflict) {
        cell[n_cells][ROW] = kR;
        cell[n_cells][COL] = kC;
        n_cells++;
        }
      } // if (grid[kR][kC]..
    } // for (int k..

  // Pick a cell of the box
  if (n_cells > 0) {
    problem_found = FALSE;
    int kE = rand() % n_cells;
    solved_cells[ROW][kB] = cell[kE][ROW];
    solved_cells[COL][kB] = cell[kE][COL];
    grid[solved_cells[ROW][kB]][solved_cells[COL][kB]] = i;
    }

  } // for (int kB..

if (problem_found) {

  // Restore the grid to its initial status
  for (int m = 0; m < 9 && solved_cells[ROW][m] >= 0; m++) {
    grid[solved_cells[ROW][m]][solved_cells[COL][m]] = 0;
    }
  }
return problem_found;
}
```

To understand how the algorithm works, you first have to be clear about the purpose of other_box and how it is structured. For convenience, I will reproduce here as Figure 15-1 the figure with the box IDs that you have already seen in Chapter 1 as Figure 1-3.

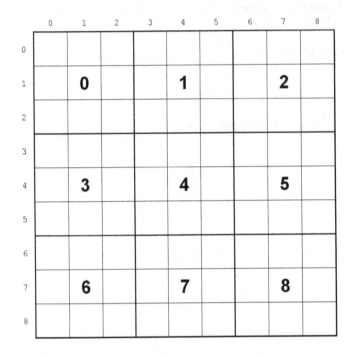

Figure 15-1. *Box IDs (repeated)*

Imagine that you want to place one number 7 (just because I like 7s) in each box. You start with box 0 and place it anywhere you like.

When you want to place a 7 in box 1, you have to ensure that it is in a row other than that containing the 7 you have already placed in box 0. And when you want to place a 7 in box 2, you are only left with one row, because what is available in box 2 depends on the rows already occupied with 7s in box 0 and 1.

The same reasoning for boxes 1 and 2 applies to boxes 3 and 6 if you replace in the previous paragraph all occurrences of the word "row" with the word "column."

Box 4 is different, because to find what cells are still available to place a 7, you have to eliminate the row used in box 3 and the column used in box 1.

You've got the idea. The most difficult box is box 8 (obviously assuming that you proceed with the boxes in order) because by eliminating the rows used in 6 and 7 and the columns used in 2 and 5, you are left with only a single cell.

In any case, a box never depends on more than two other boxes for what concerns the rows and two other boxes for what concerns the columns. The purpose of other_box is to store these dependencies. Its first index is the box ID, from 0 to 8. Its second index distinguishes between rows and columns (remember that ROW is 0 and COL is 1). Its third dimension stores the IDs of the boxes each box depends on. For example, other_box[5][ROW][0] contains 3 and other_box[5][ROW][1] contains 4 because box 5 has to avoid conflicts with the rows of box 3 and 4. Similarly other_box[5][COL][] contains 2 and -1 because box 5 has to avoid conflicts with the columns of box 2. The -1 indicates that there are no further boxes whose columns you need to consider when working on box 5. That's why the first locations of other_box[0][ROW][] and other_box[0][COL][] are both set to -1: box 0 doesn't depend on any other box.

If you are thinking that `fill_digit()` cannot ever fail, think again. What you are not considering is that as `fill()` proceeds with the numbers from 1 to 9, there are always fewer places available in the Sudoku grid. `fill_digit(1)` will always succeed, `fill_digit(2)` almost always, `fill_digit(3)` most likely, and so on. But when you arrive at the high numbers, there might be no solution available. In fact, already the placement of the second number might fail. If you are not convinced, look at Figure 15-2. Where would you place the 2 of box 8?

	0	1	2	3	4	5	6	7	8
0		2							1
1				1		2			
2	1			2					
3		1							2
4			2			1			
5				2	1				
6	2			1					
7			1		2				
8							1		

Figure 15-2. *A failed fill_digit()*

Because it can fail, it is necessary for `fill_digit()` to remember the coordinates of all the cells of the Sudoku grid that it solves, so that it can revert the modified cells to their original free state if necessary. If it didn't do so, it would have to start every time from box 0 and hope to succeed. As it is, `fill_digit()` behaves as if it tried to find a path through a maze by backtracking to the last fork rather than going back to the entrance after each dead end it encounters. The array `solved_cells` keeps track of what `fill_digit()` has already achieved: whenever it finds a solution for a box, it saves its coordinates in `solved_cells`. For example, when in the example in Figure 15-2 the algorithm places the 1 for box 7 in (6,3), it updates `solved_cells` as follows:

```
solved_cells[ROW][7] = 6;
solved_cells[COL][7] = 3;
```

For each box (i.e., for each value of kB from 0 to 8), the for-loop with control variable k saves in the array `cell` the coordinates of all the cells of the current box that have not been solved and that do not conflict with cells containing the same number in boxes the current box depends on.

As an example, let's follow what happens inside the for-loop with control variable k when `fill_digit()` processes box 5 for the number 2 in the situation of Figure 15-2.

After the processing of boxes from 0 to 4, solved_cells contains the following values:

```
           box ID:  0  1  2  3  4  5  6  7  8
solved_cells[ROW]:  0  2  1  4  5 -1 -1 -1 -1
solved_cells[COL]:  1  4  6  2  3  x  x  x  x
```

where x means undefined because fill_digit() doesn't initialize the column fields.

k == 0 sets   kR = box[5][0][ROW] (i.e., 3)
        and   kC = box[5][0][COL] (i.e., 6)

As grid[3][6] is 0, fill_digit() sets rc[ROW] to 3 and rc[COL] to 6, after which it enters the for-loop with control variable kRC set to ROW and sets kkS as follows:

kkS = other_box[5][ROW][0] (i.e., 3)

This means that

solved_cells[ROW][kkS] == 4

The cell of box 3 containing a 2 is in row 4. As rc[ROW] == 3, it means that there is no conflict. fill_digit() sets kkS to the second value stored in other_box.

kkS = other_box[5][ROW][1] (i.e., 4)

If the current box depended on a single other box for what concerns rows, this second value of kkS would be -1. As it is, you compare rc[ROW] with

solved_cells[ROW][4] == 5

The cell of box 4 containing a 2 is in row 5. Once more, there is no conflict. The for-loop continues with kRC set to COL. This time

kkS = other_box[5][COL][0] (i.e., 2)

which means that

solved_cells[COL][2] == 6

The cell of box 2 containing a 2 is in column 6. But this is identical to rc[COL]!
conflict is set to TRUE, which causes the for-loop with control variable kRC to exit and the saving of the cell coordinates into cell to be skipped.
The next iteration with k == 1 means

kR = box[5][1][ROW] = 3
kC = box[5][1][COL] = 7

This cell is free and doesn't cause any conflict. Therefore, fill_digit() can save its coordinates.

```
cell[0][ROW] = 3;
cell[0][COL] = 7;
n_cells = 1;
```

When k exceeds 8, the for-loop exits and

```
cell = (3,7), (3,8)
n_cells = 2
```

That is, `fill_digit()` has in box 5 a choice of two cells to place a 2. In the example, it picks at random (3,8), which contributes to making it impossible to place a 2 in box 8.

Removing Clues to Make a Puzzle

Conceptually, it is simple: keep removing a clue at a time as long as the puzzle has a unique solution. When you see that the puzzle has multiple solutions, go back one removal and you are done.

In practice, though, it makes sense to start by removing more than one clue at a time. First because you are not interested in puzzles with too many clues anyway and second because you can remove sets of clues symmetrically, so that the resulting puzzle looks somewhat symmetrical. There is no logical reason for preferring more symmetrical puzzles, but they are more pleasing to the eye.

You can remove some quadruples of cells and then some couples before removing individual cells. To do so, you make lists of all possible symmetrical quadruplets, of all possible symmetrical pairs, and of all cells. Then, you arrange the elements of the lists in a random order, so that when you need them, you can go through the lists in sequence. The alternative would be to pick quadruplets, pairs, and cells at random when needed, but preparing the lists in advance is neater.

Figure 15-3 shows some examples of symmetrical quadruples of cells. There are a total of 20 possible quadruplets, which you can identify by placing the top-left cell in all positions grayed in Figure 15-3.

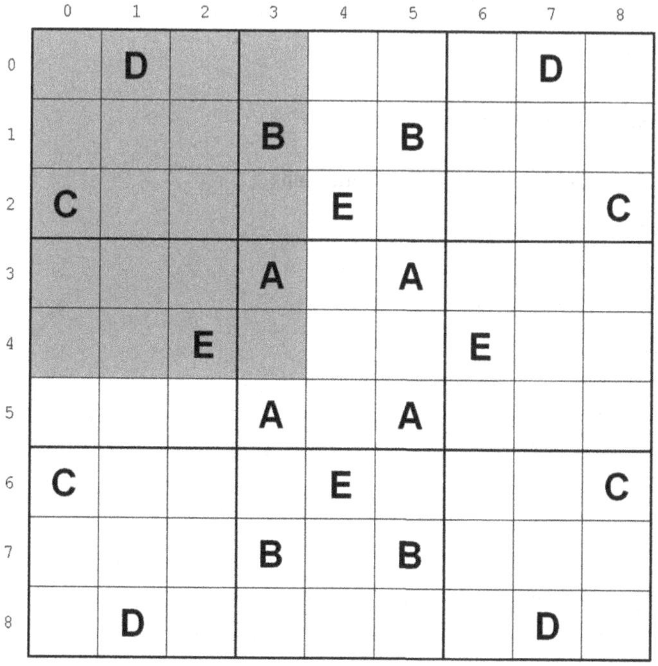

Figure 15-3. *Examples of symmetric quadruplets of cells*

Figure 15-4 shows some examples of symmetrical pairs. There are 40 possible pairs, and to identify them all, you only need to place one of the cells in the grayed area of Figure 15-4.

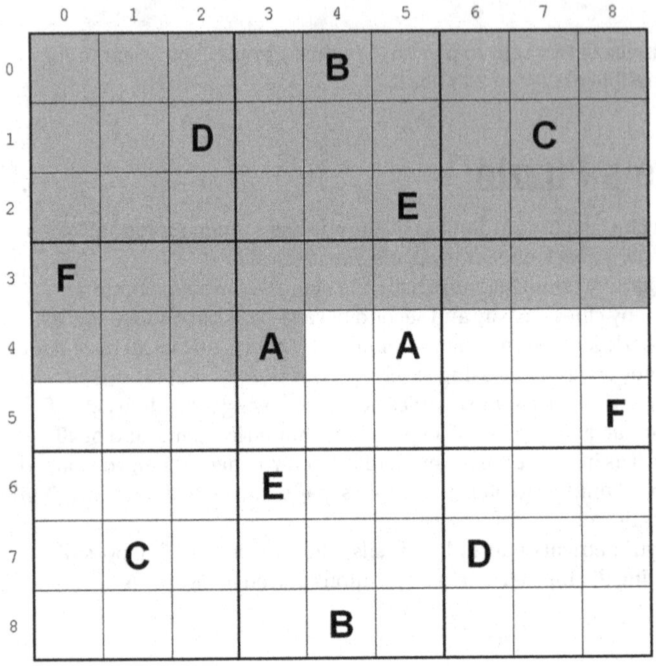

Figure 15-4. *Examples of symmetric pairs of cells*

Listing 15-6 shows the portion of the Generator that removes clues.

Listing 15-6. sudoku_gen.c—Part 2: Removing Clues from Quads, Pairs, and Cells

```
//========= Remove N_SET_QUADS quadruples of clues
if (N_SET_QUADS > 0) {
  int success = remove_quads(k_seed);
  if (!success) {
    brute_result = BRUTE_COMP_DIFFERENT;
    goto skip;                                              //==>
    }
  }


//========= Remove N_SET_PAIRS pairs of clues
if (N_SET_PAIRS > 0) {
  int success = remove_pairs(k_seed);
  if (!success) {
    brute_result = BRUTE_COMP_DIFFERENT;
    goto skip;                                              //==>
    }
  }
```

```
//========= Remove N_SET_CELLS individual clues and then some more
make_clue_list();
k_cell = 0;
if (N_SET_CELLS > 0) {
  int success = remove_clues(k_seed);
if (!success) {
  brute_result = BRUTE_COMP_DIFFERENT;
  goto skip;                                                  //==>
  }
if (ADDITIONAL_CELLS && k_cell < 81) remove_more_clues(k_seed);
```

As you can see, the Generator executes remove_quads() to remove N_SET_QUADS quadruplets, remove_pairs() to remove N_SET_PAIRS pairs, and remove_clues() to remove N_SET_CELLS individual clues. The variable k_cell is one of those defined at the beginning of the module. As you will see in a moment, the Generator uses it to keep track of how many random individual clues it has removed or attempted to remove. If, after removing N_SET_CELLS individual clues, k_cell hasn't reached 81 and ADDITIONAL_CELLS is set, it means that the Generator has not exhausted the list of clues that it can attempt to remove. Therefore, it tries to remove more individual clues by executing remove_more_clues().

Notice how I have used goto statements to break out of nested loops. For many programmers the use of goto is taboo but, to avoid goto's in this case, you would have to add four if-statements. This would increase the maximum level of indentation and, ultimately, make the code less readable. Programming is a rational activity and shouldn't become enslaved to taboos.

The goto skip statements cause jumps to the end of the big do-loop of which you still have to see the while-condition. When it is executed, the Generator restarts from the do, fills a new Sudoku from scratch, and tries again to remove first the quadruples of clues, then the pairs, and finally the individual clues.

In Listing 15-7 follow what happens within remove_quads():

Listing 15-7. sudoku_gen.c – remove_quads()

```
#define N_QUADS 20
int remove_quads(int kPuz) {

  // Build a random list of cells to be quadrupled
  int r_4[N_QUADS];
  int c_4[N_QUADS];
  {
    char quads[9][9] = {{0}};
    for (int k = 0; k < N_QUADS; k++) {
      int kR;
      int kC;
      do {
        int kk = rand() % N_QUADS;
        kR = kk >> 2;
        kC = kk - (kR << 2);
        } while (quads[kR][kC] > 0);
      r_4[k] = kR;
      c_4[k] = kC;
      quads[kR][kC] = 1;
      }
    }
```

```
// Change quadruples until you get a matching solution
int k_quad = -1;
int n_quads = 0;
while (n_quads < N_SET_QUADS && k_quad < N_QUADS-1) {
  k_quad++;
  n_quads++;
  int quad[4][2] = {{0}}; // [index][row/col]
  int kR = r_4[k_quad];
  int kC = c_4[k_quad];
  quad[0][ROW] = kR;
  quad[0][COL] = kC;
  quad[1][ROW] = kR;
  quad[1][COL] = 8 - kC;
  if (kR == 4) {
    quad[2][ROW] = kC;
    quad[2][COL] = kR;
    quad[3][ROW] = 8 - kC;
    quad[3][COL] = kR;
    }
  else {
    quad[2][ROW] = 8 - kR;
    quad[2][COL] = kC;
    quad[3][ROW] = 8 - kR;
    quad[3][COL] = 8 - kC;
    }
  if (!silent) printf("Removed quad %d:", k_quad);
  for (int k = 0; k < 4; k++) {
    int kR = quad[k][ROW];
    int kC = quad[k][COL];

    // The following 'if' is only needed when creating multi-grid puzzles
    if (kPuz == 0 || !in_box(kR, kC, overlapping_box[kPuz])) {
      grid[kR][kC] = 0;
      }
    if (!silent) printf("(%d,%d)", kR, kC);
    }
  if (!silent) printf("\n");

  // Save the Sudoku puzzle after the removal
  for (int k = 0; k < 9; k++) {
    for (int j = 0; j < 9; j++) {
      puzzle[k][j] = grid[k][j];
      }
    }

  // Solve with brute() and see whether the solution matches
  // the reference
  int brute_result = brute_comp();
  if (!silent) printf("Brute after removing quad %d: %s\n",
      k_quad, brute_comp_err[brute_result]
      );
```

```
    // If not, backtrack
    if (brute_result != BRUTE_COMP_OK) {
      if (!silent) printf("Backtracking the last quadruple\n");
      puzzle[kR][kC] = solved[kR][kC];
      puzzle[kR][8-kC] = solved[kR][8-kC];
      puzzle[8-kR][kC] = solved[8-kR][kC];
      puzzle[8-kR][8-kC] = solved[8-kR][8-kC];
      n_quads--;
      }

    // Restore the puzzle to how it was before solving it
    for (int k = 0; k < 9; k++) {
      for (int j = 0; j < 9; j++) {
        grid[k][j] = puzzle[k][j];
        }
      }
    } // while (n_quads..
  int success = n_quads == N_SET_QUADS;
  if (!silent) {
    if (success) {
      printf("%d clues left after removing the quadruples\n", count_solved());
      display();

      // Save the Sudoku puzzle after removing the quadruples
      for (int k = 0; k < 9; k++) {
        for (int j = 0; j < 9; j++) {
          grid[k][j] = puzzle[k][j];
          }
        }
      }
    else {
      printf("No unique solution when removing quadruples. Run aborted.\n");
      }
    }
  return success;
  } // remove_quads
```

The first part of remove_quads() generates the list of random cells that can be quadrupled—that is, of cells in the gray area of Figure 15-3. To do so, it keeps executing

```
int kk = random() % N_QUADS;
kR = kk >> 2;
kC = kk - (kR << 2);
```

until it hits a free place on the Sudoku grid. The shift-right-two-bits and shift-left-two-bits operations are equivalent, respectively, to dividing and multiplying by 4. I always like to replace divisions and multiplications by powers of two with bit-shifts. With optimizing compilers, it makes no difference, but it is for me a somewhat nostalgic reminder of when I had to deal with assembly language. You are obviously welcome to replace >> 2 with /4 and << 2 with *4. Incidentally, the parentheses enclosing the left-shift are unnecessary. They are only there because Eclipse otherwise issues an unjustified warning.

In any case, remove_quads() saves row and column coordinates of the cells it selects in r_4 and c_4.

The second part of the function is where remove_quads() actually removes the quadruples of clues from the Sudoku grid. It uses the k_quad variable to identify the quadruplet currently being removed, and n_quad to count the quadruplets already removed. It first saves the coordinates of the four symmetrical cells in quad[][], and then removes them with the following loop (here stripped of comments and printfs):

```
for (int k = 0; k < 4; k++) {
  int kR = quad[k][ROW];
  int kC = quad[k][COL];
  if (kPuz == 0 || !in_box(kR, kC, overlapping_box[kPuz])) {
    grid[kR][kC] = 0;
  }
}
```

The reason for making the removal of the clue from the cell with coordinates (kR,kC) conditional will become clear in Chapter 18, where you will learn about multi-grid Sudokus (of which Samurai Sudokus are a particular case). There, you will also find a description of in_box(). For now, you can simply ignore it because, when generating classic Sudokus, kPuz is always 0. Therefore, the condition is always verified and the clue at coordinates (kR,kC) is always removed.

After removing the clues, remove_quads() saves the Sudoku grid into the aptly named variable puzzle, and attempts to solve it with a brute-force algorithm (explained in the following section). If the brute-force solution does *not* match the Sudoku grid as it was before the removal (i.e., as stored in the array solved), remove_quads() restores the Sudoku grid to how it was before removing the current quadruplet and tries the next quadruplet.

To avoid confusion, perhaps I should restate here that solved stores the reference solution, grid is where the various algorithms do their work, and puzzle is where you keep the current state of the puzzle as it goes through the various phases of the generation process.

remove_pairs() (see Listing 15-8) is very similar to remove_quads().

Listing 15-8. sudoku_gen.c – remove_pairs()

```
#define N_PAIRS 40
int remove_pairs(int kPuz) {

  // Build a random list of cells to be paired
  int r_2[N_PAIRS];
  int c_2[N_PAIRS];
  {
    char pairs[9][9] = {{0}};
    for (int k = 0; k < N_PAIRS; k++) {
      int kR;
      int kC;
      do {
        int kk = rand() % N_PAIRS;
        kR = kk / 9;
        kC = kk - kR * 9;
        } while (pairs[kR][kC] > 0);
      r_2[k] = kR;
      c_2[k] = kC;
      pairs[kR][kC] = 1;
      }
  }
```

```
// Change pairs until you get a matching solution
int k_pair = -1;
int n_pairs = 0;
while (n_pairs < N_SET_PAIRS && k_pair < N_PAIRS-1) {
  int kR;
  int kC;
  do {
    k_pair++;
    if (k_pair < N_PAIRS) {
      kR = r_2[k_pair];
      kC = c_2[k_pair];
      if (grid[kR][kC] == 0) {
        if (!silent) printf("Pair %d: (%d,%d) (%d,%d) overlaps"
            " with quadruple\n", k_pair, kR, kC, 8-kR, 8-kC
          );
      }
    }
  } while (grid[kR][kC] == 0 && k_pair < N_PAIRS);
  if (k_pair < N_PAIRS) {

    // The following two 'if' are only needed when creating multi-grid puzzles
    if (kPuz == 0  || !in_box(kR, kC, overlapping_box[kPuz])) {
      grid[kR][kC] = 0;
    }
    if (kPuz == 0  || !in_box(8 - kR, 8 - kC, overlapping_box[kPuz])) {
      grid[8-kR][8-kC] = 0;
    }
    n_pairs++;
    if (!silent) printf("Removed pair %d: (%d,%d) (%d,%d)\n",
        k_pair, kR, kC, 8-kR, 8-kC
      );

    // Save the Sudoku puzzle after the removal
    for (int k = 0; k < 9; k++) {
      for (int j = 0; j < 9; j++) {
        puzzle[k][j] = grid[k][j];
      }
    }

    // Solve with brute() and see whether the solution matches
    // the reference
    int brute_result = brute_comp();
    if (!silent) printf("Brute after removing pair %d: %s\n",
        k_pair, brute_comp_err[brute_result]
      );

    // If not, backtrack
    if (brute_result != BRUTE_COMP_OK) {
      if (!silent) printf("Backtracking the last pair\n");
      puzzle[kR][kC] = solved[kR][kC];
      puzzle[8-kR][8-kC] = solved[8-kR][8-kC];
```

```
      n_pairs--;
      }

    // Restore the puzzle to how it was before solving it
    for (int k = 0; k < 9; k++) {
      for (int j = 0; j < 9; j++) {
        grid[k][j] = puzzle[k][j];
        }
      }
    } // if (k_pair..
  } // while (n_pairs..

  int success = n_pairs == N_SET_PAIRS;
  if (!silent) {
    if (success) {
      printf("%d clues left after removing the pairs\n", count_solved());
      display();

      // Save the Sudoku puzzle after removing the pairs
      for (int k = 0; k < 9; k++) {
        for (int j = 0; j < 9; j++) {
          grid[k][j] = puzzle[k][j];
          }
        }
      }
    else {
      printf("No unique solution when removing pairs. Run aborted.\n");
      }
    }
  return success;
  } // remove_pairs
```

After removing the number of quadruplets defined in N_SET_QUADS, the Generator removes pairs, but only if the brute-force algorithm executed while removing quadruplets was successful in finding a solution that matched the original one. And then, after removing the number of pairs defined in N_SET_PAIRS, the Generator removes individual clues, but, again, only if the brute-force algorithm executed while removing pairs was successful in finding a solution that matched the original one.

When it comes to removing individual clues, you need to make something slightly different (see Listing 15-9 and Listing 15-10).

Listing 15-9. sudoku_gen.c – make_clue_list()

```
void make_clue_list() {
  char singles[9][9] = {{0}};
  for (int k = 0; k < 81; k++) {
    int kR;
    int kC;
    do {
      int kk = rand() % 81;
      kR = kk / 9;
      kC = kk - kR * 9;
      } while (singles[kR][kC] > 0);
```

```
    r_1[k] = kR;
    c_1[k] = kC;
    singles[kR][kC] = 1;
    }
  } // make_clue_list
```

The first difference is that the making of the clue list and the removal of a set number of individual clues must be in separate functions. This is necessary because the Generator needs a list of random individual clues also when N_SET_CELLS == 0. The list of cells for the quadruplets is inside remove_quads() and the list of cells for the pairs is inside remove_pairs(), but if the list of cells for individual clues were inside remove_clues(), you would only make it when N_SET_CELLS > 0. This would prevent you from being able to set N_SET_CELLS to 0 and still remove additional clues by setting ADDITIONAL_CELLS to TRUE.

The second difference is that you must keep k_cell, which is equivalent to k_quad inside remove_quads() and k_pair inside remove_pairs(), outside remove_clues() because the Generator otherwise would lose track of the individual clues already removed and wouldn't be able to remove additional individual clues.

Listing 15-10. sudoku_gen.c – remove_clues()

```
int remove_clues(int kPuz) {
  int success = TRUE;
  int n_cells = 0;
  while (n_cells < N_SET_CELLS && success) {
    int kR;
    int kC;
    do {
      kR = r_1[k_cell];
      kC = c_1[k_cell];
      if (grid[kR][kC] == 0) {
        if (!silent) printf("1 Cell %d: (%d,%d) overlaps with quadruple"
          " or pair\n", k_cell, kR, kC
          );
      }
      k_cell++;
      } while (grid[kR][kC] == 0 && k_cell < 81);
    if (k_cell > 81) {
      if (!silent) printf("1 No more cells available after removing"
        " %d clues. Run aborted.\n", n_cells
        );
      success = FALSE;
      }
    // The following 'if' is only needed when creating multi-grid puzzles
    else if (kPuz == 0 || !in_box(kR, kC, overlapping_box[kPuz])) {
      grid[kR][kC] = 0;
      n_cells++;
      if (!silent) printf("1 Clue removal %d, removed"
        " cell %d: (%d,%d)\n", n_cells, k_cell-1, kR, kC
        );

      // Save the Sudoku puzzle after the removal
      for (int k = 0; k < 9; k++) {
        for (int j = 0; j < 9; j++) {
```

```
        puzzle[k][j] = grid[k][j];
        }
    }

    // Solve with brute() and see whether the solution matches
    // the reference
    int brute_result = brute_comp();
    if (!silent) printf("1 Brute after removing cell %d: %s\n",
        k_cell-1, brute_comp_err[brute_result]
        );

    // If not, backtrack
    if (brute_result != BRUTE_COMP_OK) {
        if (!silent) printf("1 Backtracking the last cell\n");
        puzzle[kR][kC] = solved[kR][kC];
        n_cells--;
        }

    // Restore the puzzle to how it was before solving it
    for (int k = 0; k < 9; k++) {
        for (int j = 0; j < 9; j++) {
            grid[k][j] = puzzle[k][j];
            }
        }
    } // if (k_cell.. else ..
  } // while (n_cells..

  if (success) {

    // Save the Sudoku puzzle after removing the individual clues
    for (int k = 0; k < 9; k++) {
        for (int j = 0; j < 9; j++) {
            grid[k][j] = puzzle[k][j];
            }
        }
    if (!silent) {
        printf("%d clues left after removing %d individual clues\n",
            count_solved(), n_cells
            );
        display();
        }
    }
  return success;
  } // remove_clues
```

For initial tests, you can set N_SET_QUADS to 5, N_SET_PAIRS to 10, and N_SET_CELLS to 0. The result before the Generator executes remove_more_clues() is a puzzle with 81 − N_SET_QUADS*4 − N_SET_PAIRS*2 − N_SET_CELLS*0 = 41 clues.

The major difference between remove_more_clues() (see Listing 15-11) and the other remove_ functions is that it keeps going until the brute-force algorithm fails to find a solution. After that, it only needs to restore the last removed clue to obtain a valid puzzle. This is how the Generator minimizes the number of clues in each puzzle.

Listing 15-11. sudoku_gen.c – remove_more_clues()

```c
void remove_more_clues(int kPuz) {
  int brute_result;
  do {
    int kR;
    int kC;
    do {
      kR = r_1[k_cell];
      kC = c_1[k_cell];
      if (grid[kR][kC] == 0) {
        if (!silent) printf("2 Cell %d: (%d,%d) overlaps with quadruple"
            " or pair\n", k_cell, kR, kC
          );
      }
      k_cell++;
      } while (grid[kR][kC] == 0 && k_cell < 81);

    // The second part of the following 'if' is only needed when creating
    // multi-grid puzzles
    if (k_cell <= 81 &&
        (kPuz == 0  ||  !in_box(kR, kC, overlapping_box[kPuz]))
        ) {
      grid[kR][kC] = 0;
      if (!silent) printf("2 Clue removal %d, removed"
          " cell %d: (%d,%d)\n", 81-count_solved(), k_cell-1, kR, kC
        );

      // Save the Sudoku puzzle after the removal
      for (int k = 0; k < 9; k++) {
        for (int j = 0; j < 9; j++) {
          puzzle[k][j] = grid[k][j];
          }
        }

      // Solve with brute() and see whether the solution matches the reference
      brute_result = brute_comp();
      if (!silent) printf("2 Brute after removing cell %d: %s\n",
          k_cell-1, brute_comp_err[brute_result]
        );

      // Restore the puzzle to how it was before solving it
      for (int k = 0; k < 9; k++) {
        for (int j = 0; j < 9; j++) {
          grid[k][j] = puzzle[k][j];
          }
        }
      } // if (k_cell..
    } while (brute_result == BRUTE_COMP_OK && k_cell < 81);
```

```
  // Restore the last clue removed
  if (brute_result != BRUTE_COMP_OK) {
    int kR = r_1[k_cell-1];
    int kC = c_1[k_cell-1];
    puzzle[kR][kC] = solved[kR][kC];
    }
} // remove_more_clues
```

brute_comp()

This function has the dual purpose of attempting to execute a brute-force algorithm to solve a Sudoku puzzle and of analyzing its results (see Listing 15-12 and Listing 15-13).

Listing 15-12. brute_comp.h

```
/* brute_comp.h
 *
 * Solves a Sudoku by executing brute() and then compares the result with
 * the reference
 *
 * See below for the return codes
 *
 * Copyright (C) 2015  Giulio Zambon  - http://zambon.com.au/
 *
 */
#ifndef BRUTE_COMPARE
#define BRUTE_COMPARE

// If you modify the following list, change brute_comp_err accordingly
#define BRUTE_COMP_OK            0
#define BRUTE_COMP_DIFFERENT     1
#define BRUTE_COMP_TIMEOUT       2
#define BRUTE_COMP_INCONSISTENT  3
#define BRUTE_COMP_IMPOSSIBLE    4
#define BRUTE_COMP_PROBLEM       5

extern const char *brute_comp_err[];

int brute_comp(void);

#endif
```

Listing 15-13. brute_comp.c

```
/* brute_comp.c
 *
 * Copyright (C) 2015  Giulio Zambon  - http://zambon.com.au/
 *
 */
```

```c
#include <stdio.h>
#include <stdlib.h>
#include <time.h>
#include "brute.h"
#include "brute_comp.h"
#include "def.h"
#include "inconsistent_grid.h"

// This messages in clear must match the codes defined in brute_comp.h
const char *brute_comp_err[] = {
    /* 0 */ "same as reference",
    /* 1 */ "different from reference",
    /* 2 */ "timeout",
    /* 3 */ "grid inconsistent",
    /* 4 */ "puzzle impossible",
    /* 5 */ "unknown result"
    };

int brute_comp() {
  int result = BRUTE_COMP_PROBLEM;
  int brute_result = brute();
  switch (brute_result) {

    case BRUTE_SUCCESSFUL:
      result = BRUTE_COMP_OK;
      for (int kk = 0; kk < 9 && result == BRUTE_COMP_OK; kk++) {
        for (int jj = 0; jj < 9 && result == BRUTE_COMP_OK; jj++) {
          if (solved[kk][jj] != grid[kk][jj]) result = BRUTE_COMP_DIFFERENT;
          }
        }
      if (inconsistent_grid()) result = BRUTE_COMP_INCONSISTENT;
      break;

    case BRUTE_IMPOSSIBLE:
      result = BRUTE_COMP_IMPOSSIBLE;
      break;

    case BRUTE_TIMEOUT:
      result = BRUTE_COMP_TIMEOUT;
      break;

    default:
      result = BRUTE_COMP_PROBLEM;
      break;
    }
  return result;
  }
```

The code of brute_comp() is almost trivial. Notice that, unlike the Solver, which relied on the analytical strategies for backtracking, the Generator adopts a real brute-force approach, thereby making it unnecessary

to include the Solver's strategies. The interesting algorithm to solve a Sudoku with brute force is in brute()
(see Listing 15-14 and Listing 15-15).

Listing 15-14. brute.h

```
/* brute.h
 *
 * Solves a Sudoku by brute force
 *
 * See below for the return codes
 *
 * Copyright (C) 2015  Giulio Zambon  - http://zambon.com.au/
 *
 */
#ifndef BRUTE
#define BRUTE

#define BRUTE_SUCCESSFUL   0
#define BRUTE_IMPOSSIBLE  -1
#define BRUTE_TIMEOUT     -2

#define BRUTE_MAX_TIME 10

int brute(void);

#endif
```

Listing 15-15. brute.c

```
/* brute.c
 *
 * Copyright (C) 2015  Giulio Zambon  - http://zambon.com.au/
 *
 */
#include <stdio.h>
#include <stdlib.h>
#include <time.h>
#include "brute.h"
#include "def.h"
#include "inconsistent_unit.h"

int brute() {
   int result = BRUTE_SUCCESSFUL;
   unsigned long start_time = clock()/CLOCKS_PER_SEC;
   unsigned long this_time;
   char initial[9][9];
   for (int k = 0; k < 9; k++) {
     for (int j = 0; j < 9; j++) {
       initial[k][j] = grid[k][j];
       }
     }
```

```
  int k = 0;
  int j = 0;
  do {
    do {
      if (initial[k][j] == 0) {
        int i = grid[k][j] + 1;
        if (i > 9) {
          grid[k][j] = 0;
          do {
            do { j--; } while (j >= 0 && initial[k][j] != 0);
            if (j < 0) {
              k--;
              if (k < 0) {
                result = BRUTE_IMPOSSIBLE;
                goto done;                                          //==>
              }
              j = 8;
            }
          } while (initial[k][j] != 0);
        } // if (i..
        else {
          grid[k][j] = i;
          int kB = k/3*3+j/3;
          if (    !inconsistent_unit("row", k, row[k])
              && !inconsistent_unit("column", j, col[j])
              && !inconsistent_unit("box", kB, box[kB])
             ) {
            j++;
          }
        } // if (i.. else
      } // if (initial[k][j]..
      else {
        j++;
      }
      this_time = clock()/CLOCKS_PER_SEC;
      if (this_time - start_time > BRUTE_MAX_TIME) {
        result = BRUTE_TIMEOUT;
        goto done;                                                 //==>
      }
    } while (j < 9);
    k++;
    j = 0;
  } while (k < 9);

done:
  return result;
  }
```

The time-out interval BRUTE_MAX_TIME of 10 seconds is completely arbitrary. I just found it boring to wait longer than that, and, in most cases, 10 seconds, even on a computer that is a few years old, are more than enough to solve a puzzle with brute force.

The algorithm is conceptually straightforward: go through all the unsolved cells in sequence and try to solve them with 1. If 1 is in conflict with some other numbers, try 2. If 2 also causes a conflict, try 3, and so on until you find a number that doesn't cause any conflict. At that point, go to the next cell and do the same. If all numbers from 1 to 9 cause conflicts, free the cell, go back to the previous one, and increase the number you find there. The algorithm goes forth and back until it completes the Sudoku. The implementation is not trivial, though. To explain how it works, refer to the example of Figure 15-5. It shows a puzzle generated after removing five quadruplets, ten pairs, and four individual cells.

	0	1	2	3	4	5	6	7	8
0	9		1		7		5		
1	5		3	8					4
2					6				
3	6	1	8	3				2	7
4	2	4		9	1	6		8	5
5		9		2		7		6	1
6					4				
7	1				3	9	8		2
8			9		2		6		3

Figure 15-5. *A puzzle to solve with brute()*

To understand brute(), concentrate on the lines of code where grid[k][j] is on the left-hand side of an assignment. They are only two and, to make your life a bit easier, I have highlighted them in bold. grid[k][j] = i is where brute() tries a number, and grid[k][j] = 0 is where it resets a cell before backtracking to the previous one.

If you insert a printf showing row, column, and number after the statement where brute() tries a number, you get the list of entries shown in Listing 15-16 (limited to the first 140 of 1,078 entries).

Listing 15-16. Tracking brute()

```
(0,1)1 (0,1)2 (0,3)1 (0,3)2 (0,3)3 (0,3)4 (0,5)1 (0,5)2 (0,5)3 (0,7)1 (0,7)2 (0,7)3 (0,7)4
(0,7)5 (0,7)6 (0,7)7 (0,7)8 (0,7)9 (0,5)4 (0,5)5 (0,5)6 (0,5)7 (0,5)8 (0,5)9 (0,3)5 (0,3)6
(0,3)7 (0,3)8 (0,3)9 (0,1)3 (0,1)4 (0,1)5 (0,1)6 (0,3)1 (0,3)2 (0,3)3 (0,3)4 (0,5)1 (0,5)2
(0,7)1 (0,7)2 (0,7)3 (0,8)1 (0,8)2 (0,8)3 (0,8)4 (0,8)5 (0,8)6 (0,8)7 (0,8)8 (1,1)1 (1,1)2
(1,4)1 (1,4)2 (1,4)3 (1,4)4 (1,4)5 (1,4)6 (1,4)7 (1,4)8 (1,4)9 (1,5)1 (1,6)1 (1,6)2 (1,6)3
(1,6)4 (1,6)5 (1,6)6 (1,6)7 (1,7)1 (1,7)2 (1,7)3 (1,7)4 (1,7)5 (1,7)6 (1,7)7 (1,7)8 (1,7)9
(1,6)8 (1,6)9 (1,5)2 (1,5)3 (1,5)4 (1,5)5 (1,5)6 (1,5)7 (1,5)8 (1,5)9 (1,1)3 (1,1)4 (1,1)5
(1,1)6 (1,1)7 (1,4)1 (1,4)2 (1,4)3 (1,4)4 (1,4)5 (1,4)6 (1,4)7 (1,4)8 (1,4)9 (1,5)1 (1,6)1
```

(1,6)2 (1,7)1 (1,7)2 (1,7)3 (1,7)4 (1,7)5 (1,7)6 (1,7)7 (1,7)8 (1,7)9 (1,6)3 (1,6)4 (1,6)5 (1,6)6 (1,6)7 (1,6)8 (1,6)9 (1,5)2 (1,5)3 (1,5)4 (1,5)5 (1,5)6 (1,5)7 (1,5)8 (1,5)9 (1,1)8 **(1,1)9** (0,8)9 (0,7)4 (0,7)5 (0,7)6 (0,7)7 (0,7)8 (0,7)9 (0,5)3 (0,7)1

Scanning the puzzle of Figure 15-5 from the top-left, the first unsolved cell is (0,1). As unsolved cells are represented by a zero, the statement

```
int i = grid[k][j] + 1;
```

sets i to 1. As i is *not* greater than 9, brute() sets grid[0][1] to 1 and prints the first entry.

But there is already a 1 in row 0. Therefore, inconsistent_unit() invoked for row 0 finds an inconsistency, and j (i.e., the column index) is not incremented. The control goes back to the beginning of the second do-statement with the same row and column IDs, where you set i to 2.

As i is still not greater than 9, brute() sets grid[0][1] to 2, prints the second entry, and executes inconsistent_unit(). This time, there is no inconsistency, and brute() increments j to 2. As initial[0][3] == 1 (i.e., the cell is solved), brute() increments j to 3 and prints the third entry of Listing 15-16.

From the entries, you see that brute() fails to solve (0,3) with 1, 2, and 3, before succeeding with 4. Similarly, brute() solves (0,5) with 3. But when brute() tries to solve (0,7), it finds out that all numbers cause a conflict. As a result, the test i > 9 succeeds and (0,7) is reset back to 0.

The two do-loops that follow the assignment grid[k][j] = 0 have the purpose of making current the cell previously solved by brute(). You cannot simply decrement j to go to the previous column, because you might be looking at the very first cell of a row. In that case, the previous cell is in the previous row. Moreover, it could be that the cell immediately preceding the current one was already solved before entering brute().

In the example, starting from (0,7), the do-loop in

```
do { j--; } while (j >= 0 && initial[k][j] != 0);
```

iterates twice, and leaves j set to 5. The current value of (0,5) is 3. That's why the entry after (0,7)9 is (0,5)4. Unfortunately, no further value can solve (0,5). Same story with (0,3). The result is that (0,1) is progressively incremented to 6 (first entry in bold).

Everything goes smoothly for a while: brute() tentatively completes the solution of row 0 (961472538) and tackles row 1. But after 81 entries, it discovers that with the current row 0, no number can solve (1,1) (second entry in bold).

This time, starting from (1,1), the backtracking do-loop

```
do { j--; } while (j >= 0 && initial[k][j] != 0);
```

exits with j set to -1.

As a result, k (the row ID) is decremented from 1 to 0 and j is set to 8. This "wrapping around" is how brute() backtracks through the beginning of a row. Notice that if k goes below 0, it means that the puzzle is unsolvable. You know that the puzzle you are looking at is solvable (because you generated it starting from a valid completed grid), but this check will become necessary when you will use brute() to thoroughly verify the uniqueness of a solution.

You had left (0,8) to be 8, and as you can see, the entry following (1,1)9 is (0,8)9. It turns out that further backtracking is necessary, but by now you should have a pretty good idea of how brute() works.

inconsistent_unit() for the Generator

As I had already done with init(), I adapted the Solver's version of inconsistent_unit() to the simpler representation of the Generator's Sudoku grid (see Listing 15-17). inconsistent_grid() essentially remains the same as that for the Solver, shown in Listing 3-17.

Listing 15-17. inconsistent_unit.c for the Generator

```c
/* inconsistent_unit.c
 *
 * Copyright (C) 2015  Giulio Zambon  - http://zambon.com.au/
 *
 */
#include <stdio.h>
#include <stdlib.h>
#include "def.h"
#include "inconsistent_unit.h"

int inconsistent_unit(char *what, int kG, char unit[9][2]) {
  int result = FALSE;
  int i_vect[10] = {0};
  for (int k = 0; k < 9 && !result; k++) {
    int kR = unit[k][ROW];
    int kC = unit[k][COL];
    int i = grid[kR][kC];
    if (i > 0) {
      if (i_vect[i] == FALSE) {
        i_vect[i] = TRUE;
      }
      else {  // we have a duplicate solution
        result = TRUE;
      }
    } // if (i..
  } // for (int k..
  return result;
}
```

Check for Uniqueness of the Solution

The removal of the clues results in a valid Sudoku puzzle. But you have to be completely sure that the solution is unique. At this point, the only verification of uniqueness is based on the fact that the brute-force solution of the puzzle and the reference solution are identical.

But it is not clear that all different ways of solving the puzzle would result in the same valid solution. To ensure that this is not a case, the Generator executes check_uniqueness() as shown in Listing 15-18. The function check_uniqueness() itself is shown in Listing 15-19.

Listing 15-18. sudoku_gen.c—Part 3: Checking for Uniqueness

```c
//========== Check whether the solution is really unique
brute_result = check_uniqueness();
```

Listing 15-19. sudoku_gen.c - check_uniqueness()

```c
int check_uniqueness() {
  int brute_result = BRUTE_COMP_OK;
  int incr = -8;
  while (incr < 9 && brute_result != BRUTE_COMP_DIFFERENT) {
    for (int k = 0; k < 9 && brute_result != BRUTE_COMP_DIFFERENT; k++) {
```

```
        for (int j = 0; j < 9 && brute_result != BRUTE_COMP_DIFFERENT; j++) {
          if (puzzle[k][j] == 0) {
            for (int kk = 0; kk < 9; kk++) {
              for (int jj = 0; jj < 9; jj++) {
                grid[kk][jj] = puzzle[kk][jj];
                } // for (int jj..
              } // for (int kk..
            grid[k][j] = solved[k][j] + incr;
            int kB = k/3*3+j/3;
            if (    grid[k][j] < 1
                 || grid[k][j] > 9
                 || inconsistent_unit("row", k, row[k])
                 || inconsistent_unit("column", j, col[j])
                 || inconsistent_unit("box", kB, box[kB])
                 ) {
              grid[k][j] = 0;
              }
            else {
              brute_result = brute_comp();
              } // if (grid[k][j]..
            } // if (puzzle[k]j]..
          } // for (int j..
        } // for (int k..
    incr++;
    if (incr == 0) incr++;
    } // while (incr..
  return brute_result;
  } // check_uniqueness
```

For each unsolved cell of the puzzle, check_uniqueness() tries all possible numbers different from the number of the reference solution. For example, with the puzzle shown in Figure 15-5, the number that solves (0,1) in the reference solution is 1. Therefore, the Generator tries to solve the puzzle with brute force after setting (0,1) to 2, then to 3, 4, and so on until it tries 9. It keeps going as long as brute_comp() does *not* return BRUTE_COMP_DIFFERENT. If and when brute_comp() returns BRUTE_COMP_DIFFERENT, it means that it solved the puzzle although one of its unsolved cells was set to a number different from that of the reference solution. Therefore, the puzzle being tested doesn't have a unique solution. check_uniqueness() then returns BRUTE_COMP_DIFFERENT, which forces the Generator to iterate through the very first do-loop of Listing 15-1—that is, to generate from scratch a brand-new puzzle while keeping the same random seed.

To be sure that all possibilities are considered, check_uniqueness() tries all possible numbers in all unsolved cells of the puzzle. For example, the puzzle of Figure 15-5 has 37 clues. This means that there are 81 – 37 = 44 unsolved cells. Therefore, check_uniqueness() tries to solve 44 * 8 = 352 puzzles, each one with 38 clues. The number of puzzles is not 44 * 9 because check_uniqueness() doesn't need to try the correct number.

To try all possible numbers, check_uniqueness() adds to the number stored in the reference solution a value between -8 and +8, and only executes brute_comp() if the resulting number is between 1 and 9 and doesn't make the puzzle impossible to solve.

Notice that check_uniqueness() only reacts when brute_comp() returns BRUTE_COMP_DIFFERENT. You might not be surprised that it ignores BRUTE_COMP_TIMEOUT, BRUTE_COMP_INCONSISTENT, BRUTE_COMP_IMPOSSIBLE, and even BRUTE_COMP_PROBLEM, but what about BRUTE_COMP_OK? Shouldn't you be concerned if the altered puzzle produces the same solution? The fact is that it cannot happen, because the solution found with brute_comp() and the reference solution will always differ at the very least in the number that check_uniqueness() altered.

You might also be concerned that check_uniqueness() only alters one cell at a time. What about swapping two cells or, more in general, rotating any number of cells? If you think about it, you will see that they would be redundant tests. For example, in the reference solution, 2 solves (2,1) and 8 solves (6,1). If you swapped the two numbers, it would mean that you would try to solve a puzzle with the same 37 clues plus an 8 in (2,1) and a 2 in (6,1). But check_uniqueness() already tried to solve a puzzle with all possible values in (2,1), including 8, and then all possible values in (6,1), including 2. Therefore, if the puzzle with the swap led to a solution, check_uniqueness() would find it (even twice, if you let it).

Completing the Generator

After checking for the uniqueness of the solution, the Generator only needs to display some messages and report the results, as shown in Listing 15-20.

Listing 15-20. sudoku_gen.c—Part 4: Closing Off

```c
//========= Check whether the solution is really unique
brute_result = check_uniqueness();

//========= Done
for (int k = 0; k < 9; k++) {
  for (int j = 0; j < 9; j++) {
    grid[k][j] = puzzle[k][j];
    }
  }
n = count_solved();
if (!silent && fp == NULL) {
  display();
  sprintf(mess, "seed %d %d", seed, n);
  display_string(mess);
  printf("The puzzle contains %d clues:", n);
  list_solved(stdout);
  }

skip:                                        // <==
  k_try++;
  printf("%d: %s\n",
      k_try,
      (brute_result == BRUTE_COMP_DIFFERENT) ? "No" : "Yes"
      );
  } while (brute_result == BRUTE_COMP_DIFFERENT);

// Save puzzle and solution into strings
int kar = 0;
for (int k = 0; k < 9; k++) {
  for (int j = 0; j < 9; j++) {
    puzzle_string[kar] = puzzle[k][j] + '0';
    solution_string[kar] = solved[k][j] + '0';
    kar++;
    }
  }
```

```
puzzle_string[kar] = '\0';
solution_string[kar] = '\0';

#ifdef SAVE_HTML_PUZZLE
    save_html(puzzle_string, seed, "p");
#endif

#ifdef SAVE_HTML_SOLUTION
    save_html(solution_string, seed, "s");
#endif
    if (fp != NULL) {
      printf("#%d\n", k_seed);
      fprintf(fp, "%s\t%d", puzzle_string, seed);
      if (brute_result != BRUTE_COMP_DIFFERENT) {
        fprintf(fp, "\t%d", n);
        list_solved(fp);
        }
      fprintf(fp, "\n");
      }
    } // for (k_seed..

  unsigned long end_time = clock();
  printf("********* done in %ld microseconds\n", end_time - start_time);
  if (fp != NULL) fclose(fp);
  return EXIT_SUCCESS;
  }
```

The output written to the file, if requested by defining LOG_TO_FILE at the beginning of the module, matches the format that the Solver expects as input.

list_solved(), shown in Listing 15-21, is a small utility function that prints out the number of times each number occurs in the puzzle.

Listing 15-21. list_solved.c

```
/* list_solved.c
 *
 * Copyright (C) 2015  Giulio Zambon  - http://zambon.com.au/
 *
 */
#include <stdio.h>
#include <stdlib.h>
#include "def.h"
#include "list_solved.h"

void list_solved(FILE *fp) {
  if (fp == NULL) {
    fp = stdout;
    }
  char spacing = (fp == stdout) ? ' ' : '\t';
  int digits[10] = {0};
```

```
for (int k = 0; k < 9; k++) {
  for (int j = 0; j < 9; j++) {
    if (grid[k][j] != 0) {
      digits[(int)grid[k][j]]++;
      }
    } // for (int j..
  } // for (int k..
for (int i = 1; i <= 9; i++) {
  fprintf(fp, "%c%d", spacing, digits[i]);
  }
}
```

Utilities for the Generator

As the Generator uses a simpler Sudoku representation than the Solver, I had to adapt some of the utilities. You have already seen the Generator's version of init() and inconsistent_unit(). In this section, you will find the listings of count_solved(), count_solved(), display(), display_string(), and save_html() (see Listings 15-22 to 15-25).

Listing 15-22. count_solved.c for the Generator

```
/* count_solved.c
 *
 * Copyright (C) 2015  Giulio Zambon  - http://zambon.com.au/
 *
 */
#include <stdio.h>
#include <stdlib.h>
#include "count_solved.h"
#include "def.h"

int count_solved() {
  int result = 0;
  for (int k = 0; k < 9; k++) {
    for (int j = 0; j < 9; j++) {
      if (grid[k][j] != 0) result++;
      }
    }
  return result;
  }
```

list_solved(), shown in Listing 15-22, prints out the number of times each number occurs in the puzzle.

Listing 15-23. list_solved.c

```
/* list_solved.c
 *
 * Copyright (C) 2015  Giulio Zambon  - http://zambon.com.au/
 *
 */
```

```c
#include <stdio.h>
#include <stdlib.h>
#include "def.h"
#include "list_solved.h"

void list_solved(FILE *fp) {
  if (fp == NULL) {
    fp = stdout;
    }
  char spacing = (fp == stdout) ? ' ' : '\t';
  int digits[10] = {0};
  for (int k = 0; k < 9; k++) {
    for (int j = 0; j < 9; j++) {
      if (grid[k][j] != 0) {
        digits[(int)grid[k][j]]++;
        }
      } // for (int j..
    } // for (int k..
  for (int i = 1; i <= 9; i++) {
    fprintf(fp, "%c%d", spacing, digits[i]);
    }
  }
```

Listing 15-24. display.c for the Generator

```c
/* display.c
 *
 * Copyright (C) 2015  Giulio Zambon  - http://zambon.com.au/
 *
 */
#include <stdio.h>
#include <stdlib.h>
#include "def.h"
#include "display.h"

void display() {
  char *h  = "   ++---+---+---++---+---+---++---+---+---++";
  char *hh = "   ++===+===+===++===+===+===++===+===+===++";
  int jBase[] = {2, 6, 10, 15, 19, 23, 28, 32, 36};
  printf("    0   1   2    3   4   5    6   7   8\n");
  for (int k = 0; k < 9; k++) {
    if (k%3 == 0) {
      printf("%s\n", hh);
      }
    else {
      printf("%s\n", h);
      }
//                  000 000 111  111 122 222  223 333 333
//                  234 678 012  567 901 345  890 234 678
    char top[42] = "||   |   |   ||   |   |   ||   |   |   ||";
    char mid[42] = "||   |   |   ||   |   |   ||   |   |   ||";
    char bot[42] = "||   |   |   ||   |   |   ||   |   |   ||";
```

```
      char *displ[42] = {top, mid, bot};
      for (int j = 0; j < 9; j++) {
        if (grid[k][j] == 0) {
          mid[jBase[j]+1] = ' ';
          }
        else {
          mid[jBase[j]+1] = '0' + grid[k][j];
          }
        } // for (int j..
      printf("  %s\n", displ[0]);
      printf("%d %s\n", k, displ[1]);
      printf("  %s\n", displ[2]);
      }
    printf("%s\n", hh);
    }
```

Listing 15-25. display_string.c for the Generator

```
/* display_string.c
 *
 * Copyright (C) 2015  Giulio Zambon  - http://zambon.com.au/
 *
 */
#include <stdio.h>
#include <stdlib.h>
#include "def.h"
#include "display_string.h"

void display_string(char *name) {
  for (int k = 0; k < 9; k++) {
    for (int j = 0; j < 9; j++) {
      printf("%d", grid[k][j]);
      }
    }
  if (name != NULL) printf(" \"%s\"", name);
  printf("\n");
  }
```

The utility function save_html() (see Listing 15-26) is specific to the Generator. Therefore, it doesn't have any counterpart in the Solver. As the Solver deals with existing puzzles, it is not important to display them graphically. Thus, the simple format provided by display() is sufficient. But for the Generator, you must be able to display the puzzles and their solutions in graphical form, so that you can print them out, add them to a web site, or send them via e-mail.

Listing 15-26. save_html.c

```
/* save_html.c
 *
 * Copyright (C) 2015  Giulio Zambon  - http://zambon.com.au/
 *
 */
```

```c
#include <stdio.h>
#include <stdlib.h>
#include "def.h"
#include "save_html.h"

void save_html(char *puzzle, int seed, char *suffix) {
  char *header_1 =
      "<!DOCTYPE html PUBLIC \"-//W3C//DTD XHTML 1.0 Strict//EN\" "
        "\"http://www.w3.org/TR/xhtml1/DTD/xhtml1-strict.dtd\">\n"
      "<html xmlns=\"http://www.w3.org/1999/xhtml\">\n"
      "<head>\n"
      "<title>"
      ;
  char *header_2 =
      "</title>\n"
      "<meta http-equiv=\"Content-type\" "
        "content=\"text/html;charset=UTF-8\"/>\n"
      "<style type=\"text/css\">\n"
      "table {empty-cells:show; border-collapse:collapse;}\n"
      "td {\n"
      "  width:50px; height:50px;\n"
      "  border-style:solid; border-width:1px; border-color:#000000;\n"
      "  text-align:center; vertical-align:middle;\n"
      "  font-family:Arial, Verdana, Sans-serif; font-size:2em;\n"
      "  }\n"
      ".c0 {border-top-width:3px; border-left-width:3px;}\n"
      ".c1 {border-top-width:3px;}\n"
      ".c2 {border-top-width:3px; border-right-width:3px;}\n"
      ".c3 {border-left-width:3px;}\n"
      ".c4 {}\n"
      ".c5 {border-right-width:3px;}\n"
      ".c6 {border-bottom-width:3px; border-left-width:3px;}\n"
      ".c7 {border-bottom-width:3px;}\n"
      ".c8 {border-bottom-width:3px; border-right-width:3px;}\n"
      "</style>\n</head>\n<body>\n<table>\n"
      ;
  char *footer = "</table>\n</body>\n</html>";

  char f_name[64] = {0};
  sprintf(f_name, "%d%s.html", seed, suffix);

  FILE *fp = fopen(f_name, "w");
  if (fp == NULL) {
    printf("Unable to open the file '%s' for writing\n", f_name);
    }
  else {
    fprintf(fp, "%s%d%s", header_1, seed, header_2);
    for (int i = 0; i < 81; i++) {
      int kR = i / 9;
      int kC = i - kR * 9;
      if (kC == 0) fprintf(fp, "<tr>");
```

```
        fprintf(fp, "<td class=\"c%d\">%c</td>",
            kR % 3 * 3 + kC % 3, ((puzzle[i] == '0') ? ' ' : puzzle[i])
            );
        if ((kC + 1) % 3 == 0) fprintf(fp, "\n");
        if (kC == 8) fprintf(fp, "</tr>\n");
        }
    fprintf(fp, "%s\n", footer);
    fclose(fp);
    }
  }
```

Several graphic packages let you generate images, but they are complex to use, and it is always advisable to use the simplest possible tools that do the job.

Strictly speaking, save_html() has nothing to do with graphics, because it stores a puzzle on a web page by means of an HTML table. But you can use it as an alternative to a drawing; it scales very well, and it uses up the same bandwidth regardless of how large you want to display the puzzle. Effectively, save_html() uses any web browser to do the heavy lifting of displaying graphics.

As you can see, the code is pretty straightforward. Most of it consists of the definition of HTML lines as strings.

An interesting bit is how you use the style of the cells to show borders of different thickness. To do so, save_html() defines a different style class for each cell of a box, from top-left (c0, with thick top and left borders) to bottom right (c8, with thick right and bottom borders). It then determines the correct position of each cell (and therefore of its style class) by calculating:

```
kR % 3 * 3 + kC % 3
```

When writing a cell to disk as an element of an HTML table with the following statement:

```
fprintf(fp, "<td class=\"c%d\">%c</td>",
    kR % 3 * 3 + kC % 3, ((puzzle[i] == '0') ? ' ' : puzzle[i])
    );
```

the string c%d results in the name of the appropriate class. What you are doing is automatically generating HTML code from C.

Note the use of new-line characters to ensure that the generated HTML code is readable. Listing 15-27 shows the resulting HTML file.

Listing 15-27. Output of save_html()

```
<!DOCTYPE html PUBLIC "-//W3C//DTD XHTML 1.0 Strict//EN" ➥
"http://www.w3.org/TR/xhtml1/DTD/xhtml1-strict.dtd">
<html xmlns="http://www.w3.org/1999/xhtml">
<head>
<title>100</title>
<meta http-equiv="Content-type" content="text/html;charset=UTF-8"/>
<style type="text/css">
table {empty-cells:show; border-collapse:collapse;}
td {
  width:50px; height:50px;
  border-style:solid; border-width:1px; border-color:#000000;
  text-align:center; vertical-align:middle;
  font-family:Arial, Verdana, Sans-serif; font-size:2em;
  }
```

```
.c0 {border-top-width:3px; border-left-width:3px;}
.c1 {border-top-width:3px;}
.c2 {border-top-width:3px; border-right-width:3px;}
.c3 {border-left-width:3px;}
.c4 {}
.c5 {border-right-width:3px;}
.c6 {border-bottom-width:3px; border-left-width:3px;}
.c7 {border-bottom-width:3px;}
.c8 {border-bottom-width:3px; border-right-width:3px;}
</style>
</head>
<body>
<table>
<tr><td class="c0">5</td><td class="c1"> </td><td class="c2">3</td>
<td class="c0"> </td><td class="c1"> </td><td class="c2"> </td>
<td class="c0">6</td><td class="c1"> </td><td class="c2">9</td>
</tr>
<tr><td class="c3">7</td><td class="c4"> </td><td class="c5"> </td>
<td class="c3"> </td><td class="c4"> </td><td class="c5"> </td>
<td class="c3"> </td><td class="c4"> </td><td class="c5">2</td>
</tr>
<tr><td class="c6"> </td><td class="c7">4</td><td class="c8">8</td>
<td class="c6">2</td><td class="c7"> </td><td class="c8">6</td>
<td class="c6">1</td><td class="c7">7</td><td class="c8"> </td>
</tr>
<tr><td class="c0"> </td><td class="c1">3</td><td class="c2"> </td>
<td class="c0">6</td><td class="c1"> </td><td class="c2">7</td>
<td class="c0"> </td><td class="c1">9</td><td class="c2"> </td>
</tr>
<tr><td class="c3"> </td><td class="c4"> </td><td class="c5"> </td>
<td class="c3"> </td><td class="c4">2</td><td class="c5"> </td>
<td class="c3"> </td><td class="c4"> </td><td class="c5"> </td>
</tr>
<tr><td class="c6"> </td><td class="c7">8</td><td class="c8"> </td>
<td class="c6">5</td><td class="c7"> </td><td class="c8">3</td>
<td class="c6"> </td><td class="c7">2</td><td class="c8"> </td>
</tr>
<tr><td class="c0"> </td><td class="c1">5</td><td class="c2">7</td>
<td class="c0">4</td><td class="c1"> </td><td class="c2">9</td>
<td class="c0">2</td><td class="c1">6</td><td class="c2"> </td>
</tr>
<tr><td class="c3">8</td><td class="c4"> </td><td class="c5"> </td>
<td class="c3"> </td><td class="c4"> </td><td class="c5"> </td>
<td class="c3"> </td><td class="c4"> </td><td class="c5">7</td>
</tr>
<tr><td class="c6">4</td><td class="c7"> </td><td class="c8">6</td>
<td class="c6"> </td><td class="c7"> </td><td class="c8"> </td>
<td class="c6">3</td><td class="c7"> </td><td class="c8">8</td>
</tr>
</table>
</body>
</html>
```

Figure 15-6 shows the screen capture of the page as it is displayed in a web browser.

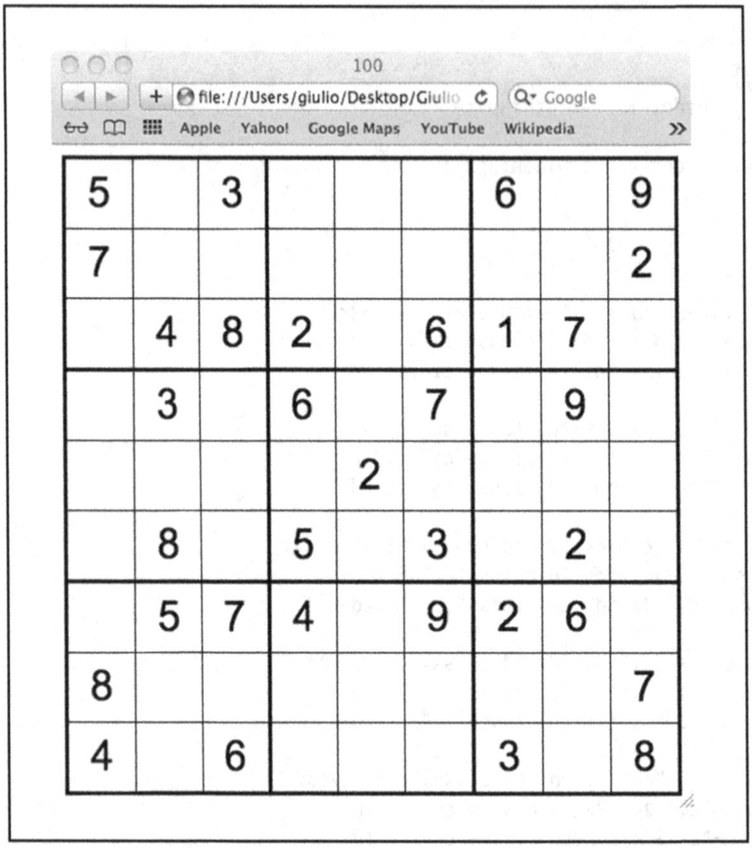

Figure 15-6. *A puzzle displayed in a web browser*

The code conforms to W3C's XHTML 1.0 and CSS Level 2.1 standards. Perhaps I went a bit overboard with that, but I wanted to be sure that you would never have problems with any browser. To be sure, I still tested it on all the browsers I could put my hands on.

Summary

In this chapter you have learned in detail how the Generator works. In particular, you have seen how you can use the different parameters to create billions of puzzles, how you can save the generated puzzles to disk, and how you can display them in a web browser. In the next chapter, you will see how difficult the generated puzzles are and how you can generate many more with some clever thinking.

CHAPTER 16

■ ■ ■

Puzzle Statistics and More Puzzles

According to Wikipedia, the total number of possible solved Sudokus is a staggering 6,670,903,752,021,072,936,960 (http://en.wikipedia.org/wiki/Sudoku, accessed on February 6, 2015). Moreover, it is possible to create many different puzzles resulting in each one of the 6.67 sextillions of solved Sudokus. Therefore, you might be disappointed that the Generator as described in the previous chapter can *only* produce up to 2,147,483,648 different puzzles because that is the number of different pseudorandom seeds you can choose from.

Although more than two billion puzzles seem enough for any practical purpose, in this chapter, besides statistically analyzing the puzzles that the Generator creates, I will also tell you how to modify the Generator to produce even more puzzles.

Statistic on Number of Clues

If you configure the Generator with

```
#define N_SET_QUADS 5
#define N_SET_PAIRS 10
#define ADDITIONAL_CELLS TRUE
```

the maximum number of clues of the puzzles it generates is 41. This is because the Generator only looks for possible puzzles when it removes individual cells. By then, it has already removed N_SET_QUADS * 4 + N_SET_PAIRS * 2 = 40 numbers, out of 81 of a solved Sudoku.

I plotted the number of clues for the first 30,000 seeds, from 0 to 29,999 (see Figure 16-1).

It looks like the lower half of a normal distribution with a mean of 41. For those of you who are not familiar with statistics and the normal distribution, I will just say that they are the bell-shaped curves that often appear when you count random events. In practical terms, it means that puzzles with a particular number of clues become less and less likely as the number of clues differs more and more from the mean. The distribution in Figure 16-1 isn't exactly normal, because its "tail" decreases more rapidly than that of a perfectly normal distribution. Not that it really matters, though.

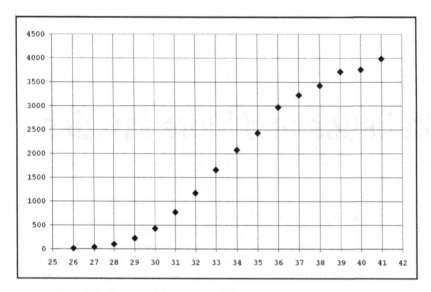

Figure 16-1. *Distribution of the number of clues—1*

Figure 16-2 shows what a puzzle with 41 clues looks like (seed 2928).

Obviously, it is perfectly symmetrical, because you obtain 41 clues when the Generator removes all the clues in quadruplets and pairs. But it does look a bit crowded. Figure 16-3 shows one of the ten puzzles the Generator made with 26 clues (seed 28288).

It looks more interesting, but much of the symmetry has disappeared, because 15 clues were removed individually.

			6	5		2		
9	4	5	2			7	6	3
	6			7	9	4	5	
			5	4	1	3		
			7	6	2			
		4	9	8	3			
	2	7	4	3			9	
3	5	6			7	1	4	2
		9		2	5			

Figure 16-2. *A puzzle with 41 clues*

212

					3			5
	1	2	8		5	4		
			2		4			8
6			5				8	
5			9		8			2
	7							
9	6		1			3		
						5		
1			3		7			

Figure 16-3. *A puzzle with 26 clues*

Incidentally, although it is true that puzzles with fewer clues are in general more difficult, this is not true for the puzzles in Figures 16-2 and 16-3. To complete the puzzle with 41 clues, the Solver needed to use rectangle, while for the puzzle with 26 clues it only needed the naked-pair strategy. Also, you will recall from Chapter 13 that you can solve most of the minimum Sudokus with unique, although they only include 17 clues.

To make puzzles with fewer clues, you can change the parameters of the Generator as follows (for example):

```
#define N_SET_QUADS 6
#define N_SET_PAIRS 13
```

By doing so, you reduce the maximum number of clues to 31. Figure 16-4 shows the new distribution of the number of clues, based on 1,000 puzzles.

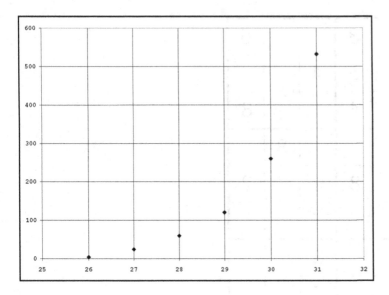

Figure 16-4. *Distribution of the number of clues—2*

For those who are interested, this matches almost perfectly the left tail of a normal distribution. Not that one can deduct anything interesting from it . . .

Statistic on Numbers

As the Generator removes the clues at random, on average, no number appears more often than any others. In each individual puzzle, though, it is a different story: the number of clues with a particular number can be anything between 0 and 9. For example, in the two puzzles in Figures 16-2 and 16-3, the distribution of the numbers is as follows:

```
Number:      1 2 3 4 5 6 7 8 9  Total
Figure 16-2: 2 6 5 6 6 5 5 1 5   41
Figure 16-3: 3 3 3 2 5 2 2 4 2   26
```

An interesting question is: are there puzzles in which a number is missing or in which a number is completely solved? It turns out that a number is missing in 521 of the 30,000 puzzles I checked, and a number is completely solved in 114 puzzles. Here is an example in which the 7 is missing:

```
Number: 1 2 3 4 5 6 7 8 9  Total
        2 5 3 3 3 3 0 5 4   28
```

and here is an example in which the number 7 is completely solved:

```
Number: 1 2 3 4 5 6 7 8 9  Total
        5 3 3 7 5 2 9 3 1   38
```

Note that there cannot ever be puzzles in which two numbers are missing, because then the solution wouldn't be unique: you could swap the two numbers and obtain two distinct and valid solutions.

Among the 30,000 puzzles, there was none with two or more numbers completely solved, but there were eight that had one number missing and one completely solved. Figure 16-5 shows one of them, in which the 6 is completely solved and the 9 is absent.

			7	6	2			
7		6			1		4	
4	8	2				7		6
	7		1	3	6	5		
5	6			2				8
	3	8		6			2	
		5				4	6	1
6			1			8		5
		7	6	4				

Figure 16-5. *Completely solved 6 and absent 9*

Statistic on Solutions

Before completing the Generator, I was very curious to find out how difficult the generated puzzles would be. As it turned out, most of them are very easy, some are easy, a sizable number are of intermediate difficulty, and a few are hard.

One big issue concerning Sudokus is the grading of their difficulty. It would be nice if there were a universally accepted method for measuring how difficult a Sudoku puzzle is, but, unfortunately, this is not the case. If you look at magazines and newspapers, you will be hard pressed to find two compatible classifications.

Ultimately, how difficult a puzzle is depends on the strategies that you need to apply in order to solve it. In Chapter 2, I grouped the strategies in five categories of increasing complexity, from 0 to 4. Clearly, if you need to apply level 3 strategies like XY-chain and rectangle, you should consider a puzzle more difficult than one you can solve with, say, unique and naked pair. The length of the series of strategies you need to apply also plays a role: if you need to use several strategies one after the other, it is fair to say that the puzzle is more difficult than one for which you only need to use a single strategy.

Table 16-1 shows how many times the Solver used the various strategies to complete 30,000 puzzles.

To better understand the figures, you need to know that in 24,374 cases the Solver completed the puzzle by doing the initial cleanup before applying any strategy. Therefore, the strategies counted in Table 16-1 refer to the remaining 5,626 puzzles.

Table 16-1. *Usage of Strategies*

Strategy	Level	Occurrences	%	Min. %
unique-loop	0	6020	73.27%	44.79%
naked pair	10	593	7.22%	21.53%
hidden pair	11	136	1.66%	12.30%
box-line	12	404	4.92%	12.40%
pointing line	13	66	0.80%	2.18%
naked triple	20	0	0.00%	0.01%
hidden triple	21	1	0.01%	0.01%
lines-2	22	92	1.12%	0.25%
naked quad	23	0	0.00%	0.00%
Y-wing	24	243	2.96%	1.20%
rectangle	30	316	3.85%	2.32%
XY-chain	31	307	3.74%	1.97%
lines-3	32	1	0.01%	0.06%
lines-4	33	0	0.00%	0.00%
backtrack	4	37	0.45%	0.98%

Table 16-1 also shows the percentages of occurrence of the strategies, and I added a column with the percentages calculated from Table 14-1 for the minimum Sudokus.

Several strategies occur in both groups in less than 0.1% (i.e., 1 in 1,000) of the puzzles: naked triple, hidden triple, naked quad, lines-3, and lines-4. In particular, naked quad and lines-4 never occur.

The generated puzzles require unique-loop much more often than the minimum Sudokus, while the minimum Sudokus require backtrack more than twice as often as the generated puzzles. This is not surprising, considering that puzzles with fewer clues often are more difficult.

Obviously, I cannot claim that this statistical analysis applies to all puzzles. Nevertheless, if you want to participate in Sudoku championships, where speed is of the essence, you might like to practice rectangle, XY-chain, and Y-wing more than the lines strategies!

It is interesting to compare the percentages of the strategies of levels 1 to 3, as shown graphically in Figure 16-6. Notice that the minimum puzzles, when compared with the generated ones, rely much more on level 1 strategies and much less on the strategies of levels 2 and 3.

These results have no practical impact on generating and solving Sudokus, but I find them intriguing. Obviously, you could do much more. For example, you could see how the usage of strategies changes when you modify the Generator's parameters to answer questions such as the following: are more symmetrical puzzles easier or more difficult?

If you do use the Generator and the Solver to study the Sudoku puzzles, I would love to hear from you!

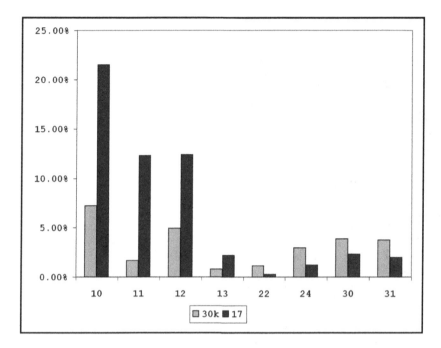

Figure 16-6. *Comparison of strategy occurrences*

I was pleased to see that the Solver needed backtrack in only 37 cases (of 30,000). To be honest, the Solver might have not needed backtrack at all if I had programmed additional strategies into the Solver. But I wanted to keep the Solver close to what a human being can hope to achieve in a real-life situation. Recognizing the pattern required to apply strategies like rectangle and XY-chain is at the limit of what normal (whatever that means) people like you and me can achieve. To clarify what I mean, I would like to show you a partially solved puzzle (see Figure 16-7).

I have listed all candidates to help you, but can you see where you can apply lines-4? Don't feel too bad if you don't and my sincere congratulations if you do!

	0	1	2	3	4	5	6	7	8
0	9	2 3	7	3 6	2 5 6	1	8	2 5	4
1	8	6	5	4	9	2 7	1	2 7	3
2	4	2 3	1	8	2 5	2 3 7	6	2 5 7 9	2 9
3	3	5	8	2 9	1	2 9	4	6	7
4	1	4	6	7	3	8	2 9	2 9	5
5	2	7	9	5	4	6	3	1	8
6	6	1 9	2 3	1 2 3	7	4	5	8	2 9
7	7	1 9	4	1 2	8	5	2 9	3	6
8	5	8	2 3	2 3 6 9	2 6	3 9	7	4	1

Figure 16-7. The Solver applies lines-4

Let's see: to apply lines-4, you have to find four rows or four columns with the same four numbers in pairs, although not all numbers need to be in all four lines. The following is what the Solver logs:

```
lines(4): the rows 1 3 4 7 let us eliminate 2 from the columns 3 5 6 7
lines: removed 2 from (6,3)
lines: removed 2 from (8,3)
lines: removed 2 from (2,5)
lines: removed 2 from (0,7)
```

The four rows 1, 3, 4, and 7 contain pairs of candidates for 1, 2, 7, and 9. The candidate for 2 is in columns 3 (rows 3 and 7), 5 (rows 1 and 3), 6 (rows 4 and 7), and 7 (rows 1 and 4). Clearly, there cannot be 2s in those columns of any other row. That's why the Solver removes 2s from (6,3), (8,3), (2,5), and (0,7).

I don't think that the Solver needs to know strategies more complicated than the jellyfish (as lines-4 is often called). Do you?

Timing

The Solver is very quick and goes through thousands of puzzles in well below a minute. It certainly takes more time to log the results than to solve a puzzle.

But the Generator, at least on my aging Mac, takes a non-negligible amount of time to create puzzles. It spent approximately 11 hours creating the 30,000 puzzles with N_SET_QUADS set to 5, N_SET_PAIRS set to 10, and ADDITIONAL_CELLS set to TRUE. This means that each puzzle required 1.32 seconds to be generated.

The amount of time the Generator needs to create a puzzle grows as you decrease the maximum number of clues. For example, it took almost three and a half hours to generate 1,000 puzzles with N_SET_QUADS set to 6, N_SET_PAIRS set to 13, and ADDITIONAL_CELLS set to TRUE, or 12.38 seconds per puzzle.

I tried to generate a puzzle with 21 clues by setting N_SET_QUADS to 7 and N_SET_PAIRS set to 16 but, after longer than half an hour, the Generator had not yet managed to create it. The same happened when I tried to generate a puzzle with 23 clues by setting N_SET_QUADS to 7 and N_SET_PAIRS to 15.

I thought that perhaps puzzles with so few clues couldn't be very symmetric. It was just a wild and unconfirmed hypothesis (well possibly wrong), but, in an attempt to generate a puzzle with not more than 21 clues, I configured the Generator to remove 60 individual clues instead of quadruplets and pairs. Unfortunately, once more, no valid puzzle was produced after longer than half an hour.

I tried removing 58 individual clues to generate a puzzle with not more than 23 clues. Checking the log, I noticed that on some occasions it attempted to remove more than 58 clues. I was not surprised, because that is how the algorithm works, but it made me realize that, by seeking to remove further clues, the program might "throw away" possible solutions. Therefore, I restarted the Generator after removing the code that attempts to minimize the number of clues. In other words, I configured the Generator to find a puzzle with exactly 23 clues, rather than 23 or less. It succeeded after 31 minutes. This obviously doesn't confirm my conjecture that puzzles with fewer clues are less symmetric, but it was encouraging. I changed the seed from 0 to 62416598 and tried again. This time, I stopped the Generator after one hour of unsuccessful attempts.

I configured the Generator to create a puzzle with exactly 24 clues by removing individual clues. With seed set to 0, it was still trying after a quarter of an hour; with seed set to 123456789, it succeeded after 1 minute. I then tried with seed set to 333333 and it succeeded after 11 minutes. Clearly the variability is too high to make some sense out of it with unsystematic tests.

In order to make more reliable projections, I made several runs of the Generator, each producing ten puzzles and removing only individual clues. I started by removing 41 clues (to obtain puzzles with 40 clues) and went up to 56 (to obtain puzzles with 25 clues), using as seeds, for no particular reason, the prime numbers (2, 3, 5, 7, etc.) and noting every time how long it took. Figure 16-8 shows the combined results of two batches of tests.

As you can see, and as was expected, the Generator takes longer and longer to create a puzzle as the number of removed clues increases. The interpolated line fits the measured points reasonably well. Therefore, I felt I could extend it to make estimates of timing outside the range of the measurements. Notice that the scale of the time axis is logarithmic. This means that a straight line in the plot represents an exponential function. As a result of this exponential behavior, the Generator can create a puzzle with 40 clues in approximately 0.1 seconds, but to create one with 26 clues, it needs 100 seconds or more.

The formula that expresses the best-fit line is

```
seconds_per_puzzle = 3*10-11*exp(0.5256*clues_removed)
```

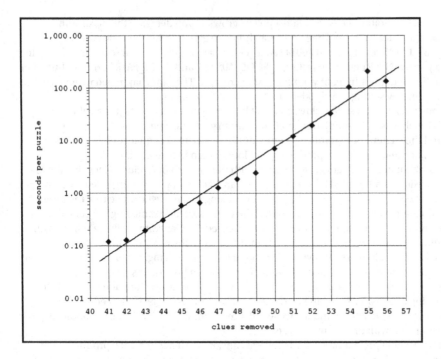

Figure 16-8. *Time profile of puzzle generation*

Obviously, this interpolation is only valid for my computer, but the behavior with newer and faster computers should be the same. You can easily repeat my analysis with your system.

Generating More Puzzles

There are several ways of generating more puzzles. I shall start with the simplest one and then move on to more complex methods.

Number Shifting

As long as all numbers are present in each row, column, and box, the rules of Sudoku only apply to individual numbers. This means that you can swap numbers without invalidating the puzzle. As each permutation of the numbers results in a different puzzle, by swapping pairs of numbers, you can generate 9! - 1 = 362,879 new puzzles from each puzzle you have, although most of them will only differ by some numbers,

You can also add a value to each number and take modulo 9 of the result (i.e., divide the result by 9 and use the remainder). In this way, considering that you can add any value between 1 and 8, you can create eight new puzzles from the original one. But the advantage of this method is that you don't leave any number in its original place. Figure 16-9 shows a puzzle you generate by adding 2 modulo 9 to the puzzle of Figure 16-3.

Figure 16-10 shows how you shift the numbers.

					5			7
	3	4	1		7	6		
			4		6			1
8			7				1	
7			2		1			4
	9							
2	8		3			5		
						7		
3			5		9			

Figure 16-9. *Puzzle of Figure 16-3 with shifted numbers*

The puzzle is for all practical purposes identical to the original one, but it looks different.

There are other methods to create sets of puzzles in which all numbers move to different places, but I am no mathematician expert in group theory, and one method is sufficient for our purposes.

You might find swapping and shifting numbers trivial and uninteresting, but I might change your mind in the next section.

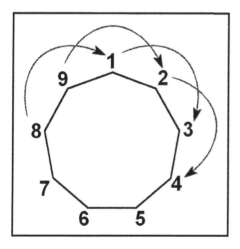

Figure 16-10. *Shifting numbers*

Rotating, Flipping, and Mirroring

Figure 16-11 shows you the same puzzle of Figure 16-3 after a rotation of 180° and Figure 16-12 shows you the same puzzle again after flipping (i.e., up-down mirroring).

			7		3			1
		5						
		3			1		6	9
							7	
2			8		9			5
	8				5			6
8			4		2			
		4	5		8	2	1	
5			3					

Figure 16-11. Puzzle of Figure 16-3 rotated 180°

1			3		7			
					5			
9	6		1		3			
	7							
5			9		8			2
6			5				8	
			2		4			8
	1	2	8		5	4		
					3			5

Figure 16-12. *Puzzle of Figure 16-3 flipped*

You will agree with me that only a Sudoku champion would perhaps recognize that the two new puzzles are equivalent to the original one.

The rotations and reflections of a square (including a Sudoku grid) form a group that the mathematicians call D_4. In practical terms, it means that you can obtain a new puzzle by doing one of the following seven operations: vertical flip (around a line in the middle of row 4, what I used to generate the puzzle of Figure 16-11), horizontal mirroring (around a line in the middle of column 4), clockwise rotation by 90°, rotation by 180° (what I used to generate the puzzle of Figure 16-10), counterclockwise rotation by 90°, diagonal flip (around the line through the bottom-left and top-right corners), and counter-diagonal flip (around the line through the top-left and bottom-right corners).

All in all, if you combine the eight possibilities you have by shifting numbers and the seven possibilities you have through rotation and flipping, you can generate 56 puzzles from the original one. Note that if you apply more than one operation, you don't necessarily obtain more puzzles. For example, a rotation by 180° followed by a vertical flip has the same result as a horizontal mirroring.

Swapping Lines and Triplets of Lines

Question: if you swap two lines (either two rows or two columns), is the resulting puzzle still valid? The answer is yes, but only if you swap lines within the same blocks.

For example, if you swap rows 0 and 1 of the puzzle of Figure 16-3, you obtain the puzzle shown in Figure 16-13.

	1	2	8		5	4		
					3			5
			2		4			8
6			5				8	
5			9		8			2
	7							
9	6		1			3		
						5		
1			3		7			

Figure 16-13. Puzzle of Figure 16-3 with the top two rows swapped

The new puzzle must be valid and have the same solution as the puzzle shown in Figure 16-3 but with the top two rows swapped. To convince yourself that this is the case, consider that there are two broad types of strategies: those that involve individual units, like the naked and hidden strategies, and those that involve alignment of cells across units, like box-line and rectangle, to name two. Clearly, the strategies based on single units are unaffected by the swapping. And as the content of the boxes remains unchanged, all alignments and chains of lines and cells will also be maintained. For example, a rectangle might become narrower or broader, but, when applicable before the swap, it will remain applicable after it.

There are six possible orderings of the three lines that cross the same three boxes (e.g., 012, 021, 102, 120, 201, and 210), and six triples of aligned boxes whose lines can be swapped in any order (boxes 012, 345, 678 horizontally, and 036, 147, and 258 vertically). This means that you can generate 36 different puzzles from each one that you directly create with the Generator. That said, be aware that the Generator might (but it is not said) generate these puzzles directly with a particular choice of pseudorandom seed. Given the number of possible puzzles, this eventuality is certainly rare, but you cannot rely on the fact that all puzzles you generate (or even directly create with the Generator) are unique. If you select a number of puzzles for a book or a web site, you have to check that they really are different from each other!

The considerations about swapping individual lines also apply to triplets of lines. For example, the puzzle shown in Figure 16-4 is the puzzle of Figure 16-3 but with boxes 1, 4, and 7 (i.e., the three central columns) swapped with boxes 2, 5, and 8 (i.e., the three rightmost columns) (see Figure 16-14).

				5			3	
	1	2	4			8		5
				8	2		4	
6			8		5			
5				2	9		8	
	7							
9	6		3			1		
			5					
1					3		7	

Figure 16-14. Puzzle of Figure 16-3 with the central and rightmost column-triples swapped

As there are six triples of aligned boxes, you can generate 36 different puzzles, by arranging the horizontal triples (Top-Center-Bottom, TBC, CTB, CBT, BTC, BCT) and then the vertical ones (Left-Middle-Right, LRM, MLR, MRL, RLM, RML) in any order you like.

You can apply as many swaps as you like of either type and in any order. Note that the operations described in the section "Rotating, flipping, and mirroring" are a subset of the swapping operations. That is, you can rotate, flip, and mirror a puzzle by applying swapping, but not vice versa. For example, if you swap the row-triples TCB -> BCT and the row swaps 012 -> 210, 345 -> 543, and 678 -> 876, you obtain the same puzzle you would have obtained by a vertical flip of the original one.

Removing Different Numbers of Clues

To make the statistical analysis of puzzles and solutions, I first generated 30,000 puzzles with N_SET_QUADS == 5 and N_SET_PAIRS == 10. That is, I left N_SET_CELLS set to zero. If you had set N_SET_PAIRS == 9 (i.e., 1 less) and N_SET_CELLS set to 2 (i.e., 2 more), the puzzles generated with the same seed in the two cases would have been completely different.

Every time you change one, two, or all three of the N_SET_ parameters, the Generator produces different puzzles because it uses the pseudorandom number generator in different ways. If you want to remove a total of between, say, 40 and 56 cells (to obtain puzzles with a maximum of between 41 and 25 clues), you have 2,845 different combinations of the N_SET_ parameters, and the Generator produces 2,845 * 2,147,483,648 = 6,109,590,978,560 different puzzles. That said, to be 100% correct, some of the parameter combinations will generate identical puzzles. But this is true for every generator based on random numbers.

Listing 16-1 shows the algorithm to calculate the number of combinations.

Listing 16-1. Calculating the Number of Parameter Combinations

```
int kount = 0;
for (int n = 40; n <= 56; n++) {
  int mq = n / 4;
  for (int nq = 0; nq <= mq; nq++) {
    int mp = (n - nq * 4) / 2;
    for (int np = 0; np <= mp; np++) {
      kount++;
      }
    }
  }
printf("kount=%d\n", kount);
```

Did you think I had used some combinatorial analysis? It would certainly be possible to do so but, as I said in Chapter 1, this is a practical book, not a scientific treaty, even if sometimes I get a bit (pun intended!) carried away by my fondness for statistics.

Summary

After reading this chapter, you know what puzzles you can create with the Generator and how you can multiply their number by a factor of thousands. Next, you will learn how to make fancy Sudokus that you never see in newspapers and seldom in bookstores.

CHAPTER 17

Special Sudokus

Now that you know how to generate standard Sudoku puzzles, it is time to learn how to make some special ones.

Designer Sudokus

By "designer Sudokus," I mean puzzles in which the clues form a particular pattern. For example, Figure 17-1 shows a "diamond Sudoku" (with difficulty level 3). I grayed the cells with the clues to highlight the pattern.

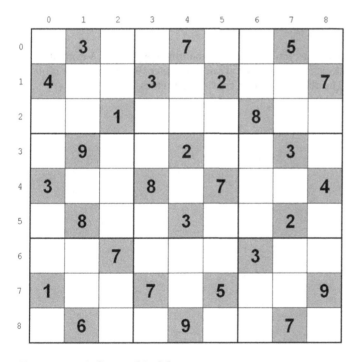

Figure 17-1. *A diamond Sudoku*

To implement designer puzzles, you need to modify sudoku_gen.c in such a way that instead of removing clues by pseudorandom choices, it removes the clues you want to have removed. You do this by replacing the code shown in Listing 15-6 with that shown in Listing 17-1.

Listing 17-1. sudoku_gen.c: code to Remove Clues for Diamond Sudokus

```
char *KEEP =
    ".1..1..1."
    "1..1.1..1"
    "..1...1.."
    ".1..1..1."
    "1..1.1..1"
    ".1..1..1."
    "..1...1.."
    "1..1.1..1"
    ".1..1..1."
    ;
for (int i = 0; i < 81; i++) {
  if (KEEP[i] == '.') {
    int k = i / 9;
    int j = i - k * 9;
    puzzle[k][j] = 0;
    grid[k][j] = 0;
    }
  }
```

These few statements let you choose what clues you keep in order to form nice patterns. A word of warning though: you have to leave at least 26 clues because, as you saw in Chapter 16, the Generator is not able to create puzzles with 25 clues or less. The diamond pattern consists of 28 clues.

If you set KEEP as in

```
char *KEEP =
    "..11111.."
    ".1.....1."
    "1..1.1..1"
    "1.......1"
    "1.......1"
    "1.1...1.1"
    "1..111..1"
    ".1.....1."
    "..11111.."
    ;
```

you obtain "smiley Sudokus" with 31 clues, like the puzzle shown in Figure 17-2 (difficulty level 2).

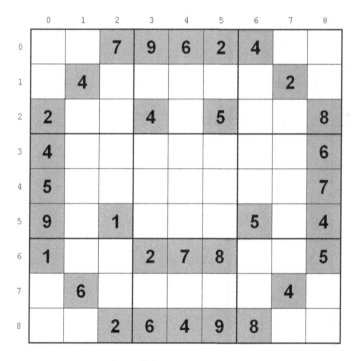

Figure 17-2. *A smiley Sudoku*

With KEEP set as in

```
char *KEEP =
    ".11...11."
    "1111.1111"
    "11.111.11"
    "11..1..11"
    "11.....11"
    ".11...11."
    "..11.11.."
    "...111..."
    "....1...."
    ;
```

you obtain "heart Sudokus" with 40 clues, like the puzzle shown in Figure 17-3 (an easy one).

	0	1	2	3	4	5	6	7	8
0		7	4				6	1	
1	6	9	5	8		2	7	4	3
2	3	1		7	6	4		8	9
3	7	3			4			2	5
4	5	6						3	4
5		4	9				8	7	
6			7	4		6	3		
7				1	7	9			
8					5				

Figure 17-3. *A heart Sudoku*

And one more example: Figure 17-4 shows you a "wave Sudoku" with 27 clues generated by setting KEEP as follows:

```
char *KEEP =
    "..1..1..1"
    ".1..1..1."
    "1..1..1.."
    ".1..1..1."
    "..1..1..1"
    ".1..1..1."
    "1..1..1.."
    ".1..1..1."
    "..1..1..1"
    ;
```

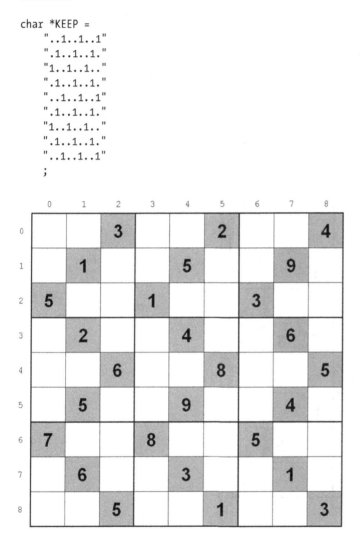

Figure 17-4. *A wave Sudoku*

If you experiment with designer Sudokus by setting KEEP to different strings, you will discover that the Generator might take a very long time to create puzzles with particular patterns. In some cases, it will not be able to generate a puzzle at all. I believe that it has to do with the logic of Sudoku puzzles, rather than with the Generator's implementation, but I see no way of proving it.

In any case, to generate designer Sudokus, you don't need to use KEEP. You can use other mechanisms to select the clues. For example, if you replace the code shown in Listing 15-6 with

```
for (int k = 0; k < 9; k++) {
  for (int j = 0; j < 9; j++) {
    if (k != 4 && j != 4 && j != k && j != 8-k) {
      puzzle[k][j] = 0;
      }
    }
  }
```

you obtain an "asterisk Sudoku" with 33 clues as shown in Figure 17-5.

	0	1	2	3	4	5	6	7	8
0	7				2				4
1		5			6			9	
2			2		3		1		
3				2	8	6			
4	2	6	9	4	1	5	7	8	3
5				3	7	9			
6			4		5		9		
7		8			9			3	
8	3				4				8

Figure 17-5. *An asterisk Sudoku*

Symbolic Sudokus

As you never perform any mathematical operation with the numbers that appear in a Sudoku, you don't really need to keep them as numbers. Any group of nine letters, symbols, or even words would do.

The Generator exploits the fact that the symbols used within Sudokus are in fact numbers from 1 to 9, but you can easily create symbolic Sudokus by "tweaking" the function save_html(). All you need to do is associate a different symbol with each number.

First, define the array to contain the association

```
char *symbols[10] = {"", "A", "B", "C", "D", "E", "F", "G", "H", "I"};
```

Then, use symbols[] as a look-up table when you insert the numbers into the HTML table. You do this by replacing

```
fprintf(fp, "<td class=\"c%d\">%c</td>",
    kR % 3 * 3 + kC % 3, ((puzzle[i] == '0') ? ' ' : puzzle[i])
    );
```

with

```
fprintf(fp, "<td class=\"c%d\">%s</td>",
    kR % 3 * 3 + kC % 3, symbols[(int)(puzzle[i] - '0')]
    );
```

With these two small changes (the code is already in save_html.c but switched off with a #define), the puzzle shown in Figure 16-5 becomes a symbolic Sudoku, as shown in Figure 17-6.

				G	F	B		
G		F			A		D	
D	H	B				G		F
	G			A	C	F	E	
E	F			B				H
	C	H		F			B	
		E				D	F	A
F			A			H		E
		G	F	D				

Figure 17-6. *A symbolic Sudoku—1*

But why stop there?
By setting symbols[] to Unicode characters as in

```
char *symbols[10] = {"", "\u260E", "\u2622", "\u262F", "\u263C", "\u263D",
    "\u2658", "\u269B", "\u2665", "\u266B"
    };
```

you can transform the same puzzle into that shown in Figure 17-7.

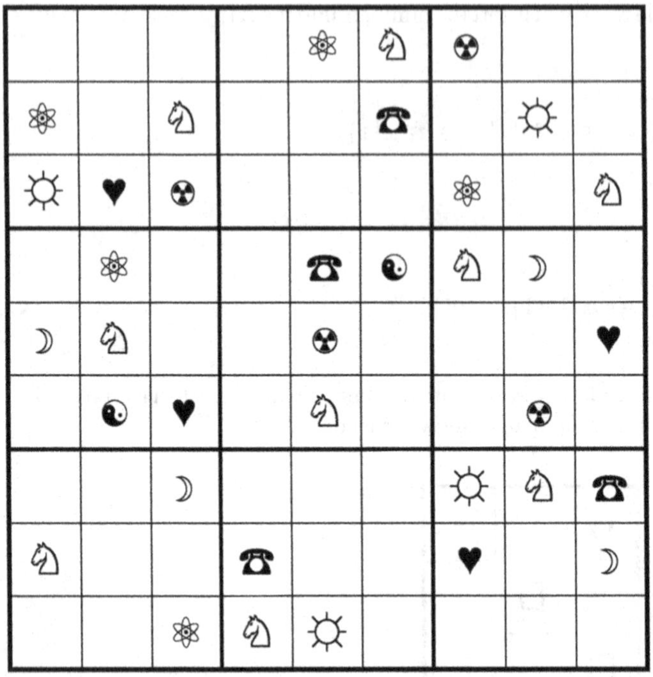

Figure 17-7. *A symbolic Sudoku—2*

You can find the list of Unicode characters on the Web (e.g., one good site is http://www.utf8-chartable.de/unicode-utf8-table.pl (accessed on February 7, 2015)).

Now, the next step is to use your own icons, isn't it? No problem at all. All you need to do is create the images (of size 50x50 pixels), name them 1.jpg to 9.jpg and store them in the same folder where you keep the puzzle's HTML pages. You will also have to create an image 0.jpg completely white. Then, replace the fprintf() statement with the following one:

```
fprintf(fp, "<td class=\"c%d\" background=\"%c.jpg\"> </td>",
    kR % 3 * 3 + kC % 3, puzzle[i]
    );
```

See an example in Figure 17-8, for which I used freely available icons I found on the Web at

http://www.smashingmagazine.com/2009/06/07/50-fresh-useful-icon-sets-for-your-next-design/

They are much nicer in color, but you get the idea.

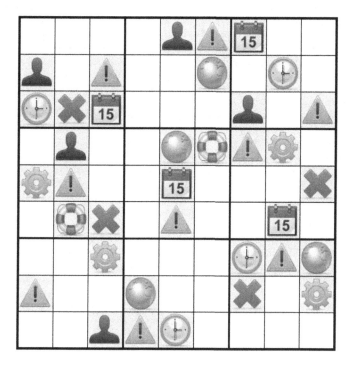

Figure 17-8. *A symbolic Sudoku—3*

Summary

This chapter has shown you how to personalize Sudokus. You can now create Sudokus with the clues that form a particular pattern or with symbols or images instead of numbers. Next, you will learn how to make complex Sudokus by joining together multiple 9x9 puzzles.

CHAPTER 18

Multi-Grid Sudokus

You obtain a multi-grid Sudoku when you combine two or more classic puzzles by partially overlapping them. For example, Figure 18-1 shows a double Sudoku.

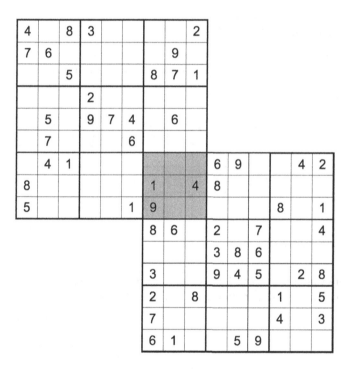

Figure 18-1. *A double Sudoku*

You solve a double Sudoku by solving the two 9x9 puzzles normally, but whenever you solve one of the cells grayed in Figure 18-1, that solution is valid for both puzzles.

There Are Many Different Multi-Grid Sudokus

To explore the way in which you can combine several Sudoku grids to form composite puzzles, let's reduce multi-grid Sudokus to the outlines of their boxes, as shown in the examples in Figure 18-2.

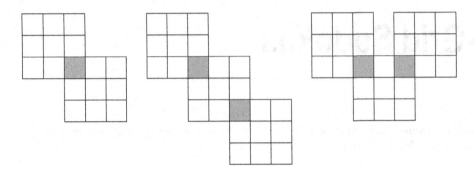

Figure 18-2. *Simplified representation of multi-grid Sudokus*

All the puzzles in Figure 18-2 overlap by one of their corner boxes, but you can also overlap two, three, four, and even six boxes, as shown in Figure 18-3.

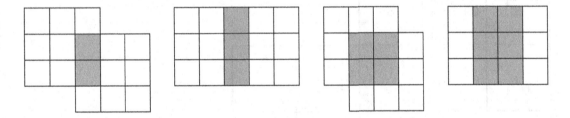

Figure 18-3. *Double Sudokus with more than one box of overlap*

You can also obtain new configurations with rotations and flips. For example, you can obtain three additional configurations by rotating the third puzzle of Figure 18-2, as shown in Figure 18-4.

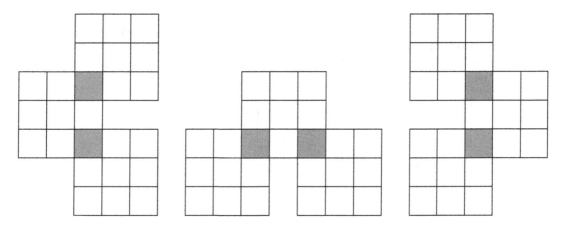

Figure 18-4. *New configurations by rotating and flipping existing ones*

Theoretically, there is no limit to the number of grids you can combine. For an example of a very complex configuration, take a deep breath and have a look at Figure 18-5 (the non-overlapping boxes are not in white because otherwise you would have had problems in seeing the holes in the grid).

Figure 18-5. *A very complex multi-grid Sudoku*

If you are interested in such "monster" Sudokus, I'm afraid you will have to make your own version of the Generator, because this book is only going to show you how you can create four configurations of multi-grid Sudokus: the first two of Figure 18-2 plus those shown in Figure 18-6 (the second one is a "samurai Sudoku"), with one-box overlapping, no rotations, and no flippings.

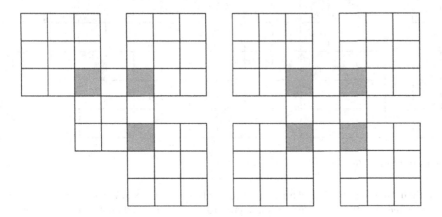

Figure 18-6. *Multi-grid Sudokus with four and five grids*

I left out the third configuration of Figure 18-2 because its shape didn't appeal to me, but also to simplify the code. I initially had also discarded the four-grid configuration on the left of Figure 18-6, but, after I completed the implementation of the two-, three-, and five-grid puzzles, I realized that exactly the same code would work for the four-grid puzzle as well. I only needed to change an if-condition from

```
(N_GRIDS == 2  ||  N_GRIDS == 3  ||  N_GRIDS == 5)
```

to

```
(N_GRIDS >= 2  &&  N_GRIDS <= 5)
```

It was too good to ignore, although I have to admit that I find the four-grid configuration even less appealing than the three-grid one shaped like a Mickey Mouse's head!

How You Join the Grids

To fully understand the code of the Generator, you need to be familiar with the issues that arise when you join grids. First of all, Figure 18-7 shows how I numbered the grids to form multi-grid Sudokus.

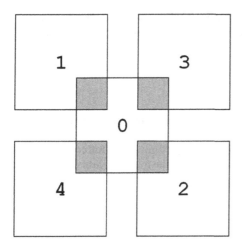

Figure 18-7. *Grid numbering*

Consider the simplest case of multi-grid puzzles shown in Figure 18-1, with only the two grids 0 and 1. Box 8 of grid 1 overlaps with box 0 of grid 0. This means that the three clues 1, 4, and 9 belong to both grids. But it also means that the content of the two boxes must remain identical when they are fully solved.

As you know, when you configure the Generator to create several puzzles (by setting N_SEEDS to a value greater than 1), the program starts working on each puzzle by filling up its grid.

But, if you generate two grids that you want to combine to form a double Sudoku, you must modify the Generator in such a way that box 8 of puzzle 1 contains the nine numbers in exactly the same order as they appear in box 0 of puzzle 0.

You have two alternatives: either you predefine box 8 of the second grid so that the match is there from the start, or you fill in the second grid at random and then "play" with the numbers to achieve the match.

The Generator, as you will see shortly, uses the second alternative. To see how it works, suppose that the box on the left of Figure 18-8 solves box 0 of puzzle 0, while the right box solves box 8 of grid 1.

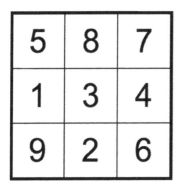

Figure 18-8. *Box 0 of grid 0 and box 8 of grid 1—not a match*

After reading Chapter 17, you should be comfortable with the idea that the Sudoku numbers are just a particular choice of symbols. Then, all you need to do is change all 3s (in the whole puzzle, not just in box 8) of grid 1 to 5s, all 4s to 8s . . . and all 1s to 6s. If you do so, the two boxes will match!

Once you have made the shared boxes of both puzzles identical, you still need to ensure that in box 8 of puzzle 1 you remove all and only the clues you have already removed from box 0 of puzzle 0. Only then can you integrate the two puzzles.

How the Generator Does It

After writing the Generator for classic Sudokus, to implement multi-grid puzzles, you need to modify sudoku_gen.c and add a couple of new modules.

To see all the changes and to understand how they work together, let's go through the full code of the main program as shown in Listing 18-1. Note that all the new code, as well as the relevant parts you already saw in Chapter 15, is in bold.

Listing 18-1. sudoku_gen.c—Modified for Multi-grid Sudokus

```
/* sudoku_gen.c
 *
 * Copyright (C) 2015  Giulio Zambon  - http://zambon.com.au/
 *
 */
#include <stdio.h>
#include <stdlib.h>
#include <string.h>
#include <time.h>
#include "brute_comp.h"
#include "count_solved.h"
#include "def.h"
#include "display.h"
#include "display_string.h"
#include "fill.h"
#include "inconsistent_grid.h"
#include "inconsistent_unit.h"
#include "init.h"
#include "in_box.h"
#include "list_solved.h"
#include "multi_html.h"
#include "save_html.h"

#define LOG_TO_FILE   NO
#define FILE_NAME "puzzles.txt"

#define SAVE_HTML_PUZZLE
#define SAVE_HTML_SOLUTION

// N_GRIDS is defined in multi_html.h.
// When N_GRIDS is between 2 and 5, it triggers the creation of multi-grid
// puzzles. With any other value, the Generator creates a classic Sudoku.
#define DO_MULTI_GRID (N_GRIDS >= 2  &&  N_GRIDS <= 5)
```

```
// Parameters
#define N_SET_QUADS 5
#define N_SET_PAIRS 10
#define N_SET_CELLS 0
#define ADDITIONAL_CELLS TRUE
#define FIRST_SEED 123456
#define N_SEEDS 1

// Global variables
char *unit_names[3] = {"row", "column", "box"};
char grid[9][9];
char row[9][9][2];
char col[9][9][2];
char box[9][9][2];
char puzzle[9][9];
int silent = FALSE;

// Variables and functions local to this module
char solved[9][9];
int r_1[81];
int c_1[81];
int k_cell;
int remove_quads(int k_puz);
int remove_pairs(int k_puz);
void make_clue_list(void);
int remove_clues(int k_puz);
void remove_more_clues(int k_puz);
int check_uniqueness(void);

// The following table identifies the box of grid 0 that overlaps with other
// grids when creating multi-grid Sudokus.
// The first box refers to puzzle0 and second one to the other puzzle:
//
// N_GRIDS  kPuz=1  kPuz=2  kPuz=3  kPuz=4
//     2     b0-b8
//     3     b0-b8   b8-b0
//     4     b0-b8   b8-b0   b2-b6
//     5     b0-b8   b8-b0   b2-b6   b6-b2
//
// Puzzle:    0   1   2   3   4
int box0[] = {-1,  0,  8,  2,  6};

//====================================================================== main
int main(int argc, char *argv[]) {
  printf("*** sudoku_gen ***\n");
  char mess[32];
  int n_seeds = N_SEEDS;
  k_try = 0;
```

```
#if DO_MULTI_GRID
  // When creating multi-grid puzzles, set n_seed to the number of
  // puzzles that you need
  n_seeds = N_GRIDS;
#endif

  // Open a file to log the results
  FILE *fp = NULL;
#ifdef LOG_TO_FILE
  fp = fopen(FILE_NAME, "a");
  if (fp == NULL) {
    printf("Unable to open the file '%s' for reading\n", FILE_NAME);
    return EXIT_FAILURE;                                                    //==>
  }
#endif

  // Try all the seeds in the given range
  unsigned long start_time = clock();

  for (int k_seed = 0; k_seed < n_seeds; k_seed++) {
    int seed = FIRST_SEED + k_seed;
    srand(seed);
    int brute_result;
    int n;

    // Keep repeating the generation until you find a unique solution
    char puzzle_string[82];
    char solution_string[82];
    do {

      // Generate a solved Sudoku
      do { init(); } while (fill());

      // Save the solved Sudoku
      for (int k = 0; k < 9; k++) {
        for (int j = 0; j < 9; j++) {
          solved[k][j] = grid[k][j];
          puzzle[k][j] = grid[k][j];
        }
      }

#if DO_MULTI_GRID
      if (k_seed > 0) {
        // You arrive here if you are creating a multi-grid puzzle and
        // have already created the first one (puzzle 0).
        int k0 = box0[k_seed]/3*3;
        int j0 = box0[k_seed]%3*3;
        int kk = overlapping_box[k_seed]/3*3;
        int jj = overlapping_box[k_seed]%3*3;
```

```
      // Build the look-up list of numbers to match puzzle 0 when creating
      // subsequent grids.
      char map[10] = {0};
      for (int k = 0; k < 3; k++) {
        for (int j = 0; j < 3; j++) {
          map[(int)grid[(kk + k)][jj + j]] =
              multi_string[0][SOL][(k0 + k)*9 + j0 + j] - '0'
              ;
          }
        }

      // Convert the numbers in the grid and save the modified grid
      for (int k = 0; k < 9; k++) {
        for (int j = 0; j < 9; j++) {
          grid[k][j] = map[(int)grid[k][j]];
          solved[k][j] = grid[k][j];
          puzzle[k][j] = grid[k][j];
          }
        }

      // Make the box that overlaps puzzle 0 identical to the
      // corresponding one of puzzle 0
      for (int k = 0; k < 3; k++) {
        for (int j = 0; j < 3; j++) {
          grid[(kk + k)][jj + j] =
              multi_string[0][PUZ][(k0 + k)*9 + j0 + j] - '0'
              ;
          }
        }
      }
#endif

    //========= Remove N_SET_QUADS quadruples of clues
    if (N_SET_QUADS > 0) {
      int success = remove_quads(k_seed);
      if (!success) {
       brute_result = BRUTE_COMP_DIFFERENT;
       goto skip;                                              //==>
       }
      }

    //========= Remove N_SET_PAIRS pairs of clues
    if (N_SET_PAIRS > 0) {
      int success = remove_pairs(k_seed);
      if (!success) {
       brute_result = BRUTE_COMP_DIFFERENT;
       goto skip;                                              //==>
       }
      }
```

```c
//========== Remove N_SET_CELLS individual clues and then some more
make_clue_list();
k_cell = 0;
if (N_SET_CELLS > 0) {
  int success = remove_clues(k_seed);
  if (!success) {
    brute_result = BRUTE_COMP_DIFFERENT;
    goto skip;                                              //==>
    }
  }
if (ADDITIONAL_CELLS && k_cell < 81) remove_more_clues(k_seed);

//========== Check whether the solution is really unique
brute_result = check_uniqueness();

//========== Done
for (int k = 0; k < 9; k++) {
  for (int j = 0; j < 9; j++) {
    grid[k][j] = puzzle[k][j];
    }
  }
n = count_solved();
if (!silent && fp == NULL) {
  display();
  sprintf(mess, "seed %d %d", seed, n);
  display_string(mess);
  printf("The puzzle contains %d clues:", n);
  list_solved(stdout);
  }
skip:                                                       // <==
  k_try++;
  printf("%d: %s\n",
      k_try,
      (brute_result == BRUTE_COMP_DIFFERENT) ? "No" : "Yes"
      );
  } while (brute_result == BRUTE_COMP_DIFFERENT);

// Save puzzle and solution into strings
int kar = 0;
for (int k = 0; k < 9; k++) {
  for (int j = 0; j < 9; j++) {
    puzzle_string[kar] = puzzle[k][j] + '0';
    solution_string[kar] = solved[k][j] + '0';
    kar++;
    }
  }
puzzle_string[kar] = '\0';
solution_string[kar] = '\0';
```

```
#if DO_MULTI_GRID
    // Save the puzzle and solution strings to be combined later into
    // a multi-grid Sudoku
    for (int i = 0; i < 82; i++) { // copy also the '\0' at the end
      multi_string[k_seed][PUZ][i] = puzzle_string[i];
      multi_string[k_seed][SOL][i] = solution_string[i];
      }
#endif

#ifdef SAVE_HTML_PUZZLE
    save_html(puzzle_string, seed, "p");
#endif

#ifdef SAVE_HTML_SOLUTION
    save_html(solution_string, seed, "s");
#endif
    if (fp != NULL) {
      printf("#%d\n", k_seed);
      fprintf(fp, "%s\t%d", puzzle_string, seed);
      if (brute_result != BRUTE_COMP_DIFFERENT) {
        fprintf(fp, "\t%d", n);
        list_solved(fp);
        }
      fprintf(fp, "\n");
      }
    } // for (k_seed..

#if DO_MULTI_GRID
  multi_html(FIRST_SEED, PUZ);
  multi_html(FIRST_SEED, SOL);
#endif

  unsigned long end_time = clock();
  printf("********* done in %ld microseconds\n", end_time - start_time);
  if (fp != NULL) fclose(fp);
  return EXIT_SUCCESS;
  }
```

The first relevant part is the inclusion of in_box.h and multi_html.h (see Listing 18-2 for in_box.c and Listing 18-3 for multi_html.c). Essentially, in_box() checks whether a particular cell belongs to a box, while multi_html() is an extension of save_html(), which you know from Chapter 15.

The line

```
#define DO_MULTI_GRID (N_GRIDS >= 2  &&  N_GRIDS <= 5)
```

allows you to easily switch on and off code within sudoku_gen.c that is only to be executed when generating multi-grid puzzles. You only need to set N_GRIDS to 1 within multi_html.h to make the Generator behave as described in Chapter 15.

Listing 18-1 highlights the four declarations

```
int remove_quads(int k_puz);
int remove_pairs(int k_puz);
int remove_clues(int k_puz);
void remove_more_clues(int k_puz);
```

because the functions I wrote for the original Generator to create classic Sudokus didn't need any argument, as each created a puzzle that consisted of a single grid.

You use the one-dimensional array

```
int box0[] = {-1, 0, 8, 2, 6};
```

to determine which boxes of grid 0 overlaps with the other grids. For example, box0[3] is 2 because grid 3 is positioned top right with respect to grid 0, where grid 0's box 2 is.

The statement

```
n_seeds = N_GRIDS;
```

is where you tell the Generator that it needs to create as many grids as are to appear in the composite Sudoku. Note that n_seeds originally allowed you to create many puzzles with a single run of the Generator. This is not possible with multi-grid Sudokus because the Generator, in the implementation I am describing, relies on n_seeds to create a single composite puzzle. If you need to create many multi-grid Sudokus, you should be able to adapt the existing code to do so. For example, you could enclose a loop that generates N_GRIDS Sudokus inside the loop with control variable k_seed. The only thing you would need to be careful with would be initializing/resetting all the affected variables.

The next block of conditional code is more substantial, but note that it is only executed when k_seed is greater than 0. In other words, the Generator creates the first puzzle of a multi-grid Sudoku (i.e., with k_seed == 0) in exactly the same way as it creates a classic, single-grid puzzle.

When DO_MULTI_GRID is true and you are creating puzzles with k_seed > 0, you need to "play with the numbers" of the current puzzle as I briefly described in the section "How You Join the Grids," so that the two overlapping boxes of the current puzzle and puzzle 0 become identical.

The two expressions box0[k_seed]/3*3 and box0[k_seed]%3*3 give you the coordinates of the top-left cell that puzzle 0 shares with the current puzzle. This is because box0[] identifies the overlapping box of puzzle 0. For example, if you are currently generating puzzle 3, box0[3] is 2, consistent with the fact that the overlapping box of puzzle 0 is the top-right one. Then, k0 is 2/3*3 = 0 (because the result of a division between integers is truncated) and j0 is 2%3*3 = 2*3 = 6 (because the remainder of 2 divided by 3 is 2).

The two definitions

```
int kk = overlapping_box[k_seed] / 3 * 3;
int jj = overlapping_box[k_seed] % 3 * 3;
```

do the same for the current puzzle. overlapping_box[] is defined in multi_html.c as follows:

```
int overlapping_box[] = {0, 8, 0, 6, 2};
```

So, for example, puzzle 3's box that overlaps with puzzle 0 is the bottom-left one. Accordingly, overlapping_box[3] is 6 and the top-left cell of the overlap has coordinates (6,6).

Once you know the top-left cells of the two overlapping boxes, you can map the numbers in the current puzzle's box with the corresponding ones in the puzzle 0's box:

```
char map[10] = {0};
for (int k = 0; k < 3; k++) {
  for (int j = 0; j < 3; j++) {
    map[(int)grid[(kk + k)][jj + j]] =
        multi_string[0][SOL][(k0 + k)*9 + j0 + j] - '0'
        ;
  }
}
```

where SOL and multi_string[][][] are defined in multi_html.h as follows:

```
#define PUZ 0
#define SOL 1
extern char multi_string[N_GRIDS][2][82];
```

multi_string[][][] is used to save all Sudoku strings (both of the solved and the unsolved puzzle) of a multi-grid Sudoku.

The map is a character array in which the position of each character corresponds to a number in the overlapping box of the current puzzle, while the character is the corresponding number in the overlapping box of puzzle 0.

For example, with the two overlapping boxes in Figure 18-8, the algorithm results in map[1] to map[9] being set to the characters 675834291. Figure 18-8 refers to a double Sudoku. Therefore, the two overlapping boxes are box 0 of puzzle 0 and box 8 of puzzle 1. Accordingly, (k0,j0) is (0,0) and (kk,jj) is (6,6). The map assignment in the first iteration of the two loops, with both k and j set to 0, then results in map[3] = '5'. The second assignment is map[4] = '8', the third map[2] = '7', etc., until the map is completed with map[1] = '6'.

Once the map is done, it is easy to convert the current puzzle with

```
for (int k = 0; k < 9; k++) {
  for (int j = 0; j < 9; j++) {
    grid[k][j] = map[(int)grid[k][j]];
  }
}
```

The last thing you need to do at this point of the puzzle-creation process is to remove from the grid the clues that were removed when creating puzzle 0. You do this by simply overwriting in grid the box of the current puzzle with the box of puzzle 0.

```
for (int k = 0; k < 3; k++) {
  for (int j = 0; j < 3; j++) {
    grid[(kk + k)][jj + j] =
        multi_string[0][PUZ][(k0 + k)*9 + j0 + j] - '0'
        ;
  }
}
```

You will recall that when I described the remove_*() functions in the section "Removing Clues to Make a Puzzle" in Chapter 15, I said that in

```
for (int k = 0; k < 4; k++) {
  int kR = quad[k][ROW];
  int kC = quad[k][COL];
  if (kPuz == 0 || !in_box(kR, kC, overlapping_box[kPuz])) {
    grid[kR][kC] = 0;
    }
  }
```

the reason for making the removal of the clue from the cell with coordinates (kR,kC) conditional would become clear in Chapter 18. You now know that when the Generator removes clues from the puzzles 1 to 4 of multi-grid Sudokus, one box of those puzzles is already identical to the corresponding box of puzzle 0. You must therefore ensure that the remove_*() functions leave those boxes unchanged. This is exactly what the condition (kPuz == 0 || !in_box(kR, kC, overlapping_box[kPuz]) does. The first part tells you that puzzle 0 is just a standard puzzle. But when kPuz is not 0, you only want to remove clues from boxes other than the preformatted (i.e., overlapping) one. As in_box() returns TRUE if a cell belongs to a given box, as shown in Listing 18-2, you only need to pass to in_box() the current cell and the ID of overlapping box to identify the cells from which you can safely remove the clues.

Listing 18-2. in_box.c

```
/* in_box.c
 *
 * Copyright (C) 2015  Giulio Zambon  - http://zambon.com.au/
 *
 */
#include <stdio.h>
#include <stdlib.h>
#include "in_box.h"

int in_box(int kR, int kC, int kB) {
  int kkR = kB / 3 * 3;
  int kkC = kB % 3 * 3;
  return (kR >= kkR  &&  kR < kkR + 3  &&  kC >= kkC  &&  kC < kkC + 3);
  } // in_box
```

The next block of conditional code needed to create multi-grid puzzles saves solved and unsolved puzzles in the array multi_string[][][]

```
for (int i = 0; i < 82; i++) { // copy also the '\0' at the end
  multi_string[k_seed][PUZ][i] = puzzle_string[i];
  multi_string[k_seed][SOL][i] = solution_string[i];
  }
```

This is necessary because you need all two to five puzzles in order to display the multi-grid puzzle and its solution with

```
multi_html(FIRST_SEED, PUZ);
multi_html(FIRST_SEED, SOL);
```

which I describe in the following section.

Displaying a Multi-Grid Sudoku

In Chapter 15, you saw how to save a puzzle to disk with save_html() (Listing 15-25). To save a multi-grid Sudoku to disk in HTML format, you need first to join the grids of the individual puzzles. The equivalent of save_html.c for multi-grids puzzle is the module multi_html.c shown in Listing 18-3.

Listing 18-3. multi_html.c

```
/* multi_html.c
 *
 * This module must be able to display all different types of multi-grid
 * puzzles (only the boxes are shown):
 *
 * +---+---+---+
 * |   |   |   |
 * +---+---+---+
 * |   | 1 |   |
 * +---+---+---+---+---+              N_GRIDS == 2 (double Sudokus)
 * |   |   |   |   |   |
 * +---+---+---+---+---+
 *         |   | 0 |   |
 *         +---+---+---+
 *         |   |   |   |
 *         +---+---+---+
 *
 * +---+---+---+
 * |   |   |   |
 * +---+---+---+
 * |   | 1 |   |
 * +---+---+---+---+---+
 * |   |   |   |   |   |
 * +---+---+---+---+---+
 *         |   | 0 |   |          N_GRIDS == 3
 *         +---+---+---+---+---+
 *         |   |   |   |   |   |
 *         +---+---+---+---+---+
 *                 |   | 2 |   |
 *                 +---+---+---+
 *                 |   |   |   |
 *                 +---+---+---+
 *
 * +---+---+---+   +---+---+---+
 * |   |   |   |   |   |   |   |
 * +---+---+---+   +---+---+---+
 * |   | 1 |   |   |   | 3 |   |
 * +---+---+---+---+---+---+---+
 * |   |   |   |   |   |   |   |
 * +---+---+---+---+---+---+---+
```

```
*           |   | 0 |   |              N_GRIDS == 4
*           +---+---+---+---+---+
*           |   |   |   |   |   |
*           +---+---+---+---+---+
*               |   | 2 |   |
*               +---+---+---+
*               |   |   |   |
*               +---+---+---+
*
* +---+---+---+   +---+---+---+
* |   |   |   |   |   |   |   |
* +---+---+---+   +---+---+---+
* |   | 1 |   |   |   | 3 |   |
* +---+---+---+===+===+===+---+---+---+
* |   |   | I |   |   | I |   |   |
* +---+---+---+---+---+---+---+---+---+
*           I   | 0 |   I              N_GRIDS == 5 (samurai)
* +---+---+---+---+---+---+---+---+---+  (the central puzzle is highlighted)
* |   |   | I |   |   | I |   |   |
* +---+---+---+===+===+===+---+---+---+
* |   | 4 |   |   |   | 2 |   |   |
* +---+---+---+   +---+---+---+
* |   |   |   |   |   |   |   |
* +---+---+---+   +---+---+---+
*
* The cell borders are defined like in save_html.c, but their position
* and the size of the HTML table depend on the type of puzzle.
*
* Copyright (C) 2015  Giulio Zambon  - http://zambon.com.au/
*
*/
#include <stdio.h>
#include <stdlib.h>
#include <string.h>
#include "def.h"
#include "in_box.h"
#include "multi_html.h"

// Define the number of rows and columns needed for the multi-grid
#if N_GRIDS == 2
#define SIZE 15
#else
#define SIZE 21
#endif

char multi_string[N_GRIDS][2][82];

// The following table identifies the box of each grid that overlaps with
// a corner box of grid 0 when creating multi-grid Sudokus.
//
// N_GRIDS  kPuz=1  kPuz=2  kPuz=3  kPuz=4
```

```
//      2      8
//      3      8      0
//      4      8      0      6
//      5      8      0      6      2
//
// Puzzle:              0  1  2  3  4
int overlapping_box[] = {0, 8, 0, 6, 2};

void multi_html(int seed, int what) {
  char *header_1 =
      "<!DOCTYPE html PUBLIC \"-//W3C//DTD XHTML 1.0 Strict//EN\" "
        "\"http://www.w3.org/TR/xhtml1/DTD/xhtml1-strict.dtd\">\n"
      "<html xmlns=\"http://www.w3.org/1999/xhtml\">\n"
      "<head>\n"
      "<title>"
      ;
  char *header_2 =
      "</title>\n"
      "<meta http-equiv=\"Content-type\" "
        "content=\"text/html;charset=UTF-8\"/>\n"
      "<style type=\"text/css\">\n"
      "table {empty-cells:show; border-collapse:collapse;}\n"
      "td {\n"
      "  width:50px; height:50px;\n"
      "  border-style:solid; border-width:1px; border-color:#000000;\n"
      "  text-align:center; vertical-align:middle;\n"
      "  font-family:Arial, Verdana, Sans-serif; font-size:2em;\n"
      "  }\n"
      ".c0 {border-top-width:3px; border-left-width:3px;}\n"
      ".c1 {border-top-width:3px;}\n"
      ".c2 {border-top-width:3px; border-right-width:3px;}\n"
      ".c3 {border-left-width:3px;}\n"
      ".c4 {}\n"
      ".c5 {border-right-width:3px;}\n"
      ".c6 {border-bottom-width:3px; border-left-width:3px;}\n"
      ".c7 {border-bottom-width:3px;}\n"
      ".c8 {border-bottom-width:3px; border-right-width:3px;}\n"
      ".c_ {border-top-width:0px; border-right-width:0px; "
             "border-bottom-width:0px; border-left-width:0px;}\n"
      "</style>\n</head>\n<body>\n<table>\n"
      ;
  char *footer = "</table>\n</body>\n</html>";

  // Puzzle offsets (row/column) for each puzzle (puzzle 0 is in the middle):
  //                    0      1      2      3      4
  int offs[5][2] = {{6,6}, {0,0}, {12,12}, {0,12}, {12,0}};

  // Combined multi-string (+1 to be able to close each string with a '\0').
  char multi_s[SIZE][SIZE + 1];
  for (int k = 0; k < SIZE; k++) {
```

```c
      for (int j = 0; j < SIZE; j++) {
        multi_s[k][j] = ' ';
        }
      multi_s[k][SIZE] = '\0';
      }


  // Copy the puzzles to the places they belong.
  // The boxes that overlap are set twice, first for puzzle 0 and then for
  // the other one. But it doesn't matter, as the two boxes are identical.
  // To set them only once, it would be sufficient to do the setting only
  // if (multi_s[baseR + kR][baseC + kC] == ' ')
  for (int kPuz = 0; kPuz < N_GRIDS; kPuz++) {
    int baseR = offs[kPuz][ROW];
    int baseC = offs[kPuz][COL];
    char *s = multi_string[kPuz][what];
    for (int i = 0; i < 81; i++) {
      int kR = i / 9;
      int kC = i - kR * 9;
      multi_s[baseR + kR][baseC + kC] = (s[i] == '0') ? '.' : s[i];
      }
    }
  for (int k = 0; k < SIZE; k++) printf("%s\n", multi_s[k]);
  printf("\n");


  // Finally, save the HTML to disk
  char f_name[64] = {0};
  sprintf(f_name, "%d_%d%c.html", seed, N_GRIDS, (what == SOL) ? 's' : 'p');
  FILE *fp = fopen(f_name, "w");
  if (fp == NULL) {
    printf("Unable to open the file '%s' for writing\n", f_name);
    }
  else {
    fprintf(fp, "%s%d%s", header_1, seed, header_2);
    for (int kRow = 0; kRow < SIZE; kRow++) {
      char *s = multi_s[kRow];
      fprintf(fp, "<tr>");
      for (int i = 0; i < SIZE; i++) {
        if (s[i] == ' ') {
          fprintf(fp, "<td class=\"c_\"> </td>");
          }
        else {
          fprintf(fp, "<td class=\"c%d\" style=\"background-color:%s\">%c</td>",
              kRow % 3 * 3 + i % 3,
              (what == SOL || (s[i] == '.') ? "White" : "LightGray"),
              ((s[i] == '.') ? ' ' : s[i])
              );
          }
        }
      fprintf(fp, "</tr>\n");
      }
```

```
    fprintf(fp, "%s\n", footer);
    fclose(fp);
    }
  }
```

The initial comment shows how the individual puzzles join to form a multi-grid Sudoku. Admittedly, as you already know multi-grid Sudokus from Figures 18-2 and 18-6, I could have omitted the comment. But, I confess, after having drawn the nice diagrams (before writing the code that generated the figures), I didn't have the heart to throw them away, with the excuse that source code should be well commented!

The first interesting piece of code is

```
// Define the number of rows and columns needed for the multi-grid
#if N_GRIDS == 2
#define SIZE 15
#else
#define SIZE 21
#endif
```

If you look at Figures 18-2 and 18-6 or at the nice diagrams in the comment at the beginning of the module, you see that the double Sudoku is 15 cells wide and 15 cells high. All the other multi-grid Sudokus are 21 cells wide and 21 cells high. By making the definition of SIZE a C preprocessor directive linked to N_GRIDS, you can define the array to store the multi-grid of exactly the size you need.

As you learned at the end of Chapter 15, save_html() defines nine styles, named c0 to c8, whose function is to render the nine cells of a box in HTML with the appropriate borders. multi_html() uses the exact same styles, because they apply to each box separately, regardless of how many boxes exist in a puzzle.

But if you left it at that, a double Sudoku, just as an example, would look like that shown in Figure 18-9.

3	9	7			2	6	4	1						
			3					2						
	2						9	3						
2			9		5	4	6							
	4		6				1							
	5	6	2		1		7							
1	3								6	9		4	2	
9			2		1				4	8				
4	7	5	1		9							8	1	
					8	6			2		7		4	
									3	8	6			
					3				9	4	5		2	8
					2		8					1		5
					7							4		3
					6	1				5	9			

Figure 18-9. *A rough representation of a double Sudoku*

255

To remove the borders of empty cells, you only need to add the c_ style and use it for the cells that contain a space instead of a number.

To make the puzzles more interesting, you can add a background color to the cells of the puzzle that contain a clue, as shown in Figures 18-10 to 18-13.

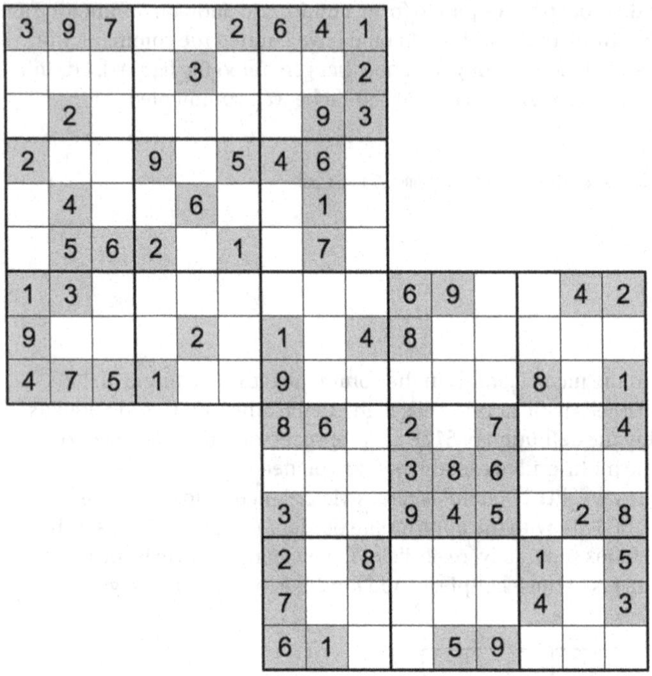

Figure 18-10. *A neat double Sudoku*

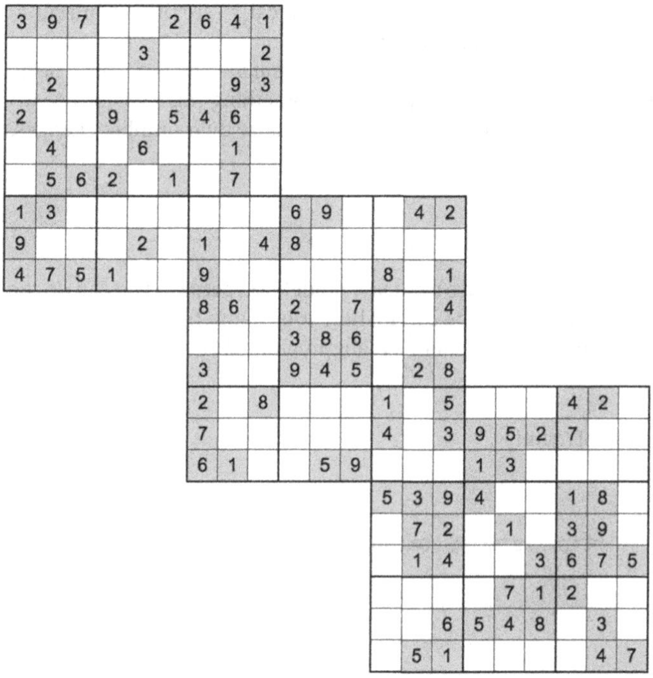

Figure 18-11. *A triple Sudoku*

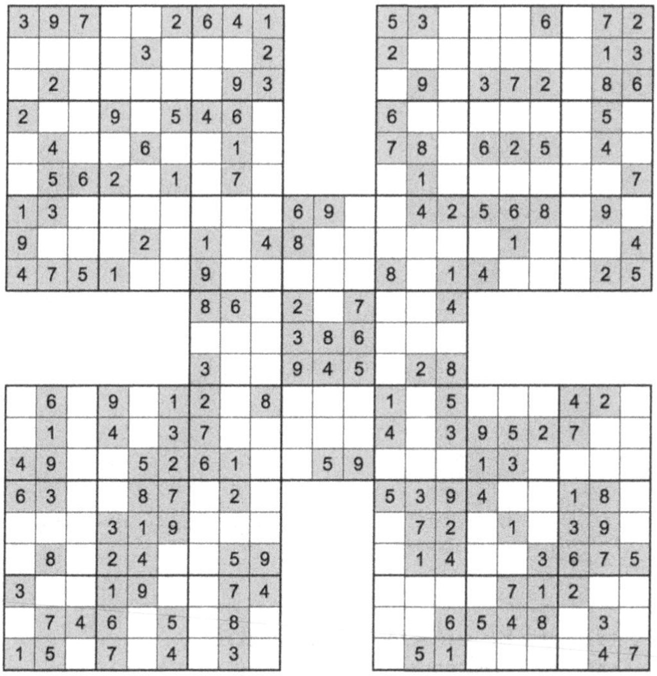

Figure 18-12. *A samurai Sudoku*

Notice that all three instances of puzzle 0 in Figures 18-10 to 18-12 are identical, as are those of puzzle 1 and, for the two larger puzzles in Figures 18-11 and 18-12, those of puzzle 2.

This tells you that all three multi-grid puzzles have been generated with the same choice of FIRST_SEED, which is defined in sudoku_gen.c (set to 123456 to create the examples). It is something you have to keep in mind when you create a multi-grid puzzle. The grids are not different simply because their number changes.

Designer Multi-Grid Sudokus

In Chapter 17, you saw how to create puzzles in which the clues formed a predefined pattern. You can do the same with multi-grid Sudokus to great effect. But you have to be careful how you choose the patterns.

Listing 18-4 shows the third (and last) version of the Generator's main program. As usual, I have highlighted the new parts.

Listing 18-4. sudoku_gen.c—The Final Version of main()

```
/* sudoku_gen.c
 *
 * Copyright (C) 2015  Giulio Zambon  - http://zambon.com.au/
 *
 */
#include <stdio.h>
#include <stdlib.h>
#include <string.h>
#include <time.h>
#include "brute_comp.h"
#include "count_solved.h"
#include "def.h"
#include "display.h"
#include "display_string.h"
#include "fill.h"
#include "inconsistent_grid.h"
#include "inconsistent_unit.h"
#include "init.h"
#include "in_box.h"
#include "list_solved.h"
#include "multi_html.h"
#include "save_html.h"

#define LOG_TO_FILE___NO
#define FILE_NAME "puzzles.txt"

#define SAVE_HTML_PUZZLE
#define SAVE_HTML_SOLUTION

#define DO_PATTERN

// N_GRIDS is defined in multi_html.h.
// When N_GRIDS is between 2 and 5, it triggers the creation of multi-grid
// puzzles. With any other value, the Generator creates a classic Sudoku.
#define DO_MULTI_GRID (N_GRIDS >= 2  &&  N_GRIDS <= 5)
```

```
// Parameters
#define N_SET_QUADS 5
#define N_SET_PAIRS 10
#define N_SET_CELLS 0
#define ADDITIONAL_CELLS TRUE
#define FIRST_SEED 12345
#define N_SEEDS 1


// Global variables
char *unit_names[3] = {"row", "column", "box"};
char grid[9][9];
char row[9][9][2];
char col[9][9][2];
char box[9][9][2];
char solved[9][9];
int silent = TRUE;

// Variables and functions local to this module
char puzzle[9][9];
int r_1[81];
int c_1[81];
int k_cell;
int remove_quads(int k_puz);
int remove_pairs(int k_puz);
void make_clue_list(void);
int remove_clues(int k_puz);
void remove_more_clues(int k_puz);
int check_uniqueness(void);


// The following table identifies the box of grid 0 that overlaps with other
// grids when creating multi-grid Sudokus.
// The first box refers to puzzle0 and second one to the other puzzle:
//
// N_GRIDS  kPuz=1  kPuz=2  kPuz=3  kPuz=4
//    2     b0-b8
//    3     b0-b8   b8-b0
//    4     b0-b8   b8-b0   b2-b6
//    5     b0-b8   b8-b0   b2-b6   b6-b2
//
// Puzzle:     0   1   2   3   4
int box0[] = {-1,  0,  8,  2,  6};

#ifdef DO_PATTERN
const char KEEP0[82] =
    "..1.1.1.."
    ".1..1..1."
    "1..1.1..1"
    "..1...1.."
    "11..1..11"
    "..1...1.."
    "1..1.1..1"
```

```
    ".1..1..1."
    "..1.1.1.."
    ;
const char KEEP1[82] =
    "..11111.."
    ".1.....1."
    "1..111..1"
    "1.1...1.1"
    "1.1.1.1.1"
    "1.1...1.1"
    "1..111..1"
    ".1.....1."
    "..11111.."
    ;
const char KEEP2[82] =
    "..11111.."
    ".1.....1."
    "1..111..1"
    "1.1...1.1"
    "1.1.1.1.1"
    "1.1...1.1"
    "1..111..1"
    ".1.....1."
    "..11111.."
    ;
const char KEEP3[] =
    "..11111.."
    ".1.....1."
    "1..111..1"
    "1.1...1.1"
    "1.1.1.1.1"
    "1.1...1.1"
    "1..111..1"
    ".1.....1."
    "..11111.."
    ;
const char KEEP4[] =
    "..11111.."
    ".1.....1."
    "1..111..1"
    "1.1...1.1"
    "1.1.1.1.1"
    "1.1...1.1"
    "1..111..1"
    ".1.....1."
    "..11111.."
    ;
const char *KEEPS[5] = { KEEP0, KEEP1, KEEP2, KEEP3, KEEP4 };
#endif
```

```
//=========================================================================== main
int main(int argc, char *argv[]) {
  printf("*** sudoku_gen ***\n");
  char mess[32];
  int n_seeds = N_SEEDS;
  int k_try = 0;

#if DO_MULTI_GRID
  // When creating multi-grid puzzles, set n_seed to the number of
  // puzzles that you need
  n_seeds = N_GRIDS;
#endif

  // Open a file to log the results
  FILE *fp = NULL;
#ifdef LOG_TO_FILE
  fp = fopen(FILE_NAME, "a");
  if (fp == NULL) {
    printf("Unable to open the file '%s' for reading\n", FILE_NAME);
    return EXIT_FAILURE;                                                    //==>
    }
#endif

  // Try all the seeds in the given range
  unsigned long start_time = clock();

  for (int k_seed = 0; k_seed < n_seeds; k_seed++) {
    int seed = FIRST_SEED + k_seed;
    srand(seed);
    int brute_result;
    int n;

    // Keep repeating the generation until you find a unique solution
    char puzzle_string[82];
    char solution_string[82];
    do {

      // Generate a solved Sudoku
      do { init(); } while (fill());

      // Save the solved Sudoku
      for (int k = 0; k < 9; k++) {
        for (int j = 0; j < 9; j++) {
          solved[k][j] = grid[k][j];
          puzzle[k][j] = grid[k][j];
          }
        }
```

```
#if DO_MULTI_GRID
      if (k_seed > 0) {
        // You arrive here if you are creating a multi-grid puzzle and
        // have already created the first one (puzzle 0).
        int k0 = box0[k_seed]/3*3;
        int j0 = box0[k_seed]%3*3;
        int kk = overlapping_box[k_seed]/3*3;
        int jj = overlapping_box[k_seed]%3*3;

        // Build the look-up list of numbers to match puzzle 0 when creating
        // subsequent grids.
        char map[10] = {0};
        for (int k = 0; k < 3; k++) {
          for (int j = 0; j < 3; j++) {
            map[(int)grid[(kk + k)][jj + j]] =
                multi_string[0][SOL][(k0 + k)*9 + j0 + j] - '0'
                ;
          }
        }

        // Convert the numbers in the grid and save the modified grid
        for (int k = 0; k < 9; k++) {
          for (int j = 0; j < 9; j++) {
            grid[k][j] = map[(int)grid[k][j]];
            solved[k][j] = grid[k][j];
            puzzle[k][j] = grid[k][j];
          }
        }
#ifndef DO_PATTERN
        // Make the box that overlaps puzzle 0 identical to the
        // corresponding one of puzzle 0
        for (int k = 0; k < 3; k++) {
          for (int j = 0; j < 3; j++) {
            grid[(kk + k)][jj + j] =
                multi_string[0][PUZ][(k0 + k)*9 + j0 + j] - '0'
                ;
          }
        }
#endif
      }
#endif

#ifdef DO_PATTERN
      for (int i = 0; i < 81; i++) {
        if (KEEPS[k_seed][i] == '.') {
          int k = i / 9;
          int j = i - k * 9;
          grid[k][j] = 0;
          puzzle[k][j] = 0;
        }
      }
```

```
#else
      //========= Remove N_SET_QUADS quadruples of clues
      if (N_SET_QUADS > 0) {
        int success = remove_quads(k_seed);
        if (!success) {
          brute_result = BRUTE_COMP_DIFFERENT;
          goto skip;                                              //==>
          }
        }

      //========= Remove N_SET_PAIRS pairs of clues
      if (N_SET_PAIRS > 0) {
        int success = remove_pairs(k_seed);
        if (!success) {
          brute_result = BRUTE_COMP_DIFFERENT;
          goto skip;                                              //==>
          }
        }

      //========= Remove N_SET_CELLS individual clues and then some more
      make_clue_list();
      k_cell = 0;
      if (N_SET_CELLS > 0) {
        int success = remove_clues(k_seed);
        if (!success) {
          brute_result = BRUTE_COMP_DIFFERENT;
          goto skip;                                              //==>
          }
        }
      if (ADDITIONAL_CELLS && k_cell < 81) remove_more_clues(k_seed);
#endif

      //========= Check whether the solution is really unique
      brute_result = check_uniqueness();

      //========= Done
      for (int k = 0; k < 9; k++) {
        for (int j = 0; j < 9; j++) {
          grid[k][j] = puzzle[k][j];
          }
        }
      n = count_solved();
      if (!silent && fp == NULL) {
        display();
        sprintf(mess, "seed %d %d", seed, n);
        display_string(mess);
        printf("The puzzle contains %d clues:", n);
        list_solved(stdout);
        }
```

```
skip:                                                                    // <==
      k_try++;
      printf("%d: %s\n",
          k_try,
          (brute_result == BRUTE_COMP_DIFFERENT) ? "No" : "Yes"
          );
      } while (brute_result == BRUTE_COMP_DIFFERENT);

    // Save puzzle and solution into strings
    int kar = 0;
    for (int k = 0; k < 9; k++) {
      for (int j = 0; j < 9; j++) {
        puzzle_string[kar] = puzzle[k][j] + '0';
        solution_string[kar] = solved[k][j] + '0';
        kar++;
        }
      }
    puzzle_string[kar] = '\0';
    solution_string[kar] = '\0';

#if DO_MULTI_GRID
    // Save the puzzle and solution strings to be combined later into
    // a multi-grid Sudoku
    for (int i = 0; i < 82; i++) { // copy also the '\0' at the end
      multi_string[k_seed][PUZ][i] = puzzle_string[i];
      multi_string[k_seed][SOL][i] = solution_string[i];
      }
#endif

#ifdef SAVE_HTML_PUZZLE
    save_html(puzzle_string, seed, "p");
#endif

#ifdef SAVE_HTML_SOLUTION
    save_html(solution_string, seed, "s");
#endif
    if (fp != NULL) {
      printf("#%d\n", k_seed);
      fprintf(fp, "%s\t%d", puzzle_string, seed);
      if (brute_result != BRUTE_COMP_DIFFERENT) {
        fprintf(fp, "\t%d", n);
        list_solved(fp);
        }
      fprintf(fp, "\n");
      }
    } // for (k_seed..

#if DO_MULTI_GRID
  multi_html(FIRST_SEED, PUZ);
  multi_html(FIRST_SEED, SOL);
#endif
```

```
unsigned long end_time = clock();
printf("********* done in %ld microseconds\n", end_time - start_time);
if (fp != NULL) fclose(fp);
return EXIT_SUCCESS;
}
```

The first difference from the previous version of the Generator's main() is the definition of DO_PATTERN. The first effect of defining DO_PATTERN is to switch on the definition of the KEEP* arrays. KEEP0 to KEEP4 determine the position of the clues in the five grids of a samurai Sudoku. But if you set N_GRIDS to 1 in multi_html.h, only puzzle 0 will be created and only KEEP0 will be used.

Once you define the clue patterns, all you need to do is use them to remove the clues. You do this with the following few lines of code:

```
for (int i = 0; i < 81; i++) {
  if (KEEPS[k_seed][i] == '.') {
    int k = i / 9;
    int j = i - k * 9;
    grid[k][j] = 0;
    puzzle[k][j] = 0;
    }
  }
```

Note that when you create designer multi-grid puzzles, you don't need to do anything concerning the overlapping boxes because you have already matched them by defining the KEEP* arrays.

Many patterns of clues do not result in valid puzzles. Therefore, defining the matching patterns for up to five grids is at times a bit frustrating. But the results can be very rewarding, as the samurai shown in Figure 18-13 convincingly testifies.

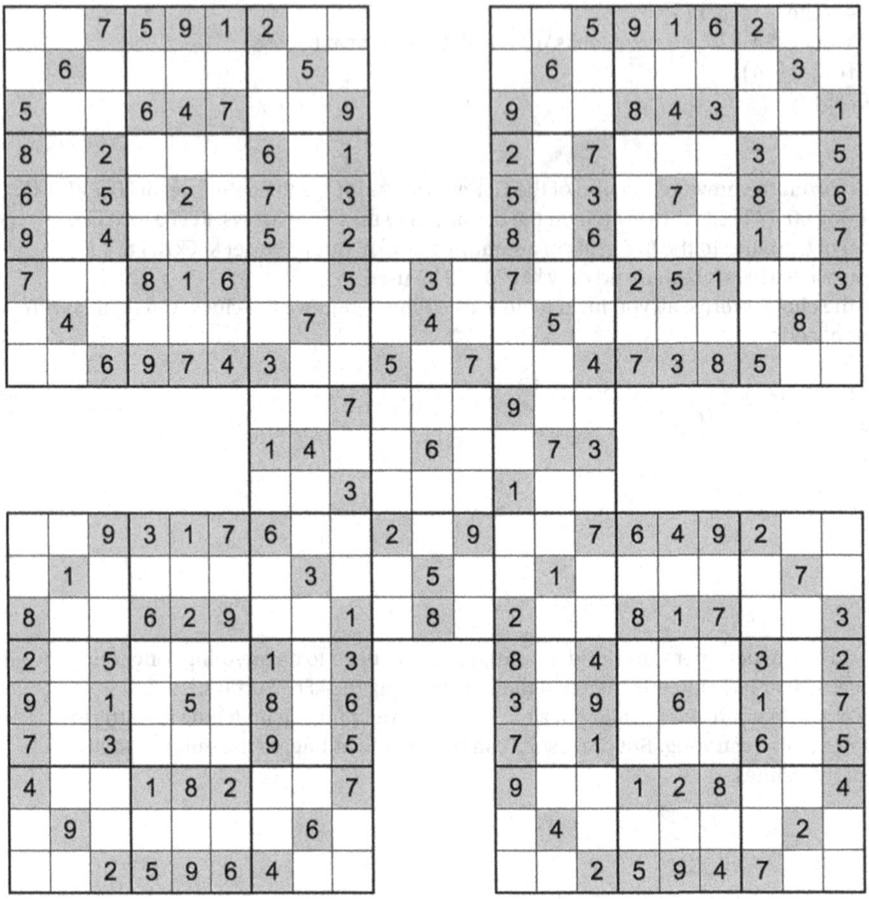

Figure 18-13. *A symmetrical samurai Sudoku*

Summary

This chapter taught you how to generate multi-grid Sudokus. It is the last chapter of the book and you now know everything I know concerning the generation of Sudoku puzzles. Appendix A will tell you how to set up the Eclipse development environment.

I hope you have enjoyed reading this book as I have enjoyed writing it. Happy puzzling!

APPENDIX A

■ ■ ■

Development Environment

I developed the Solver and the Generator on a Macintosh, but from the very start I wanted to be certain that they were portable to Windows-based PCs. That is why I chose Eclipse as an Integrated Development Environment rather than Apple's Xcode. This appendix will show you how to set up and run the Solver and Generator.

Eclipse

This section is not a user's guide for Eclipse, as you can find extensive documentation on the web, but setting it up on a PC running Windows is not entirely straightforward, and I would like to spare you at least some of the pain I had to go through!

To install Eclipse, you only need to go to `http://eclipse.org/downloads/`, download the package suitable for your operating system, and unzip it. At the moment of writing, the latest packages are `eclipse-cpp-luna-SR1a-macosx-cocoa-x86_64.tar.gz` for the Mac and `eclipse-cpp-luna-SR1a-win32-x86_64.zip` for the PC.

The installation of the Eclipse package itself is straightforward: all you need to do is expand the zip file you have downloaded and move the folder named "eclipse" to any convenient location. Any place will do but, to be on the safe side, I would choose a path that doesn't contain any folder name with spaces. In the past, Eclipse couldn't navigate through such names. Perhaps they have fixed the problem, but I haven't checked whether it is so because it is not a big deal to be conservative in this case.

Eclipse is a Java application. Therefore, before you can execute it, you need to ensure that a Java Runtime Environment (JRE) is available on your system. Also, as the Eclipse package doesn't include any compiler, it cannot do anything useful unless you also have a C compiler already installed on your system.

Once you have a JRE and a C compiler, to launch Eclipse you just double-click the icon of `eclipse.app` on a Mac or `eclipse.exe` on a PC.

With the MacOS (mine is Mavericks, 10.9.5), Eclipse is immediately ready to run, but under Windows on a PC, you need to do some preparatory work.

Setting Up Eclipse on a PC

First of all, you probably have to install a JRE. I say *probably*, because Microsoft meanwhile might have realized that a Windows PC should have a JRE or a JDK (Java Development Kit) already installed from the factory. To install Java on your PC is a simple operation: go to `http://java.com` and pick the appropriate JRE. Note that, unless you want to use Eclipse also to develop Java programs, you don't need any development kit. The JRE will suffice.

I tested the Solver and the Generator on a system with Windows 7 Enterprise. It did have a C compiler installed, but I preferred to install GNU C (call me paranoid if you like!). To do so, point your web browser to the URL http://sourceforge.net/projects/mingw/files/, click the link marked "Automated MinGW Installer" and then, when you see the new page, click the link that starts with "Download." When I did it, the link was named "Download mingw-get-setup.exe (86.5 KB)," but the name might have changed by the time you are reading this page.

MinGW means "Minimalist GNU for Windows," which SourceForge describes as "A native Windows port of the GNU Compiler Collection (GCC), with freely distributable import libraries and header files for building native Windows applications; includes extensions to the MSVC runtime to support C99 functionality" (MSVC stands for "Microsoft Visual C").

The installer asks you where you would like the program to be installed and then, after downloading several files, displays the MinGW Installation Manager's window, which lets you choose what package you want to download. If you like, you can obviously download everything available, but to compile the Solver and the Generator, you only need the package for the basic MinGW installation, named mingw32-base.

After selecting the package, you click the item "Apply Changes" of the "Installation" menu and confirm it by clicking the button "Apply" in the dialog that pops up.

Once the Installation Manager is done with the downloading of files (it will take a while), go back to the "Installation" menu and click the item "Update Catalogue."

You need the support of the C99 standard because it lets you define control variables of for-loops within the for statements, as in the following example:

```
for (int k = 0; k < 9; k++) {
```

This is a standard feature of Java that I find very good, and I almost always use this format in my coding, but it was not present in the C ANSI standard of 1990, which is the default for the GNU C compiler.

Fortunately, it was introduced into the ANSI standard of 1999 (hence the term "C99").

Although C99 is included in the basic MinGW distribution, you have to configure Eclipse to use it. Once you have created the Solver and Generator projects (I'm jumping ahead of myself here), you can configure them to use C99 by opening the projects' properties dialogue and adding the option -std=c99 to the compiler by selecting Settings ➤ GCC C Compiler ➤ Miscellaneous and adding the C99 option to the Other flags field, as shown in Figure A-1.

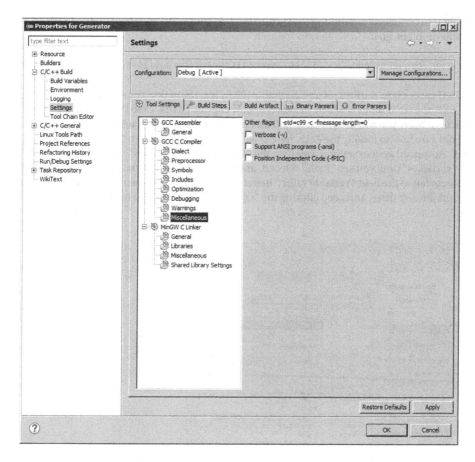

Figure A-1. *Choosing the C99 standard for a project*

I like to encapsulate variables within limited scopes, and by defining the control variable within the for-statement, I achieve that the variable is invisible outside the loop. I could have achieved an equivalent result by adding a pair of braces, as in the following example:

```
{
  int k;
  for (k = 0; k < 9; k++) {
    ...
  } // for (k...
}
```

but I find it ugly and cumbersome, as each for-loop would add two levels of indentation instead of one.

After you have installed the C compiler, you still have to install another package. Without it, you would not be able to work because you would keep getting the following error message every time you tried to run a Sudoku program:

```
12:03:04 **** Clean-only build of configuration Debug for project Generator ****
rm -rf src/inconsistent_unit.o src/display_string.d [GZ: rest omitted]
Cannot run program "rm": Launching failed
```

269

The message is caused by Eclipse attempting to execute the Unix command rm, which Windows doesn't recognize. To solve this problem, go to

`http://sourceforge.net/projects/gnuwin32/files/coreutils/5.3.0/coreutils-5.3.0.exe/download`

and download the GNU coreutils in the form of an executable (EXE) file. If you don't change any default while executing the EXE, the GNU utilities will be installed in `C:\Program Files (x86)\GnuWin32\bin`. To make them available to Eclipse, you will then need to add that path to the system variable `Path`.

In case you are not sure how to modify the `Path`, here is what you need to do: open the Control Panel System, click the link "Advanced system setting" and then the "Environment Variables" button. Scroll through the "System variables" until you see "Path," select it, and click the "Edit" button. After that, move the cursor to the extreme left of the field "Variable value," insert the new path, type a semicolon to keep it separate from the paths already there, and keep clicking the "OK" button until you are out of the control panel (see Figure A-2).

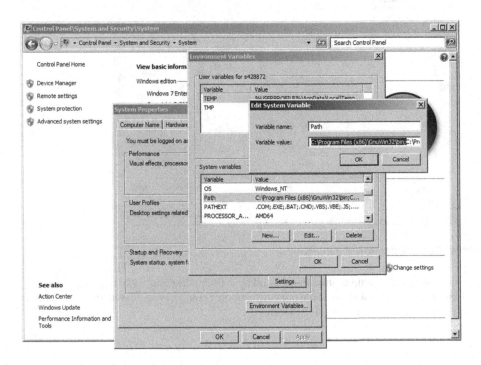

Figure A-2. *Environment variable "Path"*

Coding Style

Eclipse lets you choose many options concerning the formatting of the source code. To configure Eclipse with your own style (i.e., with your own Formatter Profile), open the project properties of any project, select `C/C++ General` ➤ `Formatter` and click the link `Configure Workspace Settings`. This opens up the Formatter dialogue that lets you define a style for all your projects. Click the `New` button and you will see what is shown in Figure A-3.

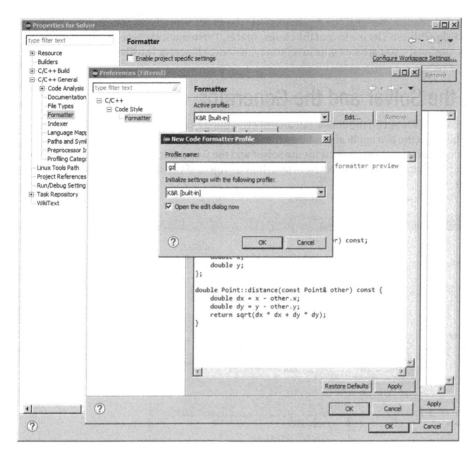

Figure A-3. *Giving a name to your coding style*

After choosing a name for your style and clicking OK, you will get access to a series of options to modify it while leaving the predefined profiles unchanged. My style, which I have used throughout this book, differs from the K&R (see Appendix B for definition) style in only two things: two spaces of indentation instead of tabs equivalent to four spaces and indenting the closing braces, so that blocks "hang" from their first lines like flags.

```
if (condition) {
  whatever();
  }
else {
  something_else();
  }
```

My style makes the block statements easier to identify when looking at the code. Besides, the closing braces *belong* to the block statements and should therefore be indented. This is apparent if you replace the block statements with simple statements, as in the following example:

```
if (condition)
  whatever();
else
  something_else();
```

Why should the indentation change if you replace a single statement with a block statement?

In any case, as Eclipse doesn't let me indent the closing braces, I systematically type two additional spaces before them. Obviously, you are welcome to reformat my source however you like!

Setting Up the Solver and the Generator

In this section, I explain how to set up the Solver, but almost everything I say will also apply to the Generator, the only difference between the two applications being that the Generator doesn't need an input string.

The simplest way to create Eclipse projects for the Solver and the Generator is to position the cursor on the Project Explorer's sidebar, right-click, select New, and then C Project. If you do so, you will see the dialog shown in Figure A-4.

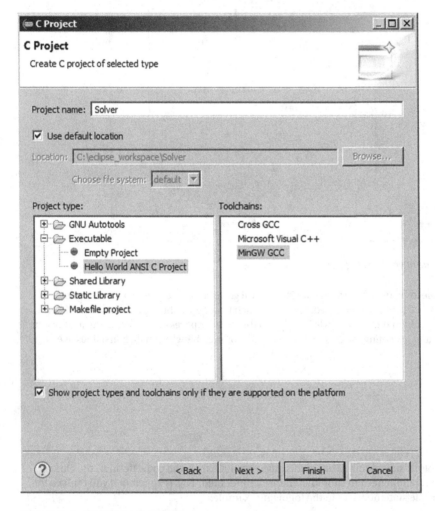

Figure A-4. *Creating a C project*

Select Hello World ANSI C Project as shown, write Solver as the project name, select MinGW GCC as the toolchain, and click Finish. A folder named Solver will appear in the Project Explorer sidebar. Copy all the Solver source files attached to this book to the subfolder Solver/src/ of the Eclipse's workspace folder. Then, within Eclipse, position the cursor on the Solver folder within the Project Explorer sidebar, right-click, and select Refresh. Open the src folder within the project Solver, which now contains all the sources of the Sudoku Solver, and delete Solver.c by right-clicking on it as shown in Figure A-5.

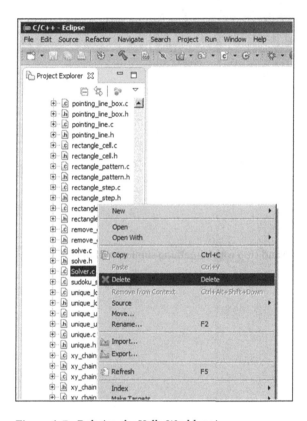

Figure A-5. *Deleting the Hello World main*

You can now build the Solver, but you are not yet ready to launch it. Open the src subfolder of the project and double-click sudoku_solver.c to open the Solver's main module. Check that USE_FILE is not set. If you find that there is a #define USE_FILE, change it to something like #define USE_FILE_NO (or whatever else you like). This will ensure that the Solver expects a single Sudoku string as the first input argument, rather than reading several strings from the disk. Also check that the global variable silent is set to FALSE, so that the Solver sends log entries to Eclipse's console.

If you right-click the project folder that you see in Eclipse's Project Explorer sidebar, select Run As, and then Local C/C++ Application, you will get in the console the following error message: You need to provide a Sudoku string. Right! You have to pass a Sudoku string to the Solver as an argument!

To do so, click Eclipse's Run menu and select the item Run Configurations. When the run configurations' dialogue appears, click the tab marked (x)= Arguments, paste or type the Sudoku string of a puzzle into the text area marked Program arguments, click Apply, and then Run (see Figure A-6).

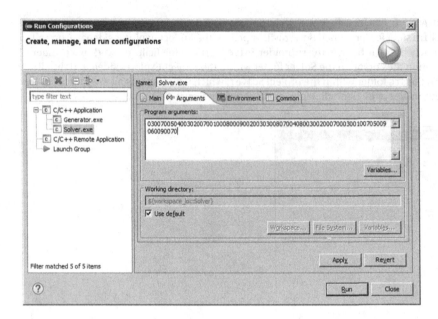

Figure A-6. *Providing a Sudoku string to the Solver*

The Solver's log will scroll up in the Console pane and stop with something similar to what you see in Listing A-1.

Listing A-1. The Solver Log

```
sudoku: the final grid contains 81 solved cells
        0   1   2   3   4   5   6   7   8
    ++===+===+===++===+===+===++===+===+===++
    ||   |   |   ||   |   |   ||   |   |   ||
  0 ||(6)|(3)|(9)||(4)|(7)|(8)||(2)|(5)|(1)||
    ||   |   |   ||   |   |   ||   |   |   ||
    ++---+---+---++---+---+---++---+---+---++
    ||   |   |   ||   |   |   ||   |   |   ||
  1 ||(4)|(5)|(8)||(3)|(1)|(2)||(9)|(6)|(7)||
    ||   |   |   ||   |   |   ||   |   |   ||
    ++---+---+---++---+---+---++---+---+---++
    ||   |   |   ||   |   |   ||   |   |   ||
  2 ||(2)|(7)|(1)||(6)|(5)|(9)||(8)|(4)|(3)||
    ||   |   |   ||   |   |   ||   |   |   ||
    ++===+===+===++===+===+===++===+===+===++
    ||   |   |   ||   |   |   ||   |   |   ||
  3 ||(7)|(9)|(6)||(5)|(2)|(4)||(1)|(3)|(8)||
    ||   |   |   ||   |   |   ||   |   |   ||
    ++---+---+---++---+---+---++---+---+---++
    ||   |   |   ||   |   |   ||   |   |   ||
  4 ||(3)|(1)|(2)||(8)|(6)|(7)||(5)|(9)|(4)||
    ||   |   |   ||   |   |   ||   |   |   ||
    ++---+---+---++---+---+---++---+---+---++
    ||   |   |   ||   |   |   ||   |   |   ||
  5 ||(5)|(8)|(4)||(9)|(3)|(1)||(7)|(2)|(6)||
    ||   |   |   ||   |   |   ||   |   |   ||
    ++===+===+===++===+===+===++===+===+===++
    ||   |   |   ||   |   |   ||   |   |   ||
  6 ||(9)|(4)|(7)||(2)|(8)|(6)||(3)|(1)|(5)||
    ||   |   |   ||   |   |   ||   |   |   ||
    ++---+---+---++---+---+---++---+---+---++
    ||   |   |   ||   |   |   ||   |   |   ||
  7 ||(1)|(2)|(3)||(7)|(4)|(5)||(6)|(8)|(9)||
    ||   |   |   ||   |   |   ||   |   |   ||
    ++---+---+---++---+---+---++---+---+---++
    ||   |   |   ||   |   |   ||   |   |   ||
  8 ||(8)|(6)|(5)||(1)|(9)|(3)||(4)|(7)|(2)||
    ||   |   |   ||   |   |   ||   |   |   ||
    ++===+===+===++===+===+===++===+===+===++
****** 639478251458312967271659843796524138312867594584931726947286315123745689865193472
Strategies used 13: 'unique-loop' 'naked-pair' 'box-line' 'lines-2' 'lines-3' 'Y-wing'
'Y-wing' 'XY-chain' 'unique-loop' 'naked-pair' 'naked-pair' 'box-line' 'Y-wing'
```

I chose a difficult puzzle for this example!

APPENDIX B

Abbreviations and Acronyms

ANSI	American National Standards Institute
app	The extension in the file names of Macintosh applications
ASCII	American Standard Code for Information Interchange
bit	Contraction of "binary" and "digit", the unit of information in computing
C99	ANSI C standard of 1999
CSS	Cascading Style Sheets
e.g.	"Exempli gratia," Latin for "for the sake of example"
exe	The extension in the file names of Windows applications
GCC	GNU compiler collection
GNU	GNU is not Unix
GUI	Graphical user interface
HTML	Hypertext Markup Language
i.e.	"Id est," Latin for "that is"
ID	Identifier
IDE	Integrated Development Environment
ISBN	International Standard Book Number
JDK	Java Development Kit
JRE	Java Runtime Environment
JSP	JavaServer Pages
K&R	*The C Programming Language, Second Edition*, by B. W. Kernighan & D. M. Ritchie (Prentice Hall Software Series)
MinGW	Minimalist GNU for Windows
MSVC	Microsoft Visual C
OO	object oriented
OS	operating system
PC	personal computer
URL	Universal Resource Locator
W3C	The Worldwide Web ("WWW" = "W3") Consortium
XHTML	HTML conforming to the XML standard
XML	Extended Markup Language

Index

Get the eBook for only $10!

> Now you can take the weightless companion with you anywhere, anytime. Your purchase of this book entitles you to 3 electronic versions for only $10.

This Apress title will prove so indispensible that you'll want to carry it with you everywhere, which is why we are offering the eBook in 3 formats for only $10 if you have already purchased the print book.

Convenient and fully searchable, the PDF version enables you to easily find and copy code—or perform examples by quickly toggling between instructions and   applications. The MOBI format is ideal for your Kindle, while the ePUB can be utilized on a variety of mobile devices.

Go to www.apress.com/promo/tendollars to purchase your companion eBook.